S P O

CYCLING

A GUIDE TO TRAINING, RACING, AND ENDURANCE
MICHAEL SHERMER

CONTEMPORARY
BOOKS, INC.
CHICAGO

Library of Congress Cataloging in Publication Data

Shermer, Michael.
 Sport cycling.

 Includes index.
  1. Bicycle racing.   2. Bicycle racing—Training
 3. Bicycle racing—Psychological aspects.   I. Title.
 GV1049.S483   1985   796.6   85-9623
 ISBN 0-8092-5244-9

I would like to dedicate this book to
a number of individuals who
have been prime movers in my life:

My Parents

for their guidance in all of my aspirations,
no matter what size or how important.

Dr. Richard C. Hardison
for teaching me how to think.

John Marino and Lon Haldeman
my competitors, business partners, and friends.

Christa Morones
for her 100-percent support and
dedication to my cycling career.

Published by Contemporary Books, Inc.
180 North Michigan Avenue, Chicago, Illinois 60601
Manufactured in the United States of America
Library of Congress Catalog Card Number: 85-9623
International Standard Book Number: 0-8092-5244-9

Published simultaneously in Canada by Beaverbooks, Ltd.
195 Allstate Parkway, Valleywood Business Park
Markham, Ontario L3R 4T8 Canada

CONTENTS

ACKNOWLEDGMENTS

COPYEDITING

I would like to thank Kecia Harris for her editing and input into the manuscript. Far more than proofreading the text, she provided valuable feedback on the flow and structure of the book.

SPONSORS

The prohibitive costs of ultra-marathon cycling make the sport highly dependent on the support of sponsors. I would like to thank the many individuals and companies who have helped me throughout the years.

Current sponsors include See's Candies, Shimano, the Great American Chocolate Chip Cookie Company, Cycles Peugeot, Power/Bata Footwear, Bell Helmets, Spenco Medical Products, Kucharik Bicycle Clothing, Wolber Tires, Boost Energy Tablets, and Richard Godbold, my step-father and owner of Hauter Ford for supplying vehicles and support.

Past sponsors include Campagnolo Components, Sidi Shoes, Skid-Lid Helmets, Motobecane Bicycles, Brooks Saddles, Veltec Pacer 2000 Computer, Hatch Gloves, Bianchi Bicycles, Body Accounting, Nautilus Plus, K.D. Naturotherapeutics, Electro-Medical Products, Health Valley Foods, Alacer Vitamins, and Hansen Juices.

SUPPORT CREWS

Ultra-marathon cycling also requires a support crew, ranging in size from five to nine people, who work and live together in the confines of a motor home for as long as 10 days, 24 hours a day. There is little money and even less glory. However, there is the satisfaction of being involved in an event as intense as an ultra-marathon race. Those who have taken the challenge with me are listed below alphabetically, with the support crew(s) of which they were members.

1980 Seattle-to-San Diego: Dan Cunningham, Kathy Dynes, John Marino, George Oakley, Joanne Penseyres, and Michael Ruvo.

1981 Seattle-to-San Diego: Larry Barber, Dan Cunningham, Kathy Dynes, Christa Morones, George Oakley, and C. J. Shank.

1982 Great American Bike Race: B. J. Anderson, Dan Cunningham, Dr. Bill Mckean, Christa Morones, George Oakley, and Michael Ruvo.

1983 Miami-to-Maine: B. J. Anderson, Michael Coles, Jeff Davis, Karen Hiner, Dave Johnson, Christa Morones, and Len Vreeland.

1983 Race Across AMerica: Dan Cunningham, Karen Hiner, Bernie Landis, Christa Morones, Michael Morones, and Robert Warren.

1984 Spenco 500: Christa Morones and Chuck Ritz.

1984 Seattle-to-San Diego: Michael Coles, Karen Hiner, Christa Morones, Angel Rodriguez, Tina Shermer, and Janice Simmons.

1984 Race Across AMerica: Michael Coles, Ben Corrington, Richard Debernardis, John Hiner, Karen Hiner, Christa Morones, Michael Morones, Buck Peacock, and Janice Simmons.

1985 San Francisco-to-Los Angeles: Christa Morones, Shawn Shermer, John Uhte, Robert Warren.

1985 Race Across AMerica: Karen Hiner, Debra Kettler, Michael Morones, Christa Morones, Shawn Shermer, Vicky Vodon, Robert Warren, Scott Gillette.

I also wish to thank Michael Grandi and Jack Artenstein, my publishing agents, for making this book possible.

FOREWORD

The assignment sounded forbidding.

The summer production schedule for ABC Sports personnel appeared in late May 1982. There was an early August listing for an event called "The Great American Bike Race," with a notation listing locations in Santa Monica, California, and New York City. The names "Lampley" and "Nyad" appeared in the announcer column. There couldn't really be a bicycle race from California to New York, could there? Yes.

ABC's "Wide World of Sports" had entered the culture of ultra-endurance sports events in 1980, with the first telecast of the Hawaiian Ironman Triathlon. At the time, the triathlon event was held on the island of Oahu, where small handfuls of fitness adventurers had finished its swim-bike-run grind in 1978 and 1979. But the arrival of television cameras coincided with a quantum leap in participation—more than 100 entrants in 1980, more than 300 when the event was moved to the big island of Hawaii in 1981.

When I had gone to Oahu to participate in that first triathlon telecast in 1980, my mind was boggled by the prospect of athletes swimming 2.4 miles in the ocean, bicycling 112 miles on island roads, then dismounting their bikes to run a marathon. But I soon began to learn that the limits of human endurance are more mental than physical. Not only could highly trained, elite athletes like former collegiate swimmer David Scott and Olympic bike racer John Howard complete the Ironman, but hundreds of others—schoolteachers, doctors, retirees, military officers—

could do it, too. Because millions of fitness-oriented Americans could identify with it, and because the commentary of the ultra-marathon swimming star Diana Nyad gave it credibility, the Triathlon rapidly became one of Wide World's most popular events. In the spring of 1982, the poignant performance of an unknown triathlete named Julie Moss helped to create one of the most memorable and dramatic segments in the program's 24-year history.

So by the time of that first transcontinental bicycle race, I was well versed in the lives and lifestyles of the small group of ultra-endurance athletes who had begun to emerge from triathlon culture as public figures. In an abstract way, I had accepted the notion that I was going to travel all the way across the United States with four bicyclists who would be racing along a prescribed route of streets and highways. They were sure to be fit. After all, one of the four, John Howard, had won the 1981 Ironman. Another, Michael Shermer, had completed it. Two nights before the race, one of the four riders told me he expected to make it to New York in less than ten days and to average less than two hours of sleep per day. I wasn't sure I believed that.

What followed remains one of the most unforgettable experiences of my eleven years as a network sports commentator. We left the Santa Monica Pier at 9:00 A.M., Pacific time. My first real understanding of what the trip would be like was formed at about midnight, somewhere in the darkness of the California desert. As leader Lon Haldeman rolled under a highway overpass, I stood looking down at him and marveled at his implacable, machine-like precision. I turned to Haldeman's girl-friend, Susan Notorangelo, and asked when he was planning to sleep. She looked at me as if I were crazy. "Sleep? We're going to New York. Aren't you going to New York?"

In three years, the transcontinental bicycle race (now called the Race Across AMerica) has become a greatly anticipated annual event on ABC's "Wide World of Sports." As the most extreme yet in the growing culture of extreme endurance events, it is the ultimate laboratory for the science which tests and expands the athlete's physical and mental limits. And Michael Shermer is one of its foremost experimenters.

This book encompasses all the elements of training, preparation, and self-discipline which are part of long-distance cycling culture. Included are personal recollections, from one who has been there, of some of the greatest events ever to take place in ultra-endurance sports. In the future, there will be many more such events, thanks to the dedication and foresight of thoughtful pioneers like Michael Shermer.

Jim Lampley

INTRODUCTION

In 1982 I was asked by ABC television to cover the Race Across AMerica. At the time I was racing in Europe so I had a good excuse not to cover it. The next year I was again asked to cover the Race Across AMerica. This time however there was no way out. I was going to have to follow a bunch of guys and one woman, who called themselves cyclists, for about ten days as they pedaled from the Pacific to the Atlantic.

What could I do? I thought to myself there must be some way out of this. These people are not bicycle racers. Sure, they taught John Howard a lesson last year but he was old, maybe even over the hill.

After the start in 1983 it took just five hours for me to realize what John Howard had discovered in 1982. I was shocked—the top competitors can HAMMER.

I rode the first 100 miles with the leaders, one of whom was Michael Shermer, and I was dead! To say that I was glad to see the ABC mobile home is an understatement. These guys were maintaining a speed of over 20 mph into a stiff head wind and the temperature was well over 100 degrees. It was a humbling experience for someone who considers himself a bicycle racer.

Over the next week and a half my respect for the leaders increased as I was continually amazed by their talent as cyclists.

In this book Michael Shermer lends his experiences of being an
endurance cyclist along with his methods for training in a unique way.
He describes not only his physical training methods but also the methods
he uses to train his mind to endure the momentus task of racing across
America. He leaves no stone unturned—from physical training to
training the mind to race across America. Shermer tells us how he and
others have done it.

This book will get any endurance cyclist down the road with a smile on
his or her face as Shermer explains how to avoid the common pitfalls and
mistakes he and others have made.

It would be a mistake to think that this book is only designed for the
endurance cyclist. Shermer's insight into training can be applied to all
sports. I would recommend an athlete in any sport to spend the time to
read it.

Take it from me, these endurance cyclists are racers to be respected
and listened to!

Eric Heiden

PART
I

PSYCHLING
ON MENTAL
FITNESS

1
THE "PSYCH" IN CYCLING

"To be nobody-but-myself—in a world which is doing its best, night and day, to make you everybody else—means to fight the hardest battle which any human being can fight, and never stop fighting."

E. E. Cummings

On a crisp, clear day late in October 1972 history was made. The setting was the mile-high metropolis of Mexico City, where enthusiasts, press, onlookers, and officials gathered to witness the spectacle. The event was one of the greatest achievements in the history of athletic endeavors—the breaking of the hour record.

Being the holder of the hour record in cycling is at least as prestigious as being the holder of the mile record in running. The cyclist mounts his expertly tooled, professionally handcrafted machine and rides for one hour around a banked, velodrome racetrack. At the end of the hour, the distance is measured. In the past this record, like all records, had traded hands many times. Before the historic 1972 record-setting date, Danish rider Ole Ritter became the first to use the new Olympic track in Mexico City, where he shattered the long-standing 30-mile barrier with a ride of 48.653 kilometers, or 30.23 miles. It was a feat of which he was justifiably proud.

On this October day in 1972 the great Belgian rider Eddy Merckx said he would break that record. Though he had already won international acclaim as the greatest rider who ever lived, had won the prestigious Tour de France five times, and was the triumphant champion of countless

Eddy Merckx, considered by all to be the greatest cyclist in history, found the psych in cycling in his victory in the 1974 World Championships in Montreal.

single-day classics, when he flashed 49.408 kilometers around the track in the allotted one hour he called it the greatest victory of his career.

Why would a superstar of so many conquests and accomplishments consider this particular event his greatest?

In July 1981 the unbelievable occurred. The 11-day barrier for traversing the United States by bicycle was crossed. When John Marino set the record in 1978 his time of 13 days, 1 hour, and 20 minutes was said to be unbeatable. But for Lon Haldeman of Harvard, Illinois, *unbeatable* was the wrong word to use. Upon hearing the news he endeavored to destroy that record and eventually set two others in the process.

In June 1981 Lon left New York City Hall in the cool, quiet hours of the early morning. His goal was to ride to Los Angeles in 12 days, then turn around and ride back to New York to break Marino's record and beat the 11-day barrier. Lon arrived in Los Angeles 12 days, 18 hours after leaving New York. After a couple of hours of rest he turned around and headed back for New York. Few people imagined that, having just ridden 3,000 miles, Lon could go on to beat Marino's time. But Lon had discovered the "psych" in cycling, and 10 days, 23 hours, 27 minutes later he sat down on the steps of New York City Hall, a little more than 24 days after he had left.

Three world records in one month. Could Lon's 10-day mark ever be bettered? Under the pressures of competition, could human beings push themselves beyond the known limits?

On August 4, 1982, four men set out to discover the limits of human endurance. Lon Haldeman, John Howard, John Marino, and I lined up for the first annual Great American Bike Race from Los Angeles to New York. Three of the four of us broke Haldeman's 1981 record, and Haldeman himself broke the 10-day barrier with an incredible time of 9 days, 20 hours, 2 minutes.

There have now been three transcontinental bike races, and a new world record of 9 days, 13 hours has been set by Pete Penseyres. What are the limits of human endurance? What motivates individuals to excel beyond the expected?

In any endeavor of the human experience there are certain individuals who rise above all others. They are, whether anyone likes it or not, sui generis: irrevocably, indubitably, intransigently individual. They simply do not care about popular opinion. They refuse to adopt current standards and norms.

The "psych" in cycling, like the "psych" to be found in any human endeavor, is that inner drive that causes an individual to strive beyond defined barriers, past previous limits, and through mental boundaries. Psych is the element that tips the scale in favor of the person who refuses to accept approximations and inexactitudes. It may be found in those who excel solely for the sake of being the best.

Sport Cycling reaches into the psychological realm behind the spinning cranks. The book shows how the principles of success in riding across the United States are the same principles that apply in riding across town. Whether you are pedaling 30, 300, or 3,000 miles, the processes of setting and attaining goals are identical.

Sport Cycling is also a guide to training, racing, and endurance. It covers the practical aspects of cycling—training for endurance events,

PHOTO BY STEVE ESSIG

There are few people with whom I share the unique relationship of competitors, business partners, and friends. On the bikes we can be fiercely competitive, yet off the bikes there is no one I trust more than these two gentlemen, John Marino and Lon Haldeman.

beginning a training program, being comfortable on a bike, understanding gearing systems for racing and touring, weight training, self-massage, stretching, and equipping yourself for both training and endurance rides. The program of training outlined here is applicable to any cyclists, from novice to professional.

Finally, *Sport Cycling* is the accumulation of six years and over 100,000 miles of training and racing experience in endurance cycling, culminating in this work. I have given a firsthand account of all the major rides I have completed, including the Great American Bike Race, the Race Across AMerica, the Seattle-to-San Diego Challenge, the Miami-to-Maine Challenge, the Ironman Triathlon, and the Spenco 500. I relate these events not merely as a travelogue and a history of ultra-marathon cycling, but also to enlighten the reader on the finer points of racing, both physical and psychological.

This book covers what I have learned about the sport of cycling and all of my experiences as a sports psychologist. I recommend nothing that I haven't experimented with myself. When I was a novice and looking for information on how to excel in my sport I sought out the experts and professionals—John Marino, John Howard, Lon Haldeman, and Jock Boyer. I read as much material on the sport as I could find and asked as many questions as my mentors would answer.

One of the greatest scientific minds in history, Sir Isaac Newton, once responded to accolades showered upon him for his work in the field of physics with these words: "If I have been able to see further than others it is by standing upon the shoulders of giants."

I have spent the last six years climbing onto the shoulders of giants such as those mentioned above. I have tried to use their experiences and knowledge to help myself reach higher levels of excellence. I shall receive the greatest satisfaction from this book in knowing that readers can take my experiences and knowledge and use them for their benefit in search of their own excellence.

2
THE IMPOSSIBLE
TAKES A
LITTLE LONGER

*"The difficult you can do right away;
the impossible takes a little longer."*

This proverb was given to me by Harley Phillips, a Hutchinson, Kansas, bike dealer, as I reached the halfway point across the United States during the Great American Bike Race.

For me, the impossible took just five days longer. As I wheeled my bicycle the final 100 feet to the finish line in front of the Empire State Building the clock read 10 days, 19 hours, 54 minutes. I had done the "impossible." I had accomplished my goal of breaking all previous United States transcontinental records. Unfortunately, so did two others ahead of me, Lon Haldeman and John Howard.

Reaching New York in record time was the final goal, the ultimate challenge. To reach that end, many smaller goals had to be set.

The principle behind setting and breaking world records is the same one behind accomplishing all tasks and feats in life—setting goals. The difficult ordeals are the small individual goals. The impossible is that ultimate goal. By setting a mark to aim for, you make realization of that goal possible.

For decades the four-minute mile stood like the impenetrable wall of an English castle—a physical barrier beyond the limits of human capacity. On May 6, 1954, however, the wall came tumbling down when a young man from England named Roger Bannister ran a remarkable 3-

John Marino, the man who set the example for me of how to set a goal and achieve it.

PHOTO BY DAVE NELSON

minute, 59.4-second mile. More significant, however, were the events following Bannister's record. *Many* people shattered the physical four-minute barrier, and the mile record continued to drop to the point where today the record ownership swaps hands so often that the record books are obsolete by the time they reach the shelves.

It was soon realized that the four-minute mile was a mental barrier rather than a physical one. Once people realize that a particular goal is attainable, the door is flung wide open to whatever limits they set for themselves.

The evolution of the marathon run exemplifies this point. The first marathon occurred in 490 B.C. when a runner was dispatched to carry the news of victory at Marathon to the city of Athens, 26 miles away. Upon delivering the message, he promptly collapsed and died. Many marathon runners wish he had collapsed at the 20-mile mark, thus shortening their agony 2,300 years later.

It wasn't long ago that running a marathon was considered an amazing feat reserved only for the incredibly fit. Only a handful could finish. Yet in 1984 over 16,000 people competed in the New York Marathon, with over 14,000 successfully completing it!

In 1978 on the island of Oahu, Hawaii, seven men got together after a barroom challenge to put together an unusual event they entitled the *triathlon*. They would swim 2.4 miles in rough open water, bicycle 112 miles around the island, and then run 26 miles, 385 yards, nonstop, with no specified break time in between. All seven finished. They were called *ironmen*. They deserved it.

Since that first triathlon the event has grown from 12 competitors in 1979 to 99 in 1980, 333 in 1981, and over 900 in 1982. Today the limit is 1,500, and applications by the dozens are being turned down daily. What can account for this phenomenal growth?

When ABC's "Wide World of Sports" aired the 1980 triathlon, people realized that this was an attainable goal since they were witnessing others successfully completing it. Today triathlons dot the landscape worldwide, including a United States series, an Australian world championship, and many European and Asian versions.

That records were made to be broken is a trite but true comment on the nature of goal setting. In March 1972 a European cyclist named Peter Duker came to the United States to see how long it would take to cross the country by bicycle. Eighteen days, 2 hours, and 30 minutes later, averaging 165 miles per day, Peter Duker became the first official record holder for the United States transcontinental. Twelve years later that record was virtually cut in half as Pete Penseyres raced across in a remarkable 9 days, 13 hours, averaging over 310 miles per day. Appendix IV at the end of this book traces the United States transcontinental record over the last 12 years.

Whenever I train for an athletic event, whether it is the Race Across AMerica, the Seattle-to-San Diego Challenge, or a triathlon, I use the "backward" approach to goal setting. I count backward from the scheduled time of the event to the day I will begin training, calculating how much time I have and how much progress I want to make. For the 1984 Race Across AMerica my goal was to ride over 300 miles a day, every day, for nine days. The race was scheduled to begin August 19, 1984. I began my serious training in March, allowing five months to build up to triple centuries. I started with 25-mile rides, then 50-mile rides, progressing to 100, 150, 200, 250, and finally 300 miles in one day. As each distance is mastered, it becomes natural to be able to cover it at any time. If you have mastered the century ride, then 50 miles is easy, 100 miles is natural, and 150 miles is challenging. The more miles ridden, the easier it becomes.

The same logic applies to triathlons, whatever the distances. Let us assume you are training for the October Hawaii Ironman Triathlon. The bicycling part of this three sport contest is a 112-mile race. Count backward from the October starting date to the date you are to begin your training, giving yourself a progression of weekly increases. By the time of the race you will already have done enough 112-mile bike rides to be physically and psychologically comfortable with the distance. Like a boxer with a repertoire of different punches and moves that come naturally to him, cranking out a 112-mile bike ride should feel natural to you.

This principle applies to the swimming and running events as well. You should have swum 2.4 miles in the ocean and run at least one marathon before the main event. My own failure to apply this principle to running was a major downfall for me in the 1981 Ironman Triathlon. Climbing out of the ocean in 189th place, I passed over 150 cyclists, only to reach the running portion, having never before run more than 13 miles in one day. I felt psychologically baffled. I had no idea what to expect. Would my muscles cramp? Would I have to walk? Could I even finish?

These worrisome thoughts alone were enough to prevent an efficient performance. In fact, being so unprepared for the run, I found many of the same 150 people passing me in the end.

If you apply these principles of training, you will have a psychological edge before the race even begins. In the triathlon, for instance, you will already know you can complete the required swim, bike ride, and run because you will already have done so in training. Then it becomes just a question of how fast you can complete it.

WRITE DOWN THE GOAL

Writing down the goal of accomplishing whatever task you have set for yourself restructures your thinking from "I wonder if I can accomplish it" to "I wonder how long it will take me." Having the goal written down in front of you drives you beyond your present limits and is half the battle in accomplishing it. The higher you set your goals, the greater your acccomplishments. Whether it's a world record, a triathlon, making money, or getting high grades in school, the higher you aim, the further you will go. If you aim for straight As, for instance, you will perform at a much higher level than if the goal were Bs. Even if you fall short of the goal and finish with one B and several As, you've still accomplished a lot more than you would have with a lesser goal.

PHOTO BY DAVE NELSON

When your goal is a monumental one, select smaller goals along the way that lead unwaveringly toward that ultimate goal.

The actual process of writing down your goals can have an almost magical effect on reaching them. By way of analogy, when you go to the supermarket without a shopping list, you inevitably forget a few items you wanted. When you shop with a list, however, you efficiently collect everything included on the list as well as other products. This is how accomplishing goals works. If you write them down, you'll get everything on the list and then some!

You can have more than one list as well. For instance, I have a list of major goals I would like to accomplish over the next several years. To reach those goals I then make a list of smaller goals for the year that will help me reach those further down the line. I then break the year up into months and make a list of what needs to be done in each particular month in order to attain the yearly goals. I also carry a pad of paper with a list of things to do every day in order to arrive at the long-range objectives.

An example of this chain of events in my life might look like this:

LONG-RANGE GOALS

1. Establish the Race Across AMerica (RAAM) as a major sporting event in the world, on a par with Wimbledon, the Indianapolis 500, the Super Bowl, the World Series, and the Tour de France.

2. Make the Race Across AMerica a profitable company.

3. Win the Race Across AMerica.

4. Write and publish several books on cycling and motivation.

5. Open a chain of Shermer Cycles bike and fitness shops.

YEARLY GOALS

1. Build the RAAM's publicity in markets other than cycling.

2. Build a strong women's field in the RAAM.

3. Win the RAAM.

4. Win the Spenco 500.

5. Write and publish this book.

6. Begin research on future books.

7. Increase sponsorship for both RAAM and myself.

8. Continue part-time career as a college professor in psychology and biology.

9. Develop a new course in astronomy.

10. Open another Shermer Cycles of America.

MONTHLY GOALS

1. Ride 1,500 to 2,000 miles.
2. Run three days a week with dog "Patton" in local hills.
3. Swim three days a week to build strength in upper body and neck.
4. Write four chapters in this book.
5. Give one or two talks.
6. Maintain contact with sponsors for product design, marketing, future sponsorship ideas, and personal relations.
7. Lead Shermer Cycles Century Club ride.
8. Work one day a week at Shermer Cycles.
9. Teach classes Tuesday and Thursday mornings and Tuesday evening.
10. Read one book.

DAILY GOALS

1. Run five miles with Patton.
2. Work on chapter for book.
3. Swim one mile.
4. Call Dr. Spence of Spenco re other sponsorship ideas.
5. Contact Lon Haldeman re ultra-marathon cycling clinic.
6. Ride two to three hours, including group ride at Griffith Park.
7. Give lecture in evening to psychology class.
8. Read current bike magazines and/or book.
9. Play time.

The last goal on this list is a subjective one that is determined by time and each individual's need for play time. No matter how ambitious you are, the value of play time cannot be overlooked. My mentor in college and the man who contributed a great deal to my teaching career, Dr.

Richard Hardison, taught me to work hard and play hard. After working feverishly for five straight hours at the college, lecturing, writing his book, writing computer programs, and planning his next summer expedition around the world, Dick would depart in a whirlwind flash, declaring, "I'm off to play hard!"

Hardison would then rush to the golf course to play a round or two, or to the tennis courts for five or six sets of tennis, and then home to spend time with his wife and friends. Not content with just a brilliant academic career, Dick became an excellent golfer, shooting below par on any given day on some of the toughest courses around the world.

Even toward the end of his career, Dick showed no signs of slowing down. Only two years before his retirement, he took his sabbatical leave. While most professors would use this as an opportunity to travel or just to waste time, Dick took courses at UCLA in computer programming, then returned to Glendale College the following year to write programmed learning courses for astronomy, psychology and economics. Finally, in his last year of teaching, when most would be content to drift until the fun begins, Hardison wrote a book entitled *Upon The Shoulders Of Giants* about the most influential people in history. He then designed a course based on the book, which he and I taught in his final semester.

Did retirement slow him down? Not at all. Three months after I last saw Dick, in June 1984, I received a newspaper clipping from the big island of Hawaii, with a short note attached which read, "Mike—hardly up to your feats of endurance, but . . ."

Just for kicks, Dick Hardison blazed through 236 holes of non-stop golf on July 31, 1984, from 6:00 A.M. to 6:00 P.M. on a regulation-size course at Punalu'u. He averaged 55 minutes per 18 holes, with an average score of 76, only 4 strokes above par! Most people take four to five hours to play 18 holes, and to shoot nearly par under such frantic conditions is incredible. To top it off he shot an unbelievable 4-under-par 68 in just 50 minutes in the second round, with a near miraculous score of 30 in just 24½ minutes on the back side. Very few pros ever shoot a 30 in their careers, let alone in 24½ minutes.

The point is that setting goals properly, including goals that allow for play time, can lead to a very successful and happy life. If you have all the riches in the world and sacrificed your health, I feel you paid too high a price. If you have fame and notoriety but sacrificed family and friends, I think you paid too high a price. We know from psychological studies that free time, when combined in the correct proportions with work and stress, is healthy.

GOAL SETTING

Though the goals you set should be high, they should also be within the realm of physical, intellectual, and mental possibility. Should you select goals that are unattainable, frustration could lead to negative side effects and the inevitable demise of the goals.

There are two ways to win a race. You can be first across the line, or you can do your absolute best. When Vince Lombardi said, "Winning isn't everything; it's the only thing," he was correct, but it all depends on your definition of winning.

To win is to perform at the highest level you are capable of reaching, to use every resource available to you, to give 100 percent of your energy and effort to that task. If it so happens that someone else has also done this and his or her capabilities are higher than yours, then there is only one conclusion: you both won. Your opponent just happened to cross the line ahead of you. Your respect for that person, and for yourself, should be elevated.

POSSIBILITY THINKING

Whether by the natural evolution of change or by careful design and planning, schools, colleges, unions, governments, and other bureaucracies tend to stifle creativity and "possibility thinking" in individuals.

It is refreshing to listen to children tell of their dreams—of whom they want to be, what they want to do, and where they want to go when they grow up. Their minds are fresh and open, not yet tainted by the "reality thinkers" of the adult world. Children's minds are creative, idealistic, and filled with possibilities of how the world should be and can be. Then, as Western culture dictates and reality thinkers demand, children are directed in their thinking: "No, that is the wrong way to do it." "No, that is not how to draw a building; this is how it should look." "Let me show you how it is done properly."

Fortunately, not everyone succumbs to reality thinking. At the turn of the century, two possibility thinkers working in a bicycle shop in Dayton, Ohio, refused to accept the known limits of the Victorian Age. They weren't educated men; neither had even finished high school. But when Wilbur and Orville Wright braced themselves against the stiff wind on that cold December morning in 1903, they saw a possibility become a reality. Orville positioned himself on the wing of the flying contraption they had built in their shop and, with Wilbur sprinting alongside, felt the craft lift off the ground and into the sky. For an invigorating 12 seconds, they defied gravity, reality, and the stifling concept of impossibility.

3
ON MENTAL FITNESS

"Man's mind stretched to a new idea never goes back to its original dimension."

Oliver Wendell Holmes

Setting goals is only the first step toward success. Accomplishing these goals is equally necessary for progression. To make anything work, you must want it to happen. The mind directs the body. Control the mind, and you control the body.

In preparation for the 1981 Seattle-to-San Diego bicycle challenge, I realized that strictly physical training wasn't sufficient to attain the average speed of 300 miles per day that I had set as my goal. I would have to condition my mind as well as my body for the arduous task that lay ahead. To accomplish this task, I attended one of the most enlightening courses in my academic career, a class entitled *Voluntary Controls Of Internal States*, by Jack Schwarz.

This course, a weekend seminar held in Klamath Falls, Oregon, was intended to teach the principles of mind control through meditation. It also taught that one can learn to control voluntarily such bodily functions as pulse rate, blood pressure, pain, fatigue, and even bleeding.

In a dramatic demonstration of control over his circulatory system, Jack took a rather large and corroded knitting needle, and while talking in a casual conversational style, proceeded to push the needle through the inside of the bicep of his left arm until it emerged on the other side, with absolutely no sign of pain or bleeding. Even more incredible, upon the removal of the needle, the two holes sealed themselves without a trace of blood, much to the amazement of an observer who tried to "wring" blood out of the arm.

Mind control is a skill and, like any skill, it can be improved through practice. A friend of mine, Bernie Landes, who served as my nutritionist during the 1983 Race Across AMerica, took a class in order to learn how to walk on hot coals.

The name of the course is "The Mind Revolution," taught by Anthony Robbins through the Robbins Research Institute in Beverly Hills, California. The purpose of the course is to teach mind control by mentally stretching you beyond your present limits and expectations. The entire class dramatically demonstrates this at the end of the course by walking barefoot across red-hot coals, with Robbins at the head of the procession!

In Robbin's own words, "The firewalk is a metaphor. What I'm really here to teach people is a series of very specific skills to break through any limitations they have created in their lives. Fear of failure, fear of success, rejection, or public speaking—what the fear is doesn't matter. I teach people to change the way they feel about themselves and how to operate effectively in their worlds."

Bernie Landes is an intelligent, skeptical man who is not prone to such extremes of behavior as fire-walking. Yet, in one short weekend course he successfully gained control over his body through his mind and walked across the coals, incurring absolutely no damage.

How does mind control work? The answer lies in what psychologists call *altered states of consciousness.*

Altered states of consciousness can be reached without sleeping. When an awake person closes his eyes and relaxes, for instance, his brain waves characteristically show a slow, regular pattern of *alpha waves* or *alpha rhythms.*

There have been many biofeedback experiments showing how control of autonomic functions can be learned. For example, it is possible to change the blood distribution in the two hands so that the temperature in one hand is increased and the other decreased. Oxygen consumption and carbon dioxide elimination can also be controlled by meditation in the alpha state.

Learning to control internal bodily processes such as pulse, respiration, blood pressure, or even bleeding and pain is not a skill restricted to yogis and mystics. Anyone can learn to control his or her state of consciousness, most commonly through hypnosis, meditation, or a process called *visualization.*

This involves distracting or detaching the mind from the body by visualizing something other than the pain. When the body experiences pain or fatigue it sends messages to the brain indicating the state of affairs. If you ignore these messages or distract the mind so that the message is blocked, the pain disappears.

I use this technique during my ultra-marathon bicycle races, when my body undergoes tremendous pain and fatigue for long periods of time. To be competitive, I have to ride 20–22 hours per day, for 9–10 consecutive days. There is ample time for thinking, daydreaming, visualization, or any other mental activity. Imagine staying awake for 220 out of 240 hours with nothing to do but think and pedal. Whether the competitors realize it or not, they all use various forms of visualization to deal with the pain and fatigue.

I might visualize myself in another location, perhaps a pleasant scene where I am comfortable and without pain. This process is greatly enhanced by the use of a portable stereo cassette player. Listening to music can be either relaxing or invigorating, depending on the style of the music, and has the effect of filling the mind with enough stimulation that messages of pain and fatigue are diminished or blocked.

I would estimate that during the Race Across AMerica I listen to music 10–12 hours per day. In addition to music, during the Great American Bike Race I took an entire course in archaeology on tape. During the 1983 RAAM I studied astronomy and U.S. history. In order to concentrate on the lecture material, I had to block other incoming stimuli such as pain.

During those hours of listening and visualization, the time passed peacefully until I suddenly realized that my feet, hands, or rear no longer hurt. In fact, much to my dismay, this realization renewed my perception of the pain.

Visualization of a goal makes it that much more attainable. Regardless of what goal one chooses—a world record, straight As in school, or even making money—visualization assists in the realization of that goal. In the RAAM I had a general visualization of the ultimate goal: Atlantic City, New Jersey.

With the starting line 3,000 miles away in Los Angeles, however, that goal becomes a little overwhelming. Consequently, I chose smaller geographic goals along the way, such as crossing the Mojave Desert or the Rocky Mountains. State borders and small towns each become a goal in and of itself.

Visualization also creates possibilities never before considered. In 1981, before my first Seattle-to–San Diego record was reduced from 7 days, 8 hours, to 4 days, 22 hours, I had planned to attempt the ride again, this time in fewer than 6 days. When I heard about the new record I was shocked but determined to come up with a way to cover the distance even faster. Thus, the process of visualizing a 4½-day record forced me to devise new ways to cut down on time—less sleep, shorter breaks, eating while riding, and more self-discipline. Had I not visualized the new record, I wouldn't have created the circumstances to make such a new record possible.

John Marino used an interesting twist on this process in his transcontinental bike trips. John visualized a "workshop," a hypothetical place where he could go for rejuvenation when fatigue set in.

While riding the bike, John would visualize himself in this workshop. As weariness and exhaustion worked their way to the surface, John looked into his "mirror of reality," where he could visualize a perfect body—every muscle toned and nourished and every organ in excellent working order.

When his legs got tired John would visualize blood rushing to them for energy. When he became extremely exhausted, almost to the point of collapse, John would envision himself on a table in the workshop with a team of the world's best doctors working on his body, replacing organs, revamping muscles, and refurbishing the body to perfection. "This visualization helped tremendously," John recalled after his 1980 record-setting ride. "I would think nothing but positive thoughts about my body."

Immediately before the 1982 Great American Bike Race I underwent hypnosis training from a professional hypnotherapist named Gina Kuras. In order to fill my mind with positive, victorious thoughts, she employed a unique visualization process in which she had me, while hypnotized, picture myself on a television screen riding my bike. As an objective observer of myself on the screen, I could easily see how I could successfully climb any hill, cross the desert regardless of the heat, ride through rain, headwinds, crosswinds, or traffic without fear or failure.

The examples of feats accomplished by people in alpha states are numerous. Even certain factions of the medical profession have turned to altered states of consciousness for cures.

HOW TO ALTER YOUR STATE OF CONSCIOUSNESS

For those who have never experienced an altered state of consciousness, or at least were not aware that they did, there are two means by which the alpha state can be reached.

PHOTO BY JONI MARINO

The "father of ultra-marathon cycling," John Marino started it all in 1978 with his first transcontinental crossing. He has currently suspended his racing career (after four crossings) in order to devote his energy to serving as executive director for the Race Across AMerica.

The first is a progressive relaxation technique. Find a comfortable position in an easy chair or a couch where your legs, arms, and head are supported. Close your eyes and begin breathing deeply. Notice the tension throughout your body. Focus on the muscles in your legs, arms, and back. Some or many may be tensed without your awareness. This is particularly noticeable after a day at work.

Now, beginning with your toes and working your way up through the feet and legs, concentrate on making all the muscles relax. Repeat "relax" to yourself several times. If it does not seem like the muscles are relaxing, try contracting them first. Squeeze your toes down toward the balls of your feet. Then relax and repeat the word "relax" several more times.

Using this method, work your way up through the legs, torso, arms, shoulders, neck, and head until you feel completely relaxed. At this point you are in an alpha state, unless you have fallen asleep. Begin concentrating on whatever goal you are aiming for. Picture yourself reaching that goal over and over again. Think of victory and tell yourself: "I can do it, I can do it."

This method would be particularly useful immediately prior to the challenge at hand. Typically, you would be somewhat tense beforehand, so this would help alleviate any complications arising from that tension and anxiety.

The visualization process was used quite extensively by the United States Olympic ski team during the 1984 Winter Olympics. ABC Sports showed members of the team sitting at the top of the ski run moments before they were to race down the hill. They were sitting with their eyes closed and their hands moving back and forth in front of them. The commentator then explained that the skiers were using a visualization technique in which they would picture themselves skiing down the slopes, successfully negotiating each and every turn. When it came time to race they had already done it in their minds, so it just became a matter of carrying it out physically.

Thought always precedes action. When you turn a page in this book the muscular contractions and relaxations that occur in sequence originate in the brain. Neurons are firing and sending their electrochemical messages to the muscles. To visualize a muscular movement before making it can only enhance the process of actually moving the muscle.

We know from research in physiological psychology that the brain is a package of billions of individual cells called *neurons*, which communicate with one another chemically via connections called *synapses*. The more synaptic connections, the more communication between cells is made possible. A thought may arise in the cortex of the brain, ordering a deeper breath to be taken. This message is sent chemically to the brain stem, where there is a synaptic connection with another neuron. This connection takes the message and sends it chemically down to the muscles in the chest to order a stronger contraction of the muscles, thus causing inhalation of extra air.

All communication depends on these synapses. Since thought always precedes action, and all thought is produced by neurological synaptic connections, there must be a physiological change that occurs when you learn something new.

In fact, this physically takes the form of new synaptic connections growing between existing nerve cells. The more you practice a new skill, the stronger those connections become. Practice, then, does indeed make perfect. Experimental evidence supports this.

Rats that were raised in enriched environments exhibited brains that were far denser in synaptic connections than rats raised in impoverished environments. The enriched environment provided much external stimuli, thus there was a need for more communication between the nerve cells.

This phenomenon also has a reverse effect. When you do not practice a learned skill, the synaptic connections actually atrophy. If you neglect to practice for long enough, the connections may disappear completely. This may explain how and why we forget.

Kittens that were raised in rooms painted with horizontal stripes and were deprived of ever seeing "verticalness," actually became blind to seeing vertical objects in the natural environment. When put into a room to walk around, the kittens would bump into table legs because they simply did not see them.

Your thoughts, which control your actions, can be controlled, strengthened, and molded into almost any shape you would like. The more you practice a skill, the stronger the synaptic connections become. Practicing a task or movement in your mind does help to later translate that thought into muscular movement. The brain, like the body, must be used and exercised, or it will, like an unused muscle, atrophy.

ENDORPHINS: THE MIND DRUG

In the past few decades there has been a trend in academic circles to overlap fields of study, and in recent years biologists and physiologists have stepped into the field of psychology to create psychobiology. These psychobiologists search for the physiological correlates of behavior discussed above.

One of the most startling finds in recent years was the discovery of a morphinelike drug, produced naturally by the brain, called *endorphins*. Endorphins are released during emotionally arousing situations when a person experiences aggression, fright, sex, pain, or fatigue. Endorphins act as an anesthesia in relieving pain, and it was recently found that people who suffer chronic pain have very low concentrations of endorphins. It was also recently revealed that people diagnosed as having depression have low levels of endorphins. Similarly, when someone is excited, elated, or aroused, endorphin production is increased, resulting in a corresponding elevation of mood.

Endorphin levels have also been tested in hypnotized subjects in various situations. In one, the subject is told that when he places his hand over a flame no pain will be experienced. Indeed, it is not only a painless experience, but no tissue damage occurs, and endorphin levels increase. When I underwent hypnosis with Gina and she had me visualize climbing a hill successfully, crossing 120-degree deserts, or winning the entire race, the charge of elation that I felt was probably due to an increase in endorphins.

Thus, endorphins are directly related to psychological experiences such as depression, elation, and the blocking of pain. Endorphins can also be connected to the principle of placebos. A placebo is a harmless, noneffective substance that, when administered as "medicine" to a subject with a particular complaint, frequently has an effect. Recent studies involving the administration of placebos for pain relief, followed · by testing for endorphins, showed that pain was relieved and endorphin levels increased in some of the subjects. This implies that just the thought of pain relief can actually produce the painkilling endorphins.

CYCLING AND STRESS

Few people would argue with the statement that stress is a negative element in our lives. Both psychologists and physicians spend a great deal of money and time researching the effects of stress. Research shows that excess stress can cause ulcers, high blood pressure, asthma and an assortment of other diseases. Psychologists show how too much stress can hinder performance, lead to the breakdown of normal social functioning, and even cause mental disorders.

A number of years ago a classic study, known as the "executive monkey syndrome," was conducted in the field of stress psychology. Two monkeys were strapped to chairs side-by-side and attached to electrodes that could deliver a mildly painful shock. A light would come on, followed by a mild shock a few seconds later. However, one monkey, the "executive" monkey, had the opportunity to avoid the shock for both monkeys by flipping a switch after the light came on and before the shock was delivered. In other words, the executive monkey was the decision maker for both monkeys, while the other had to depend on the skill and reliability of the executive. Which position would you prefer?

The executive monkey developed ulcers, nervous disorders, abnormal feeding and mating behavior, and died at an earlier age than the dependent monkey. The researchers concluded that the executive monkey was under psychological pressure to be responsible for avoiding the shock for both monkeys. This excessive stress, with little or no time for rest, produced the same symptoms we observe in today's business executive.

It's important to realize, however, that certain factors that come into play can change the negative results of stress. In fact, in some instances stress itself is not necessarily bad, and a certain amount of stress is unavoidable in the everyday world. The curve in the graph on the following page shows the hypothetical relationship between level of stress

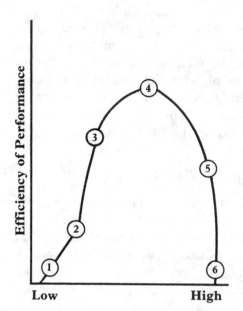

1. Deep sleep

2. Point of waking

3. Increased alertness

4. Optimal level

5. Increasing emotional disturbance

6. Disorganization

arousal and efficiency of performance. It can be seen that a certain amount of stress, somewhere between low and high, leads to an optimal level of performance efficiency.

Many psychologists go so far as to say that, not only do we need a certain amount of stress, but most of us strive to find it! Dr. Howard A. Rusk has noted:

"Stress is really an integral part of life. We set our pattern of life by our stress end point. If we hit it exactly, we live dynamic, purposeful, useful, happy lives. If we go over, we break. If we stay too far under, we vegetate."

When you think about it, many of the fun things in life do involve a certain amount of stress. This is part of the fun. Skiing, for instance, has an element of danger. You could fall and break a leg or suffer frostbite. In fact, the tremendous popularity of skiing gives testimony to our need for stress.

Most of us tend to choose situations that will provide enough stress to make the task interesting but not so stressful as to cause physical or psychological problems. The most enjoyable tennis games, for example, are those played against opponents who are equal to or better than yourself. There is that built-in element of suspense, wondering if this will be the time you finally win. When victory does come, it is quite a satisfying feeling. Either extreme of stress would be mentally destructive. An opponent who is too easy to beat would lead to boredom, one too difficult would leave you with a feeling of total frustration.

It seems we are all striving to reach a balance in life whereby all needs are met and there are no problems to overcome. Yet in this scenario there is but one possible outcome—boredom.

Insurance statistics reveal that the probability of living a long life is greatly reduced for men who retire promptly, compared to men who continue working long past the retirement age of 65. Psychologists speculate that when a man retires he is transported from an active, intellectually stimulating working environment filled with problems, challenges, crises, and rewards to a "utopia" of retirement: money in the bank, free time, and no problems. The result is boredom.

The evidence leads to the conclusion that one must maintain both physical and mental fitness in order to be truly healthy. Concentration on either extreme leads to an excess on one side and a deprivation on the other.

AUTOGENERATIONAL ACQUISITION THEORY

Gordon Smith is an individual who has utilized to the fullest the capacities of both mind and body. While in the Marines, Gordon Smith set the intermilitary Marine Corps record for the most push-ups in 1½ hours—2,010. He is a concert pianist; speaks numerous languages, which he learns in an average of four to six weeks; and went through the UCLA undergraduate program with a 4.0 grade point average.

Clearly, Smith is a genius. However, he attributes his spectacular accomplishments to a positive mental attitude that he developed through his Autogenerational Acquisition Theory, literally translated as knowledge gained through a self-generating process. Smith has taught courses for individuals who wanted to improve themselves both mentally and physically. John Marino took Smith's course before his first transcontinental bicycle attempt in 1978.

Basically, Smith's position is that thoughts range on a continuum from positive to negative. He labels positive mental attitude as *attitudinal expectancy*, or *AE*. Negative attitudes are known as *attitudinal deprivation*, or *AD*.

When you set out to accomplish something, you should always expect success. Think success and expect results. This is attitudinal expectancy. Setbacks will, of course, occur, but these should be looked upon as learning experiences. For instance, taking the wrong route when driving is not necessarily a mistake that should be considered negative. It shows which way not to go, and you never have to consider that direction again.

Smith outlines several methods for increasing AE and decreasing AD. He uses what he calls *alpha tapes*. They are motivational tapes to remind you that you can accomplish anything and that you can achieve your goal. Smith recommends making these tapes yourself. Sit down and record such positive thoughts as "I can do anything"; "There are no limits to my capabilities"; "I can attain all of my goals."

Marino tried this method when he trained for the 1978 transcontinental trip. "One night I strapped a tape recorder to my back with the microphone attached to my jersey and recorded what I felt as I rode around a one-mile course. I rode around and around until fatigue set in. The more fatigued I became, the more often I repeated, 'I can do it, I can do it.' I recorded whatever came out. I tried to visualize New York City Hall and kept telling myself that I could make it. I got so emotional that I almost started crying right there on the bike!"

The advantage of this method emerges when listening to the tape later. "One day I really felt fatigued," John recalled. "So I played the tape back, and it pumped me up."

Marino extends this principle even further when he recommends the tape recorder as an aid to all activities. "I think that whenever you feel good you should sit down and record all the great things you do and have done in your life. That way, whenever you get down, just play the tapes back and they can really motivate you to great heights."

Smith also suggests reading passages from inspirational books that you feel will motivate you. We all have read a quotation or passage from a book that has moved us. Record those passages on tape and listen to them later when that extra push is needed. Two come to mind that I have called upon for that extra lift:

From Teddy Roosevelt:
   Far better it is to dare mighty things, to win glorious triumphs, even though checkered by failure, than to take rank with those poor spirits who neither enjoy much nor suffer much, because they live in the gray twilight that knows not victory nor defeat.

From Ayn Rand's *Atlas Shrugged:*
   In the name of the best within you, do not sacrifice this world to those who are its worst. In the name of the values that keep you alive, do not let your vision of man be distorted by the ugly, the cowardly, the mindless in those who have never achieved his title. Do not lose your knowledge that

man's proper estate is an upright posture, an intransigent mind and a step that travels unlimited roads. Do not let your fire go out, spark by irreplaceable spark, in the hopeless swamps of the approximate, the not-quite, the not-yet, the not-at-all. Do not let the hero in your soul perish, in lonely frustration for the life you deserved, but have never been able to reach. Check your road and the nature of your battle. The world you desire can be won, it exists, it is real, it is possible, it is yours.

In addition to alpha tapes, Smith suggests the development of a pseudoenvironment. Unlike Marino's hypothetical workshop, this should be an actual room or a place where you can go that has physical artifacts reminding you of the specific goals you have set. For instance, when Smith began to learn a language, such as French, he would fill a room, his pseudoenvironment, with French posters, French books, and French music playing in the background.

If a century ride is your goal, put up signs in the designated room, saying "100 miles" or "I can ride 100 miles." Put up posters of heroes who have accomplished great tasks to spur you on to greater motivation. If you have trophies and awards, put them in the room to remind you of the things you have accomplished. In short, the pseudoenvironment is your place to go to concentrate on your goals and focus on accomplishing them.

Before the Great American Bike Race I set up such a room. I had posters of two of cycling's greatest heros: Eddy Merckx and Bernard Hinault. In addition, I put up posters of my competitors: Lon Haldeman, John Howard, and John Marino. I set these up on the wall facing my rollers and stationary bike so that I could stare at them and concentrate on beating them mentally as the sweat was pouring down my face and fatigue was burrowing in. During the race itself, this all came back to me, and I could feel that inner drive to win imprinted on my brain.

AUTOGENIC TRAINING

Gordon Smith's techniques have the effect of forcing positive thoughts or attitudinal expectancies into the mind so strongly that negative thoughts, or attitudinal deprivations, cannot enter. This technique was developed to the extreme in a process known as *autogenic training*, as developed by a man named Hans Linderman, a German athlete whose goal was to row a boat across the entire Atlantic Ocean. Imagine what a task this would be. The rower would have to keep the boat heading in the correct direction at all times, or he would never reach the destination. However, since sleep soon becomes a necessity, he would have to steer and sleep simultaneously.

Linderman learned to do this by means of autogenic training, or concentration and meditation on a single subject with so much intensity that nothing else can enter the mind.

"Keep going west," Linderman would repeat to himself. From this he learned to sleep while steering the boat with his foot.

Through a process similar to meditation and self-hypnosis, Linderman practiced his autogenic process across the Atlantic to a successful conclusion. He also forced positive thoughts into his mind: "I can do it, I can do it." His accomplishment proves the success of the method.

Whether he knew it or not, Muhammad Ali employed the same methods in boasting continually of his greatness. The best test of a method is its results, and Ali was certainly successful.

CYCLING AS PLAY

"All work and no play. . . ."

We have all heard that expression, and, like most clichés, it has a certain element of truth in it. Human beings need play. If looked at as being the opposite of work, play becomes an activity that is different from the normal routine of everyday life.

Cycling is a sport for everyone, even for the toughest guy in Hollywood—Mr. T.

PHOTO BY CHRISTA MORONES

People work for various reasons, such as money, reward, satisfaction, and the achievement of goals. Most people play for one reason: to receive a new form of stimulation that is different from and less stressful than the activity of work.

By this definition, play for one person may be work for another. Most professional athletes eventually find their sport to be a job that they have to go to in order to earn a living. It becomes work, and they engage in other activities when playing. Many of us engage in these very sports as our form of play.

The medical value of play has been documented by studies showing that the negative physical effects of stress could be prevented when stressful responsibility was relieved by periodic playtime.

For me, cycling has had the unique advantage of being both my work and my play. Being on a bicycle gives me the feeling of freedom. Alone on an open road, there is a beautiful interaction between man and machine; the body controls the bike, and it responds to every command. The bicycle does not pollute, litter, or clutter a landscape. To me seeing a bicycle nestled in a scenic landscape is a tribute to the interaction of the beauty of nature and the glory of man.

The psychological benefits of exercise as play are many. In addition to relieving stress and providing a feeling of freedom, cycling enhances mental concentration, acuity, and control.

Riding a bike is a long-term activity that can be simple and repetitious enough to clear the mind for lucid thinking. A long bike ride on an uncrowded country road leaves you to your thoughts. This is an opportune time to work out problems. Many a time I have had long talks with myself, discovering solutions to nagging problems while 50 miles out of town on a lonely highway.

Cycling also increases one's sense of self-worth. You are getting good exercise, improving the mind, accomplishing goals, and clearing thoughts. As self-worth increases, feelings of depression and anxiety tend to be eliminated. You cannot, at one and the same time, be both elated and depressed, satisfied and frustrated. If you are confident and in control, depression and anxiety have no place to rear up.

Cycling creates a feeling of oneness within. We typically think of the body and mind as separate entities. We are usually working at either improving our bodies or improving our minds. But the mind really is part of the body, and the body is part of the mind. The mind controls the body, but the body gives the mind an outlet. The senses are the mind's windows to the world. Without a body, the mind would be helpless and senseless.

Cycling creates a union between body and mind. They are functioning together and in unity. Racing down a hill at a good clip awakens all of the senses. The sights and smells from the environment, the wind blowing on the face, the smooth vibrations of the road below, and the beautiful hum of the chain as it propels one through time and space combine in a single unity of purpose to create a whole individual.

4
IN SEARCH OF SELF
DISCOVERING MOTIVATIONS AND CHANGING SELF-PERCEPTIONS

"Man does not hunt in order to have killed, he kills in order to have hunted."

Aristotle

MOTIVATION

Indubitably the most frequently asked question I hear in regard to ultra-marathon cycling is, "Why?" Why would anyone put himself through such an exhausting, traumatic experience of riding a bicycle 3,000 miles across the United States in 10 days or less?

An unusual answer to this question came to me during a talk at the University of Missouri with Lon Haldeman and John Marino, when the above quote from Aristotle sprang to mind from a psychology lecture I had given months before. I had used the quote in context with the topic of existentialism, a subject dealing with a person's purpose and meaning in life.

I suddenly realized that the theories on goal setting and striving to accomplish tasks are only partially correct. There is more to motivating a person than merely goals.

It isn't just the goal of the kill that motivates a person, it's the hunt, or what leads up to the kill that is the true motivator. In many ways, I suspect that the goals are an excuse for the act of conquest. It isn't just the glorious feeling of crossing the finish line—it's the process of training, organizing, and going through the experience that is so meaningful.

Setting a goal actually sets the stage for the process of the chase. Without a specific goal in mind, it becomes difficult to find motivation to continue with tasks that seem to be leading you nowhere. Just this morning in fact, I picked up the *Los Angeles Times* sports section and read the following headline: Wills Says Depression Had Him Near Death. Maury Wills, one of my childhood heroes, said that losing his position as Seattle Mariner manager three years ago pushed him into a state of depression that nearly cost him his life.

"I just went home to Los Angeles and locked myself up. I had no reason to go to bed at night and no reason in particular to wake up. It was devastating to be breathing, living and not have an objective or goal or principle in life."

The lack of a purpose led this once great professional baseball player into a state of near suicidal depression. How can this possibly happen? Yet this type of story is not at all uncommon. One of the most famous astronauts in U.S. history became an alcoholic upon retiring from the space program.

Even one of the most successful musicians in history, Paul McCartney from the Beatles, described in an interview in the December 1984 edition of *Playboy* magazine how devastated he was upon the breakup of the group:

"For the first time in my life, I was on the scrap heap, in my own eyes. An unemployed worker might have said, 'Hey, you still have the money. That's not as bad as we have it.' But to me, it didn't have anything to do with money. It was just the feeling, the terrible disappointment of not being of any use to anyone anymore. It was a barreling, empty feeling that just rolled across my soul, and it was . . . I'd never experienced it before. In this case, the end of the Beatles, I really was done in for the first time in my life."

To those who do not have it, money may seem like a motivator in life. But as McCartney explained:

"No, it isn't the money. It's doing well. And really, that's all I'm ever trying to do. I still like writing songs. It still gives me a thrill. If I had been asked at 15 why I wrote, I would have answered, 'Money.' But after a while, you realize that's not really your driving motive. When you get the money, you still need to keep going; you don't stop. There has to be something else. I think it's the freedom to do what you want and to live your dreams."

At any point in your life you can change the course of your destiny by changing your existence. You are constantly in the process of writing your own epitaph. What would you like it to say? As the motivation speaker Dr. Mark Victor Hansen noted, "If you want to know when you are done with your life's work—if you're still alive, you're not done!"

William Ernest Henley summed up this idea in the following excerpt from his poem Invictus:

> Out of the night that covers me,
>   Black as the pit from pole to pole,
> I thank whatever gods may be
>   For my unconquerable soul.
> It matters not how strait the gate,
>   How charged with punishments the scroll,
> I am the master of my fate:
>   I am the captain of my soul.

When I am in a bike race, nothing in the world is more important. I don't think about anything else, and the rest of life takes a back seat to the race. When the race is over, however, its importance is gone and the next day's activity takes over in its subjective purpose.

The renowned psychologist and philosopher Victor Frankel noted in his book on meaning in life that everyone must have a purpose for living, for if they don't, death becomes the imminent reality. Frankel's conclusions originate from years of study in a Nazi concentration camp of which he was an inmate for nearly the entire duration of World War II. He became interested in the personal and subjective meanings that the inmates created in order to stay alive.

Frankel discovered that it didn't really matter what their individual purposes were. As long as they had some sort of goal, it was enough to keep them alive. The people who simply gave up soon died.

The conclusion is that every man's meaning in life is as valid as the next. To create purpose is to create a fuller life.

Vince Scully, the Los Angeles Dodger's radio and television announcer, once related a story of an experience with the late great Jackie Robinson. They were about to go ice skating together when Robinson challenged him to a race. Even though Robinson had no experience in ice skating, he bet a steak dinner on the outcome. When they got on the ice Robinson could hardly stand, and of course, lost. Scully asked: "Why would you race me when you knew you were going to lose?" "Don't you understand?" Robinson replied. "It's the only way I'd be able to learn!"

Arthur C. Clark, author of *2001: A Space Odyssey,* wrote in a lesser known work, *Childhood's End,* that the enemy of all utopias is boredom. Humans need challenges and goals. Without them, what is the reason for living? Man kills in order to have hunted. It is the kill that gives the rest of his actions meaning and purpose.

As I sit here at my Apple II Plus word processing computer I am reminded of a story I read about the well-known *Los Angeles Times* columnist, Jack Smith, who was reflecting on how the computer has changed his life.

Before computers, Smith's daily routine consisted of driving down to the *Times* offices, writing for several hours, dining with his fellow workers, writing for a few more hours, taking a short break with the guys, more writing, then the drive home. With the current technology of computers, Smith can now write his columns at home, call the office and plug his home computer into the main terminal at the *Times,* and presto—the job is done. But what fun is that? What purpose is there in working? Jack Smith now writes articles at home on his word processor, sends it in to the *Times* via computer, drives down to the offices and has lunch with the boys, only to turn right around and drive back home!

For myself, I participate in the Race Across AMerica in order to be a cyclist. I am not a cyclist in order to compete in the RAAM. I enjoy being an athlete and a cyclist. I enjoy the training, the day after day regimen, special diet, massages, long bike tours and races, and the camaraderie of fellow cyclists. Few things are as enjoyable as rolling down a deserted, scenic highway on a clear, warm day with the wind at your back. Bicycling allows you to experience the environment you are in—the weather, hills, wind, road conditions, sights and smells of the local flora and fauna. When you are on a bike you actually feel where you are. That is what being a cyclist is all about and doing the Race Across AMerica helps me justify this full-time existence. The goals you set for yourself are only part of the reason for riding. Whatever you are aiming for—3 miles, 30 miles, 300 miles, or 3,000 miles—don't lose sight of how you got there and how you define your real purpose.

SELF-PERCEPTION

The perception of oneself can be changed radically depending on the role one is currently playing. We usually think of ourselves in terms of traits: shy, assertive, outgoing, intellectual, sensitive, or athletic. Typically we think of these traits as immutable characteristics that are pervasive and

unchanging throughout our lives. However, psychologists now think that
a person's perception of him- or herself can be changed dramatically
over time by playing out new roles.

In Irving Goffman's book on role playing, *The Presentation of Self in
Everyday Life*, he quotes Shakespeare in reference to a general conclusion
drawn by many social psychologists today.

*"All the world's a stage, and all the men and women merely
players. They have their exits and their entrances, and one man
in his time plays many parts."*
—Shakespeare, As You Like It, *Act II, Scene VII*

When I began cycling in 1979 I was teaching college psychology part-
time, working as a writer for a bicycle publication, and was an amateur,
weekend tennis player. Now over six years later I still teach college part-
time; however, I am drawing 90 percent of my income from racing
bicycles. My perception of myself is no longer that of an amateur
weekend athlete. I now consider myself a full-time professional cyclist.
What happened in those six years can only be explained by the concept
that our self-perceptions change as our roles change.

In 1979 my first assignment as a writer for the bicycle publication that
employed me was an interview with John Marino, who had just ridden
from Los Angeles to New York. I thought he was interesting but a little
exotic. I knew for sure that I could never accomplish such a feat.

In 1980 I established the Seattle–to–San Diego record as a fund raiser
for a close friend who had been paralyzed in an auto accident. John
informed me that year that he hoped one day to have a race across
America between three or four cyclists and call it the Great American
Bike Race. I told him it was a great idea but I couldn't imagine where he
would be able to find three or four cyclists to take him up on the
challenge.

In 1981 my self-perceptions began to change. My Seattle–to–San
Diego record was demolished twice by a couple of bike racers, so I went
out in 1981 to reclaim my record. This time it was not to be a charity ride.
This was purely an athletic event. My self-perception had changed
somewhat beyond the amateur weekend athlete role, but I still looked at
full-time cyclists as being in another league. I had visited the Coor's
Classic in Colorado and had seen how the pros really ride, and the image
of myself was cemented in my mind that year in an amateur role.

This set the stage for the 1982 Great American Bike Race. Three years earlier I would never have dreamed (or nightmared) of being in a race against such giants as Lon Haldeman, John Marino, or John Howard. I remember to this day standing on the Santa Monica pier with those men, the ABC "Wide World of Sports" camera crews filming, Jim Lampley and Diana Nyad commentating, and thinking to myself: "My God, what am *I* doing here? Am *I* in the same class as these guys?"

Upon arrival in New York City I had acted out my greatest role and knew in my heart that, as the "Chairman of the Board" Frank Sinatra says in the song "New York, New York," "If I can make it there, I'll make it anywhere." The acting out of the role of professional cyclist had indeed completely changed my own self-perception.

I am reminded of the rather humorous story about one of the head National Football League referees who was escorted to a game one day in a brand new Rolls Royce. One of the other gentlemen in the car queried: "Have you ever ridden in a Rolls Royce before?" "Yes," replied the ref, "But never in the front seat!"

The inescapable conclusion is that you can become almost anything you want just by taking on the characteristics of that role. Note the fictional character of Rocky Balboa from the movie *Rocky*, changing his self-perception from a "ham and eggs" fighter to the champion of the world just by acting out the role.

If you want to become a serious racing cyclist, just start racing. If you want to be a top athlete in any sport, play the role—train every day, purchase the appropriate equipment, work out with the top athletes in the sport, and compete as often as possible. If you play the role, you just may become the role.

To those who enjoy competition, all the world is a race and all the men and women merely competitors. They have their victories and their defeats, and one man in his time plays many sports.

PART
II

THE HUMAN ENGINE

5
ON THE
ROAD AGAIN

"These are the times that try men's souls. The summer soldier and the sunshine patriot will, in this crisis, shrink from the service of his country; but he that stands it now deserves the love and thanks of man and woman. Tyranny, like hell, is not easily conquered; yet we have this consolation with us, that the harder the conflict, the more glorious the triumph. What we obtain too cheap, we esteem too lightly. . . ."

Thomas Paine, The American Crisis, no. 1, 1776

Discovery of the outdoors is one of the most rewarding and enjoyable aspects of the sport of cycling. Unlike a runner, a cyclist can explore a great deal of land in a reasonable amount of time. A good cyclist can cover 20–25 miles in an hour and thus should be able to travel over 60 miles in three hours. Under favorable conditions, 100 miles of highways and country roads may be explored in less than five hours; that is, of course, under the "right" conditions. No one minds training in 85-degree temperatures, under clear blue skies, and in a gentle breeze. No one I know complains about the rigors of training during the summer.

To be in competitive shape for the summer, however, requires dedication and hard work in the winter and spring. Summer cyclists and sunshine athletes are a dime-a-dozen and easy to find—they are usually at the back of the pack or at home in front of the television, discussing how they could have won the race if they had been in the final sprint. I'll never forget the comment I overheard while two cyclists were talking in a bike shop this summer, immediately following the Olympic cycling road race. One noted that he couldn't believe American Thurlow Rogers didn't make the final breakaway at the end of the race and thus finished

The principles of stretching discussed in Chapter 9 are particularly important in spring training, when your muscles are not as prepared for the load of a long training ride as they would be in the summer. Also, temperatures are usually lower; therefore, a proper warm-up is critical.

only sixth. "If I had been there, I would have caught the wheel in front of me and made that break," he told his friend!

He wasn't in the Olympic road race, though, and when I queried as to his cycling plans for the off-season since he seemed to be such a serious cyclist, he replied: "Well, I'm taking a few months off because I worked so hard this season." As it happens, he had joined some local training rides, and I recognized him as a "wheelsucker" and a "pack filler." I was quite amused at his Olympic observations. I wonder what Thurlow Rogers would think?

To advance to the top of any sport requires year-round training and concentration. Winning is never obtained too cheaply and is therefore never esteemed too lightly. To be a victorious summer cyclist necessitates a winter and spring training program. Assuming that you have maintained your fitness during the winter by weight training, swimming, running, skiing, or pursuing some other sport, your serious training for cycling must begin in early spring.

Spring. It's the time of year when farmers and golfers begin their plowing. The cold winter months are over, flowers are blooming, and the roads are no longer coated with ice. Wind trainers and rollers are packed away in favor of riding a bicycle on the road. No matter how many miles are logged in front of "Star Trek" and "Twilight Zone" reruns, training on indoor bicycles just isn't the same.

Those of us from the Sun Belt states, particularly along the coasts, never really face the long cold winter riding sessions. But for most folk, spring means cleaning cobwebs off the spokes of their road machines and adjusting the body to highway riding.

Lon Haldeman, who hails from the northern midwestern town of Harvard, Illinois, explained how he started his spring training program. "No matter how much I ride my rollers and my wind trainer, I just don't use the same muscles in the arms, shoulders, and back as I do on the road. I can be in top shape aerobically and still feel sore and exhausted after a mere 100 miles."

Spring training allows you to develop solid habits that can be carried through the summer. The old Spanish proverb, "Habits are first cobwebs, then cables," applies here. One must ease into road riding, establishing a progressive goal system over the three or four months preceding summer, so that not only the legs, but also the arms, back, hands, shoulders, and neck are properly strengthened for the longer tours, races, and training rides ahead.

For me, turning cobwebs into cables means strengthening the weakly enforced training habits of the past into "cables" of good habits, such as maintaining strength during the off-season and formulating a program of successive goals in the spring. In other words, the more your body relaxes in the off-season, the tougher the spring's discipline will be. As Somerset Maugham said, "The unfortunate thing about this world is that good habits are so much easier to get out of than bad ones."

SPRING PROGRAM

Working out your spring riding program will depend almost entirely on the type of riding you intend to do. For racers, serious triathletes, ultra-marathoners, and cross-country tourists, spring is a crucial time for building up mileage that will later lend an advantage in competition. You can either design a program for yourself or join a local cycling or triathlon club that has a general program of rides throughout the spring. The latter is the easiest, the most efficient, and the most enjoyable for training. Usually, cycling and triathlon clubs include as members serious competitors who have a good deal of experience in training. If you are a novice to the game of training, their help will be invaluable.

Riding with other cyclists is usually better than riding alone. The pace is quicker, the time seems to pass faster, and a more efficient workout is had by all. In this pack, during the 400-kilometer RAAM Building Ride, are John Howard, Pete Penseyres, Scott Fortner (RAAM '84), and me.

In addition, it is much better to train with others than by yourself. Most of us have the bad habit of slacking off when riding by ourselves, coasting when we should be pedaling and easing up when there is a headwind. However, it seems almost a law of human behavior that when two or more people are riding together, city limit signs and the tops of hills become the finish line of the Tour de France. A better workout is had by all.

In my spring training program I am involved with two groups, the Montrose Cycle Club and the Race Across AMerica. Many years ago the Montrose Cycle Club in southern California started a ride every Tuesday and Thursday evening around the Rose Bowl in Pasadena. Another club, the North Hollywood Wheelmen, meets on Wednesday evenings at 6:00 P.M. to ride through the rolling hills of Griffith Park for an hour or more. These rides force me to pedal fast to keep up with the group or even faster to catch breakaways; thus I benefit from a much harder workout than I would have received had I been riding alone.

Participating in these rides every week, coupled with a series of rides staged by the Race Across AMerica of 200, 300, 400, and 600 kilometers in length in January, February, March, and April, culminating in the

The first of the RAAM building rides was a 200-kilometer ride/race. Anyone can enter, and it is up to the participants whether they want to race or just ride. Awards are given for finishing times, and points can be earned toward the ultra-marathon points contest. In this nationwide program the Ultra Marathon Cycling Association sanctions various rides around the country, in which points can be earned toward awards for total points at the end of the year.

700-mile John Marino Open qualifier for RAAM in May, gives me the optimal combination of both speed and endurance.

Although not everyone wishes to attain such speed or to ride so many miles, we all aim at a successive progression toward a goal of higher speeds and more miles of conditioning.

For the novice, many touring clubs have shorter and less intense rides every weekend. Your local bike shop is a good place to check for organized rides. Last year I purchased a bike shop in Arcadia, California, Shermer Cycles, in partnership with Jim and Mary Harrod, my aunt and uncle, and Jerry DeAngelo, my cousin, none of whom were cyclists. To get them involved in cycling, as well as to encourage southern California novice cyclists, I began the Shermer Cycles Century Club. Beginning in February, I organized a series of rides and clinics, starting with a 20-mile ride, then a 35-miler in March, 50 in April, and so on, culminating in a century ride at the beginning of August. Seminars and workshop topics included nutrition, training, adjusting a bike, proper pedaling, maintenance, and sports psychology. Each of these rides is accompanied by a clinic that I lead in an attempt to convince people that anyone can complete a century ride if he or she trains properly.

I firmly believe in the above statement. While we all have certain genetic limitations, most people underrate themselves. With an organized training program incorporating gradual increases in mileage and intensity, anyone can improve his cycling far beyond his expectations. The only limitations are those self-imposed.

PHOTO BY J.G. HOOVER

Shermer Cycles of America, located in Arcadia, California is co-owned by Jim and Mary Harrod and me, and managed by Jerry DeAngelo (pictured here). It has been a unique opportunity to further understand the business side of the sport of cycling. At times business can be as difficult and frustrating as racing. It can also be as rewarding.

SAMPLE TRAINING PROGRAMS

A spring training program should be plotted carefully in advance to produce the greatest efficiency and self-discipline in sticking to the plan. Write the training program down on paper, plotting the overall goals for the spring, the number of miles for each month and week, and even a general day-by-day plan for any given week. A sample training schedule may look like this:

SPRING TRAINING: MARCH, APRIL, AND MAY

Spring Training: March, April, and May

March: 1,000 miles, 250 miles/week

April: 1,200 miles, 300 miles/week

May: 1,600 miles, 400 miles/week

March: 1,000 miles, 250 miles/week

Monday:	25 miles—medium speed, high cadence, low gear
Tuesday:	30 miles—medium speed, medium cadence, medium gear
Wednesday:	50 miles—high speed, high cadence, medium to high gear
Thursday:	20 miles—medium speed, high cadence, low gear
Friday:	Day off
Saturday:	50 miles—medium speed, medium cadence, medium gear
Sunday:	75 miles—high speed, high cadence, medium to high gear

April: 1,200 miles, 300 miles/week

Monday:	25 miles—medium speed, high cadence, low gear
Tuesday:	30 miles—medium speed, medium cadence, medium gear
Wednesday:	60 miles—high speed, high cadence, medium to high gear
Thursday:	25 miles—medium speed, high cadence, low gear
Friday:	Day off
Saturday:	60 miles—medium speed, medium cadence, medium gear
Sunday:	100 miles—high speed, high cadence, medium to high gear

April: 1,600 miles, 400 miles/week

Monday:	25 miles—medium speed, high cadence, low gear
Tuesday:	50 miles—medium speed, medium cadence, medium gear
Wednesday:	80 miles—high speed, high cadence, medium to high gear
Thursday:	40 miles—medium speed, high cadence, low gear
Friday:	Day off
Saturday:	80 miles—medium speed, medium cadence, medium gear
Sunday:	125 miles—medium speed, medium cadence, high gear

This is one example of a spring training program for the serious cyclist who is preparing for road racing, ultra-marathon racing, triathlons, or long-distance touring. Obviously, the schedule should be arranged to suit your own life-style or working hours. To cover more miles on working days, split the ride into two sections, one in the morning and one in the evening. Jonathan Boyer uses this method and told me that he does so in order to log in many miles to break up the day so that boredom doesn't set in and to be able to maintain high speeds over two workout periods, which would be more difficult to do over one long period.

Simply writing out such a schedule reinforces determination, but it can be flexible. Frequently things come up that may interfere with your riding schedule—overtime work, illness, inclement weather—but you can rearrange the schedule to accommodate the changes. For instance, if you miss the 30-mile ride on Tuesday, then tack it on to the 20-mile ride on Thursday, or just extend the longer 75-mile ride on Sunday.

The average number of miles per week is just that—an average. Remember, the goal is to reach approximately 1,000 miles for the month. If you have a short week in that month of March, stretch out the other weeks in order to make that goal. If you are an active club cyclist, or train with a racing group, rides frequently come up that are longer than those you had scheduled for that day or week. You might hear of a double-century that you would like to do on a Saturday, when you had scheduled a 50-mile ride for that day. This adds an extra 150 miles to the week, so you can reward yourself with an extra day off that week or a few shorter

PHOTO BY DAVE NELSON

On long rides in the spring, it may start off cold in the
morning but become quite warm by the afternoon. I
recommend arm and leg warmers that can be taken off
quickly and stuffed into jersey pockets.

rides the following week, or you can just cycle a greater number of miles
for that month. For most of us, riding extra miles is not damaging to the
training schedule. While overtraining does occasionally occur in the
novice fanatic who wants to race in the Tour de France or Race Across
AMerica in his first year of cycling, most cyclists in this country tend to
undertrain. Boyer told me that it is not at all unusual for professionals in
Europe to train 500–600 miles per week, frequently behind a motorpace
vehicle or in a pack so that the speeds are quite high. I have trained with
local racers in southern California, and they are shocked at the thought
of riding 500–700 miles a week, which I do while training in the racing
season. They reason that those distances are reserved for ultra-marathon
zealots preparing for sitting in the saddle 20 hours a day. In reality, the
level of competition in the sport of cycling and in triathlons in this
country has become so high that the best really are training by riding

more than 500 miles per week. It is quite time-consuming—500 miles in a week is approximately the equivalent of working a 40-hour work week. Most of the people logging this many miles are sponsored professionals, amateurs, students, or working people with little or no social life.

Many triathletes I know who also work have a very tight schedule; each hour and minute of the day is accounted for by work, training, eating, and sleeping. They train in the morning from 5:00 A.M. to 7:00 A.M., during lunch hours, immediately after work, and in the evenings. Weekends are reserved as long training days. For racing cyclists, the weekend provides the time necessary to ride or race 100–150 miles. For triathletes, the weekend is simply an opportunity to combine all three events—running, swimming, and cycling—to simulate the actual competition.

When I was training for the 1981 Ironman Triathlon in Hawaii, I was also working at a full-time job with Hester Communications, which publishes *Bicycle Dealer Showcase* magazine, a bicycle trade publication for dealers. I worked the standard eight hours per day, Monday through Friday, with an hour for lunch. A typical training week ran like this:

Monday

5:30–6:00 A.M.	Stretching and warm-up
6:00–7:30 A.M.	Run, cool-down, and stretch
8:00 A.M.–Noon	Work
Noon–1:00 P.M.	Swim at local Y.M.C.A.
1:00–5:00 P.M.	Work
5:00–7:00 P.M.	Bicycle
7:30–9:30 P.M.	Weight training at local gym

Tuesday

5:30–7:30 A.M.	Bicycle
8:00 A.M.–Noon	Work
Noon–1:00 P.M.	Run
1:00–5:00 P.M.	Work
5:00–7:00 P.M.	Bicycle
7:30–9:00 P.M.	Swim

Wednesday
Same as Monday

Thursday
Same as Tuesday

Friday
Same as Monday

Saturday

7:00 A.M.–1:00 P.M.	Bicycle
2:00–4:00 P.M.	Swim
5:00–7:00 P.M.	Run
7:00 P.M.–On	Play, relax

Sunday

Sleep in	
9:00–11:00 A.M.	Run
11:00–4:00 P.M.	Bicycle
4:00 P.M.–On	Play, relax

Like the previously outlined spring training schedule, this program can be flexible. Things may come up at work that prevent a lunchtime workout, or the boss might request that you work late that night. Time off should also be flexible. This will depend on how you feel at any given time during the week. Feeling tired, sluggish, or basically run-down may demand a day off during the week or even on the weekend. If there is a triathlon race on Sunday, it may be best to rest on Saturday or at most to undertake a very light workout. When I was training for the Ironman in 1981, there weren't any other triathlons that I could compete in. Today, almost every weekend of the year is filled with several choices of triathlons of varying distances.

Training for bicycle racing while working at a full-time job is much easier than training for triathlons under the same conditions. There is only one event to concentrate on, and the need to fill every waking moment with athletic activity isn't quite as necessary as it is for triathlon training. Pete Penseyres serves as an excellent example of training around a full-time job. A nuclear engineer at the San Onofre Nuclear Power Plant, Pete lives 35 miles away from the plant and doesn't own a car. His mode of transportation to and from work, day in and day out, rain or shine, for the past 20 years has been a bicycle. Nothing stops Penseyres from riding his bike. Illness, crashes, injuries, and inclement weather have never thwarted his daily training ride. He has ridden to work the day after having had surgery. His bicycle was once washed out from under him by a flash flood—he bought a new bike and was riding to work the next day.

His minimum weekly average, then, no matter what the circumstances, is 350 miles. In preparing for the Race Across AMerica, the Spenco 500, or other races, Pete simply leaves earlier in the morning and takes a longer route to work, or he arrives home later in the evening, taking a longer route home. He also uses the weekends for century and double-century rides and in the heat of training even leaves work on Friday evening and rides continuously until Saturday evening, compiling a 400-mile ride; then he takes Sunday off for rest and relaxation.

Notice that Penseyre's schedule incorporates the European method of riding twice a day that Boyer described. Pete can ride as hard as he can, 35–50 miles each way, and have an eight-hour rest period in between in which to recover. The weekend becomes the time to adjust to sitting in the saddle for long periods of time, which ultra-marathon cycling requires.

There is another blessing in this "training around work" schedule. When you don't own a car and the only means of transportation is a bicycle, such human frailties as procrastination, laziness, fatigue, and rationalization cannot interfere with the schedule. The training goes on— no matter what. There are times when I wish I had to go somewhere, just so that I would have to put in the miles. In fact, frequently I call a friend and make plans to meet him at a certain place and time for lunch or to ride together, just so that I can't turn around on the way, if I don't feel like riding far. My training partner Michael Grandi and I will occasionally make plans to leave at the same time and ride toward each other on the same road, from which point we then ride together for a while, then ride back home alone. Since Michael lives 50 miles away, we are both guaranteed a certain base of miles before and after we ride together.

Another trick for getting in extra miles is to ride to the start of a club ride. Take, for instance, the Rose Bowl ride I described earlier in the chapter; I will usually ride to the Rose Bowl and ride home, adding 40 miles to the 32 miles ridden there. During the summer, when training for the Race Across AMerica, I will sometimes ride 100 miles before the Rose Bowl ride, then ride the 32 miles at top speed, then ride the 20 miles home for a 150-mile day. This is a much harder workout than riding 150 miles alone as the 32 miles are done at speeds between 25 and 30 miles per hour, whereas the 100 miles ridden alone are completed at more moderate speeds of 19–21 miles per hour.

Whatever your program, remember that it will take a while to perfect it to your liking. It has taken me several years to acquire a suitable year-round routine of training for fitness and competition. Adjustments need to be made as your fitness levels increase over the years. Your goals will also affect the training program. The higher the goal, the more intense the training program is going to be.

Table 1 is a graphic description of my training/racing schedule for 1984. On the horizontal axis is the year of 1984, broken down into months and weeks. The months that have 31 days are represented by five weeks while the rest are represented by four weeks. This evens out the months as spread out on this particular graph with the exception of December, which has 31 days but is represented by four weeks. The months are represented for the purpose of orienting the reader to the time of the year. It is the weeks that are important for logging the miles ridden. An exact duplication of the graph appears in Appendix V at the end of the book for your personal use.

This graph is reproduced so that you can see how to use the blank graph in Appendix VI as well as to support the ideas on training given in this chapter. It is important to note that all individual training programs are going to vary, depending on when important races are to take place, physical conditioning, weather, and any personal or work-related emergencies that might interfere with a preprogrammed schedule. I have broken down the graph into two colors, gray and black. The gray bars are pure training weeks that do not include any races. The black bars are racing/training weeks. The Spenco 500 week, for instance, is 800 miles, as I had ridden 300 miles that week before the start of the race on Friday.

The 200k, 300k, 400k, and 600k signify the kilometer distances of races that the Race Across AMerica put on in 1984 as training for the John Marino Open 800-mile RAAM qualifier in May. The Seattle–to–San Diego and the Race Across AMerica bars are almost purely racing miles. The two triathlon bars are relay triathlons of only 24 miles in which I

The 300-kilometer RAAM Building Ride covers part of the John Marino Open course to give riders a chance to become familiar with the route they will be riding during the competition in May.

competed as the cyclist. El Tour de Tucson is a 106-mile road race around the perimeter of Tucson, Arizona.

A pattern can be seen of building up to an event, cycling in the competition itself, and taking a rest period afterward. The Spenco 500, for instance, is dramatically followed by a mere 80-mile week. The two large bars that follow are a training ride I took from Savannah, Georgia, to San Diego, California, a distance of 2,400 miles. I was part of the crew for Michael Coles, who was setting a record for the southern transcontinental United States, which he did in 11 days. I was able to log 1,160 miles in those two weeks, a high-quality training period!

You will also notice a very short week of only 200 miles before the Race Across AMerica. This race is so demanding that it is necessary to taper down the miles in order to rest the body for the inflicted torture that is about to come. The gradual climb in the months following the RAAM is a good indication of the length of time it takes to recover from this event.

TABLE 1: 1984 TRAINING/RACING LOG

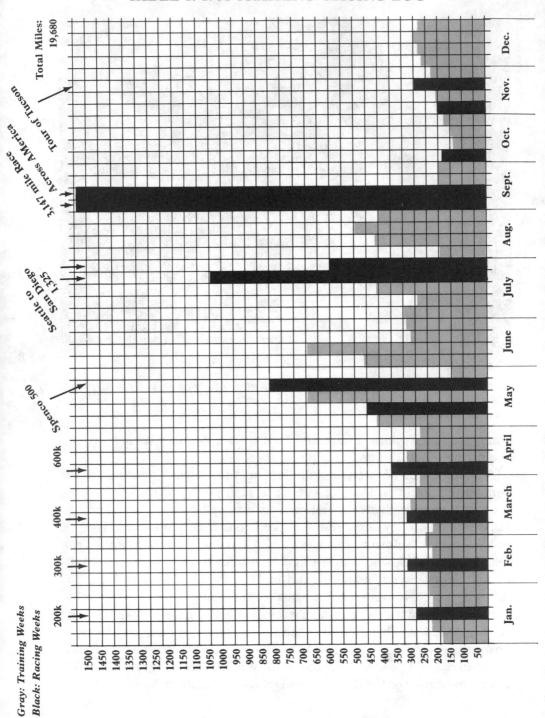

Gray: Training Weeks
Black: Racing Weeks

Total Miles: 19,680

Tour of Tucson

3,147 mile Race Across AMerica

Seattle to San Diego 1,325

Spenco 500

600k

400k

300k

200k

Jan. Feb. March April May June July Aug. Sept. Oct. Nov. Dec.

1500 1450 1400 1350 1300 1250 1200 1150 1100 1050 1000 950 900 850 800 750 700 650 600 550 500 450 400 350 300 250 200 150 100 50

6
A MATTER OF DEGREE

Training for ultra-marathon cycling or for relatively long distances is a matter of degree. This does not, however, mean simply the ability to ride a certain quantity of miles. Rather, it means the ability to attain a degree of excellence in riding those miles.

With the exception of questioning why—"Why do you do the Race Across AMerica?" for example—how to train for long distances is the most frequent question asked of me in discussions of cycling. My answer is not a simple one and has changed radically over the years. The more years I have spent racing, the more experiments I have performed in the "laboratory" of sports physiology.

QUALITY vs. QUANTITY

From *Webster's Ninth New Collegiate Dictionary:*

quan•ti•ty/¹kwan(t)-et-ē/n
1d: a considerable amount or number 2a: the aspect in which a thing is measurable

qual•i•ty/¹kwäl-et-ē/n
2a: degree of excellence

For years I thought that training for long-distance cycling was simple: riding long distances was enough. I told myself, "Ride as far as you can. Day after day, accumulate as many miles as possible." Mike Secrest summarized this philosophy on ABC's "Wide World of Sports" in a prerace interview before the 1983 Race Across AMerica when he said: "I always train alone. I never ride with anyone else." In 1984, Secrest was reportedly covering a staggering 900–1,000 miles per week before the RAAM and the Spenco 500.

Many other ultra-marathoners adopt this training philosophy. I know Pete Penseyres and Jim Elliot have both logged in as many miles as Secrest. Intuitively, this does make sense. If you want to be a piano player, then play the piano. If you want to be a great swimmer, then swim. So if you want to be a long distance cyclist, then. . . .

However, reflecting on some experiments I have conducted on myself over the past two years, riding a large quantity of miles is not necessarily the best training method. Quality training can make a difference. Quantity is just a "considerable amount" of something—in this case, miles. Quality is a degree of excellence—in this case, not just a considerable number of miles, but *excellent* miles of training.

On a bike, unlike in other activities, it is very easy to slack off and relax, particularly when you are by yourself. You can pace yourself on the uphills, coast on the downhills, and maintain a steady, easy pace on the flats. This type of riding, while quite enjoyable, is not likely to produce many positive conditioning results.

Riding in a pack, on the other hand, can make an hour of training worth three hours of solo riding. Riding with others always makes you ride more energetically. Riding with others creates a competitive atmosphere that makes you go faster and work harder. In southern California I participate in a weekly training ride, a 3.2-mile flat loop around the Pasadena Rose Bowl. About 150 riders congregate every Tuesday and Thursday evening to ride the 10 laps, which takes a little over an hour, maintaining an average speed of over 28 miles per hour. Comparing my physical state after that ride to my condition after a two-hour training ride alone, I would say that they are nearly equivalent. The quality of those 32 miles ridden in such a short time can easily replace a 40- or 50-mile solo ride. Cyclists in training can best benefit from these pack rides by staying near the front and taking a good share of pulls. This is far superior to sitting in for the entire ride, which can be fairly easy with over 100 riders in the pack.

THE SCIENTIFIC EVIDENCE

What evidence supports the subjective feeling that you're getting a better workout in a shorter period of time by riding in a pack? Sports physiology provides the answer. Monitoring your heart's pulse rate can give you valuable feedback on your body's condition. Sports physiologists discuss something called the *target heart zone* in reference to training feedback. This refers to the range within which your pulse should fall during training to maximize the time spent working out. It is a simple calculation. Subtract your age from 220, then multiply that figure by .60 and .80. These two figures are the minimum and maximum values of your target heart zone. Your pulse rate should be between these values during the majority of your training. For instance, my age is 30:

$$
\begin{array}{ccc}
220 & 190 & 190 \\
-30 & \times .60 & \times .80 \\
\hline
190 & 114 & 152
\end{array}
$$

TARGET HEART ZONE = 114–152

Thus, at age 30, I should maintain a heart rate of 114–152 beats per minute for maximum benefit during a training workout. This is much easier for me to do by riding in a pack at 30 miles per hour than it is by cruising along at 18–22 miles per hour by myself.

Your pulse rate can be calculated by counting the number of beats in your neck's carotid artery for 6 seconds, then multiplying this number by 10. To be more accurate, count for 10 seconds, then multiply the number by 6.

In my own personal training program, I try to participate in this ride at least once or twice a week, along with an organized group century or double-century ride or a long training ride with friends. Even riding with just one other person provides superior practice. My training partner and friend, triathlete George Yates, and I can cover a 70-mile loop through the foothills of the Los Angeles basin in a little over three hours, an average of 22 miles per hour. When I ride by myself, that time usually increases to three and a half hours for an average of 20 miles per hour.

A recent record ride I completed, the Seattle–to–San Diego course, supplies further evidence for the quality theory of training. My personal best time for the 1,325 miles was 4 days, 14 hours. The existing record was 4 days, 2 hours. My major objective was to break that record, but I also wanted to arrive in San Diego from Seattle in *less* than four days. To give myself a boost, I chose the departure time of 6:00 A.M., Saturday, June 23, 2 hours after the starting time of the annual Seattle to Portland double-century. This is a well-organized, popular ride in the Northwest, with several thousand cyclists participating. I purposely left two hours later than these cyclists so that I wouldn't get caught up in packs, as drafting is not allowed in this form of ultra-marathon racing. But I also chose a later starting time in order to catch and pass riders, giving myself a psychological boost.

This experiment was successful. Without drafting, I covered the first 100 miles in 4 hours, 30 minutes, a personal best and a positive note on which to begin a 4-day race. In the end I felt that my speed training had paid off. I beat the old record by 2 hours but was very doubtful as to whether I could crack the 4-day barrier. With 15 miles to go, when I could see the buildings of downtown San Diego, I was averaging between 23 and 27 miles per hour and came into the City Hall at 3 days, 23 hours, 49 minutes. Only 11 minutes to spare!

TESTING THE THEORY IN LONG-DISTANCE RACES

Though the cycling world is still undecided as to whether my theory of quality and excellence in training can make a difference in ultra-marathon cycling, further light can be shed by the 1983 Race Across AMerica and the Spenco 500.

I began to apply this theory soon after my third-place finish in the original Great American Bike Race. It was quite obvious that my weakness lay in a lack of depth of strength and speed. At that time I vowed to begin weightlifting for strength and pack riding for speed and to do the East Coast and West Coast ultra-marathon races for endurance. I felt this would give me the balance I would need to win the RAAM.

For the past two years I have spent the six months from September through February on a three-day-per-week weight training program to build strength. In addition, I rode in short races and participated in group rides to increase my speed. The ultimate objective of both years was to win the Race Across AMerica. In 1983 I established a record from Miami, Florida, to Portland, Maine, as a part of my endurance training. The course was 1,900 miles long, and I covered it in 6 days, 1 hour, and 55 minutes, an average of 315 miles per day.

I believe that this program worked quite well for the year, in spite of my having to drop out of the RAAM in Ohio because of an injured neck. I returned a much stronger contender the following year, hoping for victory over Lon Haldeman, considered by most to be the world's greatest endurance cyclist. The first thousand miles in the Great American Bike Race took me 3 days and 18 hours to cover and left me over 9 hours behind Haldeman. In the RAAM '83 I covered 1,000 miles of a much more difficult course, from sea level to the 12,000-foot top of Loveland Pass in Colorado, in exactly 3 days—only 1 hour behind Lon.

As for Secrest, Penseyres, and the others who adhere to the quantity theory of training, by the halfway point in Nebraska I was well over 125 miles ahead of them. Admittedly, the race finishes at the East Coast, not in Nebraska, and perhaps a slower pace would have found me farther behind and a finisher instead of stranded in Ohio with a neck injury.

In the Spenco 500 I was pitted once again against most of my fellow ultra-distance racers, but also against traditional road racers. It was the first time in cycling history that endurance racers and road racers were able to compete on the same battlefield. Though drafting was allowed, it was apparent from the beginning that this was more a road race than an endurance contest. Nevertheless, it was a fine battle, with the road racers, led by John Howard, taking an early lead, followed by myself in a pack with Penseyres, Secrest, Elliot, Rob Templin, Bernie Hansen, and other long-distance cyclists. By the 150-mile mark, however, I had dropped all of them and was beginning to chase down the lead pack, which was nearly 1 hour ahead. By the 275-mile mark in Comfort, Texas, I had closed to within 10 minutes of Howard and his adherents. I felt my quality theory was well supported by this performance.

Ultimately, however, riding alone in a race for 350 miles while trying to catch the lead break, which was working together to cut the wind, became an impossible task, and my finishing time was once again an hour behind the winner, Steve Speaks, and 40 minutes behind the second finisher, Howard.

TIME OFF

Finally, it should be noted that taking days off from training is not only sound advice but should be programmed into a training schedule every week. I know many athletes who are horrified at the thought of taking time off. When I mention the idea to them they wrinkle up their faces in amazement and reply, "It would be like starting over, back to square one!"

I don't agree. Taking a day or two off on a regular basis is crucial to a sound training schedule, both physically and psychologically. It breaks up the boredom and sameness of a training regimen, gives the body a chance to recover and heal itself, and gives the mind something else to think about once in a while. Long-distance cyclists often fall prey to boredom on long rides, and time away from the sport maintains their interest and can be very valuable psychologically.

Athletes also benefit physiologically from this practice. Use the heart rate as a monitor of physical condition, and you will see this for yourself. Taking your resting pulse rate every morning before getting up (try to do it at the same time every day for consistency) indicates your body's progress. If your normal resting pulse is 50 beats per minute on any given day, and after six days of hard workouts it rises to the 70s or 80s, watch what happens when you take a day or two off. It will immediately drop down to its normal rate.

The reason is simple. With so much stress on the body from so many days of working out without a break, the muscles and tissues need more oxygen and nutrients from the blood to help recover and to build up to their former condition. The heart accomplishes this by beating faster. A faster resting pulse, then, is an indication that the body is repairing itself and probably needs a day or two to recover.

Some people must concentrate wholly on their sport to maintain excellence, while others benefit from distractions and activities unrelated to their sport. This depends on individual personality. I enjoy the diversion from cycling that my career in academics allows me. When I am bored with the daily routine of training or just tired of the unidimensional thinking that many athletes are locked into, I can turn to teaching as a healthy diversion, affording new topics of discussion and new people with whom I can interact. This makes me eager to return to training when I have been relaxing for a day or two. The time I spend on other activities makes the short break seem like an age spent away from my bike.

My workouts are of better quality after a rest, and it is easier to stay on the bike longer because I enjoy it more. During the summer when I am not teaching, I must get up every morning, day after day, and decide which hundred miles to ride, which turns cycling into a job instead of a joy. Obviously, too many deviations are detrimental to your athletic prowess. Time away from cycling can be abused until you lose ground in your training. You must be careful not to let your mind rationalize time away from training, especially when the workouts are difficult and painful. In psychology we define *rationalization* as "the mind in service of the will." Do not let your will dictate when you should divert your attention to another activity. Use your rationality, not rationalization.

Ron Skarin, a past Olympic road racing team member and 10-time United States National Champion, once told me that the best years of racing in his career were the years during which he was also involved in a completely different profession. He said that all the years of doing nothing but cycling day in and day out had really exhausted him. Having something else to think about gave him a new perspective on the sport. He said he went into workouts with a new freshness and excitement, and the results on race day proved his assertions.

Other temperaments are more suited to a 100-percent focus on one and only one activity. Distractions are just that—distractions from the most important task at hand. For these people the best strategy is living, eating, breathing, and sleeping cycling. They ride every day, no matter how they feel or what the conditions. If they read, they read cycling books and periodicals. Every activity throughout the day is carefully planned to revolve around cycling. Diet, sleep, stretches, naps, social activities, and even sexual activities are all carefully plotted to fit neatly into the training program. For many people this disciplined approach brings the best results.

Ron Skarin (left), 10-time national champion, is flanked by Rick Denman, a nationally ranked trackie or track racer. Note the difference in these track bikes, compared to the standard road-racing machine. Track bikes have no brakes or gears, are designed with stiff frame geometry for greater efficiency, and have a fixed gear set-up for constant pedaling.

PHOTO COURTESY OF RICK DENMAN

QUALITY TRAINING ALTERNATIVES

If riding in a pack is not your "cup of tea" or is simply not available to you, then here are a few alternatives that may provide the same quality of training in a given period of time.

FIXED-GEAR TRAINING

Fixed gears are usually found only on velodrome track bikes, the type Olympic track racers use. The bikes have no gears, derailleurs, or brakes and are built for high-speed racing. Many cyclists, however, convert their road racing bikes to fixed gear bikes for training during the off-season. They keep the brakes on, of course, as they ride them on streets and in traffic, but the derailleurs and freewheel are replaced by a single chainring in the front and a single cog in the back. When you have a fixed-gear setup there is no freewheeling or coasting. When the bike is moving the pedals are moving. There is no opportunity to rest. Many claim that this greatly enhances their workouts as they actually complete more pedal revolutions per minute on the average than they would with a regular bike. More pedal revolutions, more exercise per unit time. It makes sense. Rick Denman, a nationally ranked road and track racer, swears by fixed-gear training. "When I ride my fixed-gear bike on the road my speed on the track during races really increases," Denman observed. "Just a couple of weeks with fixed gears and the guys at the track can't believe it. They want to know who's really on the bike!"

Many of the cycling coaches and top racers recommend this method. Even Jim Elliot, one of the top ultra-marathon cyclists in the country, trains with a fixed gear. Even if you concentrate on pedaling as much as possible on your regular bike, you still coast much of the time. The fixed gear doesn't allow you to do this. If the bike is moving, you are pedaling.

HIGH RPM

If you don't wish to convert your road bike to a fixed gear, you can obtain quality training by spinning high rpms. Revolutions per minute of the pedal cranks can easily be calculated by counting the number of times one leg makes a complete circle per 10 seconds, then multiplying by six. This rpm reading can be used as a feedback on your training program. If a fixed gear is effective because it forces you to pedal more, using a smaller gear and spinning higher rpms can have the same effect, if you have the discipline and concentration to maintain that cadence. David Brinton, an aspiring junior racer (under age 18), constantly spins high rpms in training. I have observed in training rides with him that he is constantly over 120 revolutions per minute. To maintain this cadence requires a monumental output of energy if you are also trying to maintain speed. The terrain will dictate your speed, of course, but using the pulse rate feedback described earlier in this chapter, coupled with counting the rpms, can net you a very effective workout in a limited period of time. Most professionals recommend maintaining a 90- to 120-rpm cadence in training. Many of the bicycle computers on the market today have cadence or rpm hookups for your bike. This is the easiest way to monitor this function.

MOTORPACE

An effective and enjoyable method of quality speed training is motorpacing. The cyclist rides behind a moped, motorcycle, or small automobile to attain relatively high speeds. The method works on the drafting effect—riding in the slipstream of the vehicle in front so that the cyclist doesn't have to battle against wind resistance. The faster you go, the wider and longer the slipstream behind the vehicle. At 10 miles per hour a cyclist expends 66 percent of his energy cutting through the air. At 20 miles per hour this rises to 80 percent. At 30 miles per hour over 95 percent of a cyclist's energy is spent fighting the wind. To be able to tuck in behind a vehicle allows a very fast ride. In fact, the current land speed record for a bicycle drafting behind a race car, set by Dr. Alan Abbott on the Salt Flats in Utah, is 139 miles per hour!

This method of training not only familiarizes you with riding at high speeds but also forces you to spin the pedals at a high cadence. This latter part is crucial here. Riding fast behind a vehicle doesn't necessarily constitute better training. Going fast with a high cadence does, however, contribute quality conditioning. Jonathan (Jock) Boyer, the first American ever to ride in the Tour de France and one of the greatest cyclists this country has ever produced, swears by this method. In fact, during the 1984 Race Across AMerica he joined me in riding up Loveland Pass in Colorado as part of his training session for the World Championships the following weekend. He explained to me that he motorpaces regularly and that aside from the benefits of high-speed and high-cadence training, the vehicle's constant speed forced him to maintain a steady, fast pace, which was excellent for his conditioning schedule. There is no room for slacking off. The day before I arrived in Colorado Jock had ridden 220 miles behind a Volkswagen Rabbit and completed that distance in a mere 7½ hours! That would normally take 11–12 hours for a well-conditioned athlete. That is quality training!

During my training for the original Great American Bike Race in 1982 I drafted at least once a week behind a moped at speeds of 30–35 miles per hour. At that speed, even in top gear, the rpms are well into the 100s. Not only did this increase my speed, it also broke up the monotony of training individually. My training for the 1985 season will also incorporate this method of quality training.

CIRCULAR REASONING

Cyclists often forget that they are the engines of their bicycles and that smooth transmission of power is as important to a bike racer as it is to a race car driver. Revolutions per minute is the key factor here, and once you acquire a few simple techniques you'll be cranking them out with all the even consistency of a high-performance engine with a tachometer attached.

The significance of good pedal technique is apparent as soon as you consider the astronomical numbers involved. In last year's Race Across AMerica, for example, I ground out more than 660,000 revolutions during the 3,000-mile trip. If you ride 100 miles in six hours (a comfortable 16.6 mph), averaging 60 rpm of the cranks, you'll have completed 21,600 circles with each leg!

This is all worth knowing because the body works more effectively if it expends energy at a comfortable and consistent rate, especially over long distances. Therefore, the first point of proper cycling technique is to pedal smoothly, as close to the same rate as possible, changing gears instead of pedal rpms.

To calculate revolutions per minute, count the number of revolutions you make with one leg in one minute: try it several times on easy terrain while cycling at a comfortable pace. Average the numbers and you have a good idea of your natural rpms. Most serious cyclists will push 90–120 rpm while in training to get the heart working at an optimal rate.

CIRCLES vs. SQUARES

Pedaling in circles is a skill developed over time and thousands of miles. Just as it sounds, it's the process of turning the cranks in a smooth, circular motion. You might think it's impossible to do anything else, given that the chainring connecting the cranks is round, which would force the legs to pedal in a circle, but that's not true. In fact, newcomers to the sport often pedal in squares.

Pedaling in squares is an uneven pedal stroke in which pressure is applied to the pedals unevenly, resulting in a jerky motion. Sometimes you can see this in the motion of a bike jumping itself along in quick movements forward. To understand how to correct this, a brief explanation of the mechanics of pedal stroke is in order.

UP, DOWN, AND GOING AROUND

Pedaling may be divided into the downstroke and the upstroke. The downstroke, also known as the power stroke, begins at the top of the revolution, with the leg at the 12 o'clock position. It ends at the bottom of the revolution, with the leg at 6 o'clock. The upstroke is then from 6 o'clock to 12 o'clock.

In a smooth, circular pedaling motion, you not only push down on the pedals, you pull up as well. You might think you're already doing this, when you're actually just riding up from the impetus of the power stroke. It's easier to push down than to pull up. That's because of the angle of your body over the pedals and the relatively greater strength of your quadriceps over your hamstrings (back of the legs) at that angle. Concentrate on the up portion of the stroke—it will feel awkward at first, but after a while it becomes quite comfortable. Visualization will help you perfect this technique and translate it into reality. Picture your legs going around in circles by themselves, not in the pedals or toe straps. Feel the motion of going around.

CLIPS AND STRAPS

Toe clips and straps are a must for spinning in circles. The top clip itself holds the shoe in the pedal while the toe strap keeps the foot tightly in place. If you're wearing a cleated shoe, the slot on the sole will catch the pedal and lightly hold your foot in place. Properly adjusted, toe clips and cleats allow you to exert force throughout the pedaling revolution without loss of energy. You can pull back and up for the upstroke and press forward and down for the downstroke, without fear of slipping. All that would be impossible without toe clips.

HILL WORK

The change from riding the flats to riding the hills changes the process of pedaling in circles. If you're climbing out of the saddle, you're dropping your body weight into the downstroke as you "rest" the other leg. If you've learned to pedal in circles, though, you'll notice that your climbing abilities will be greatly enhanced if you remain sitting. Keeping a smooth, spinning motion makes for a steady climb. If you waver at all, the forces of gravity that are working hard against you will quickly make you lose forward momentum.

Remember that, if you've been performing a technique incorrectly, it will be difficult at first to change the old habit. But by isolating a certain phase of your cycling and working to perfect it—in this case the circular motion of pedaling—your training will soon become cleaner and far more efficient. Your training will become a matter of degree.

7
POWER PLAY

"He didn't carve his career—he chiseled it."

Walter Winchell

"Old age is like everything else. To make a success of it you've got to start young."

Felix Marten

If I had to select one individual whom I know best fits the two quotations above, the search would not be a difficult one. Phil Guarnaccia, an intense, serious young man of 70, is among the most outspoken individuals in the cycling industry concerning the promotion of total fitness through weight training.

He detests the bodybuilding image he sometimes portrays, claiming that bodybuilders are not fit athletes. He doesn't like young athletes who rely on their youth and in the process abuse their bodies with drugs, poor nutrition, and improper training. He loathes the braggadocio displayed by jocks who have more muscle than brains—and he is willing to put his money where his mouth is. In short, he declares with unblinking modesty, "I challenge anyone to follow me through my daily routine and last an entire 45 minutes. I've got $5,000 in a special account waiting for that day. No one has made it yet, and no one will." He means it.

A dark-haired, balding man with penetrating eyes, Phil Guarnaccia, at 70 years of age, has a body that any 25-year-old would be proud to bare. Through 45 years of nonstop aerobic exercise and weight training, Phil has quite literally chiseled a body and a lifestyle to be envied and emulated.

In 1952, when Phil Guarnaccia was a younger man, his orientation to athletics was unidimensional. Weightlifting and bodybuilding represented the only sport "real men" should undertake. Phil dove into the sport with the vigor and intensity that was to become his trademark in years to come. He won the Mr. California title in 1952 but was not satisfied. He then won the Mr. Physical Fitness contest, which convinced him that he was one of the most physically fit men around—until he met the San Francisco Wheelmen one morning.

Phil Guarnaccia was working out in the gym one Sunday morning when he noticed a pack of cyclists flash past the gymnasium windows. He didn't take too much notice, however, since they appeared to be lean, sinewy athletes, without much muscle mass to push the pedals around. After all, he was Mr. Physical Fitness! To prove himself right once again, Phil joined the San Francisco Wheelmen the following Sunday for a short 30-mile jaunt through the rolling hills around the bay area.

"I couldn't believe it," Phil lamented. "I was dropped on the first hill, and it wasn't even that steep! And here I was, Mr. Physical Fitness, being thrashed by a bunch of skinny cyclists."

Since that unforgettable day Phil has taken up bicycle racing, accumulating more than 200 first-place finishes and hundreds of second- and third-place finishes. He competes and wins in the United States Cycling Federation Grand Masters category against men 55 years of age and older. Very few even approach the age of 70. Always eager to meet a challenge, Phil often competes in the Masters category against men 45–54 years of age. Once in a while during a race, and frequently while on training rides, Phil Guarnaccia finds himself head to head with the best cyclists in the country—Olympic and national team members.

To demonstrate the respect Phil commands in the sport, you can find individuals from the Olympic or national team training with Phil in his personal gym and seeking any advice he may wish to give.

The respect he has earned, however, didn't accrue overnight. Times have changed. Not too many years ago, weightlifters were few in number, and they practiced their craft in dingy, dark gyms. Now, with the advent of the aerobics age, business is booming at stylish health clubs and gyms featuring carpeting, mirrored walls, chrome-plated dumbbells, scientifically designed Nautilus and Universal weight machines, stationary bikes, treadmills, saunas, whirlpools, and sports physiology test equipment.

"I remember when there were very few of us around who took weight training seriously," Guarnaccia recalled. "Besides Jack La Lanne and myself, there were only a handful that truly understood the benefits of a total fitness program."

One must remember that in the decades of the '40s and '50s it was not only acceptable to smoke, drink, and lead a sedentary lifestyle; it was stylish. The movie stars and athletic heros all smoked, and having several drinks after the big game was common. Staying in shape during the off-season for a professional athlete was unusual, and such programs as weight training, crosstraining, nutritional programs, and the like were completely unheard of.

If you wanted to be a good cyclist, you went out and rode your bicycle day in and day out, piling up as many miles as possible. Today's cyclists, however, have discovered the benefits of weight training. One of the factors contributing to the plethora of gold and silver medals in the 1984 Olympic Games for U.S. cyclists was a well-designed training program with an especially heavy emphasis on weight training for the velodrome track racers.

Weight training builds muscle strength; increased muscle strength contributes to increased speed and endurance. The secret of creating a successful training program combining weight training and cycling lies in finding the right balance. Weight training, for most competitive riders, is concentrated during the off-season, with half-workouts becoming the norm during race season. Developing certain muscle groups through year-round weight work can increase strength, resulting in the ability to pedal faster. For racers, that means a competitive edge. For nonracers, weight training is a way to improve their condition—to feel and look good both on and off the bike.

HOW TO BEGIN

Before beginning a weight program, check with your physician. Some people have physical problems that limit their exercising capacity. A doctor can advise you on what exercises you should and shouldn't do and whether you may proceed to a full program or begin slowly and work up to a complete routine.

Next, find a gym that is equipped with modern weight machines, has a pleasant atmosphere with clean and spacious workout areas and locker rooms, and is fully staffed with knowledgeable instructors. It is best to find a gym close to your home or workplace so you're less likely to skip a session. Go to gyms that offer trial visits and ask members what they think. Weigh their recommendations against your observations before making a final decision.

When you're ready to begin, set aside consistent time blocks of 45–90 minutes per day, 3 or 4 days per week. Set goals for yourself and do the exercises, allowing at least 1 day between workouts for recovery. Remember to take it easy at the start. An out-of-shape body takes time to return to top form. Exercising too vigorously will cause soreness and quickly sour your attitude toward weight training. Stay in tune with your body. In addition, learn to breathe properly. The basic rule is to exhale when reaching the point of greatest resistance and inhale when hitting the place of least resistance. Gradually, this breathing pattern will come naturally.

Monitor your workouts by keeping a training log. Write down the repetitions, the number of sets, the number of pounds you lift, and try to describe what is happening to your body. Refer to your training log frequently; it will provide encouragement when you become discouraged about your progress.

Wear comfortable clothing. It should allow you to move without restriction. Outfits made from cotton or other natural fibers absorb perspiration, dry quickly, and are easy to care for.

There are as many different theories on weight training as there are different sports that use it as a training tool. For cycling, concentrate on the lower-body muscle groups. Some cyclists also work the upper body, especially track sprinters, flat criterium racers, and triathletes.

In general, if you are going to work the upper and lower body, do so on alternate days. George Yates, a consistently top-rated triathlete and one of my regular training partners, does upper-body lifting Monday,

PHOTO COURTESY OF GEORGE YATES

Since George Yates's early days of bike racing, he has conditioned himself into a highly rated triathlete through a complete weight training program. George attributes his added strength and stamina to weight training.

Wednesday, and Friday and lower-body lifting Tuesday, Thursday, and Saturday, with Sunday as a rest day. Yates has a well-toned body, and his muscle groups strike a balance of strength and endurance. His endurance stems primarily from daily running, swimming, and cycling; his strength results from weight training.

The reason for alternating days is to rest muscle groups between workouts, enabling each muscle to rebuild itself, each time becoming stronger than before. If you don't wish to build your upper body, the off-days can be used for hard workouts on the bike. For most competitive cyclists who do not participate in triathlons or track racing, extra upper-body muscle is just extra weight to carry up hills. Whatever arm strength is needed for out-of-the-saddle climbing can easily be developed just by riding.

WARM UP FIRST

The first step in your weight routine should be a warm-up. There is no surer way to invite an injury than to walk in cold and begin lifting weight without adequate warm-up. Warm-up entails two processes. The first is elevating the heart rate through aerobic exercise; the second is stretching. (See Chapter 5 for information on stretching for cyclists.) Stretching prepares the muscles for strenuous work and heavy loads.

The best aerobic warm-ups consist of running, cycling, or stair climbing. Any of these activities, conducted for 10–15 minutes before lifting weights, will enrich the muscles with the blood and nutrients they will need for the routine. Many health clubs have both stationary bikes and stair-climbing devices for a warm-up. Warm-up should be undertaken at a medium pace.

THE WELL-PLANNED WORKOUT

Your workout plan should be designed by someone who knows and understands cycling and the specific muscle groups you want to work on.

You don't need to overdo the number of repetitions at the weight station; it's best to do two or three sets of each exercise. Complete the full routine, one set at each station, then repeat. Some people prefer to do all their sets at a station before moving on. Either way is acceptable, though the former may provide a little more variety and thus prevent boredom.

The amount of weight you use should be determined by an expert working at the gym, who can tell you where to begin. It is better to start with too little weight than too much. Once you have established your starting weights, begin to slowly and systematically increase them as the weeks and months go by. If you suffer pain and stress in joints, decrease the amount or type of exercise rather than be macho by forcing the motion. An injury can delay your weight training program for a long time.

The following weight training exercises are depicted in photos, each with a brief descriptive caption. They were taken in Phil's personal gym in the warehouse of his electrical company in Brea, California. Phil has slowly built up his gym over the years, adding new equipment from Nautilus and Universal, as well as many stations of his own design. This includes a motorized stair-climbing device, which at full speed can take the fittest of athletes to complete exhaustion in less than a minute!

In a weight training program, as in most sports, consistency is fundamental. Phil attributes his success to this factor more than any other. He states as a fact that you can count the number of days he has missed exercise in the past 35 years on one hand and have several fingers left over! There is a sound lesson to be learned here.

There may be many exercises, besides those represented here, that are applicable to cyclists and triathletes. Each one's value should be weighed by the effects it will have on your overall performance on the bicycle.

Leg Curls: *On a Universal leg machine lie flat on your stomach with padding under your thighs if needed; curl the weights up toward your buttocks. This is a difficult exercise, and I recommend starting with a small weight as Phil is demonstrating here, perhaps 20 pounds. Try for 15–20 repetitions, three sets for the day. The leg curl builds your hamstring muscles on the back of your leg.*

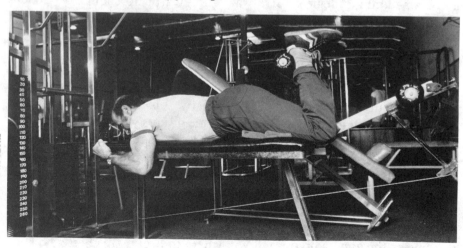

PHOTO BY JIM CASSIMUS

Leg Press: *Leg presses build the quadricep muscles so critical for cycling. Use an amount of weight that will only allow you to repeat approximately 25 repetitions before fatigue and pain cause muscle failure. As Phil demonstrates on his own machine, he has two options on where to place his feet. The upper foot pegs make the exercise much more difficult. Repeat three sets for the day.*

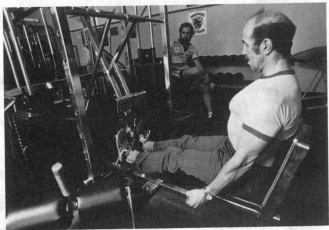

PHOTO BY JIM CASSIMUS

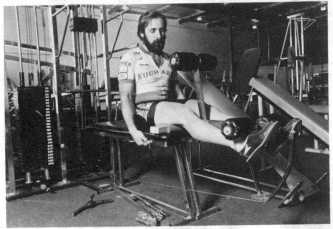

PHOTO BY JIM CASSIMUS

Leg Extensions: *Also excellent for building strength in the quadriceps, the leg extension exercise should be repeated in three sets for the day, aproximately 25 or more repetitions in each set.*

Squats: *Phil shows the proper position from which to begin the squat, which is excellent for building strength in the quads as well as in the back and shoulders. Most track and criterium racers use this weight training exercise for improvement in performance. In general, proponents of free weight exercise feel that the overall balance and muscular development is superior to weight stations such as Universal and Nautilus. Repeat the squat 10 times, three sets for the day.*

PHOTO BY JIM CASSIMUS

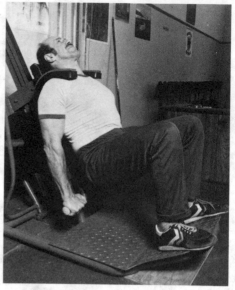

Squat Machine: *The squat machine provides many of the benefits that the squat exercise does, but utilizes the arms, back, and shoulders in a different manner. This can be repeated 15 to 20 times, three sets for the day.*

Lunges: *Begin with a weight in each hand, 20 or 30 pounds each, and "lunge" each leg forward, left, then right, then left again. To begin the exercise it is good to "walk" the lunges through slowly, then as you build your strength and balance, increase the speed to the point where each lunge is only about a second long. Repeat 25 lunges for each leg for a total of 50 each set, three sets a day.*

Toe Raises: *With a couple of hundred pounds on the bar and your toes and the balls of your feet positioned on the board, raise yourself up a couple of inches, then lower again. Repeat 25–30 times, three sets for the day. This is probably the best exercise for your calves and ankles.*

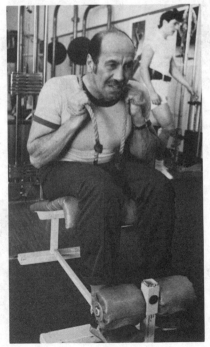

Abdomen Raises: *Hanging from a chin-up bar, Phil executes a move that will have your stomach and abdomen muscles burning—bring your legs straight up to the bar as many times as possible (which will be quite limited until you have been doing this exercise for some time).*

Extended Sit-ups: *A further variation on the sit-up, Phil positions himself in front of a weight station and, with ropes, pulls an additional 70 pounds each time he sits up. I recommend this for advanced use only. The number of repetitions will depend on the amount of weight and your ability. Start with 10 reps for each of three sets.*

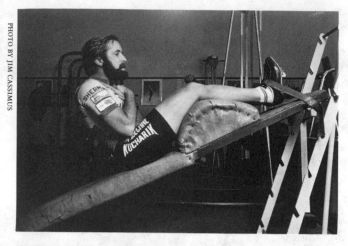

Slant Board Sit-ups: *Sit-ups, particularly on a slant board, are great for the abdomen, stomach, and upper thighs. Like the Roman chair, repeat 30 to 40 times each of three sets for the day.*

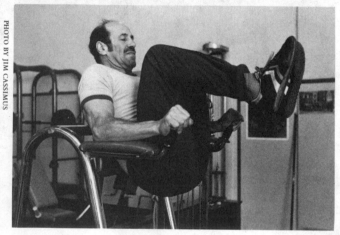

Advanced Roman Chair: *Phil demonstrates a more difficult, advanced use of the Roman chair by drawing the legs all the way up to the chin. You will not be able to repeat as many times as the standard Roman chair. I recommend starting with 15 reps in each of three sets.*

Roman Chair: *The abdomen, stomach, and upper thighs get a good workout with this exercise as you draw your knees up toward your chest as close to touching as possible. Repeat for 30 to 40 times each of three sets.*

8
HEALING HANDS
THE ART OF
SELF-MASSAGE

"Everyone should be his own physician. We ought to assist, and not force nature."

Voltaire

One of the newest, fastest-growing, and yet most confusing areas in all athletics is the area of sports medicine. The field exploded into public awareness during the 1972 and 1976 Olympics when it became apparent that the Eastern Bloc countries, especially Russia and East Germany, were collecting most of the medals. Their athletes were the product of a well-oiled sports training machine. They all had individual coaches, they trained full-time, and their lives were devoted to a single sport from a very early age. Their governments support prospective medal winners.

What made these athletes stand out, however, was the *type* of program in which they were trained. It was a scientifically designed sports medicine program. Daily blood samples were drawn to analyze lactic acid levels, hormone deficiencies, vitamin and mineral needs. Injuries were treated immediately and with the most sophisticated technology— ultrasound, electrical muscle stimulators, and all manner of scientific gadgetry.

Americans were somewhat baffled and shocked at the research emerging from the labs and locker rooms behind the iron curtain. The field is now known as *sports medicine*, and Americans have mastered the art of individual specialized training programs. The recent Los Angeles Olympics, at which the United States won an unprecedented number of gold, silver, and bronze medals, provides evidence of this. Teams employed trainers, coaches, doctors, chiropractors, and massage therapists.

For the average weekend athlete, however, the area of sports medicine can be very confusing. What type of nutritional program should you adopt? Should you take vitamin and mineral supplements? What about liver tablets? How about steroids? Should you take cortisone shots for injuries? Does ultrasound really work? Are muscle stimulators really effective in accentuating the healing process? If you have back problems, should you go to a chiropractor? What about massage therapy? Does it help?

This list could continue indefinitely, but I will stop with massage. Of all the various gimmicks, remedies, scientific potions, and treatments that I have tried over the past six years, none has been more effective and powerful in its power to rehabilitate than massage therapy. I have tried colonics, liver flushes, fasting, vitamin and mineral programs, seaweed, kelp, ultrasound, the Electric Accuscope (an electric muscle stimulator), vitamin B injections, electrolyte replacement drinks, natural stimulants, hot springs, mud baths, iridology, hypnosis, chiropractic, and massage therapy. This last has produced the most noticeable effects in my performance. I have reached great heights with it and fallen into much despair without it. My massage therapist in the 1982 transcontinental race saved me from disaster several times, while the therapist in the 1983 race left for home early and subsequently I developed a neck problem so crippling that I had to abandon the race.

It is always best to consult the experts when seeking help, especially in regard to your own body. A properly trained massage therapist can work wonders with a battered body. Unfortunately, you get what you pay for, and good massage therapists are not exempt from this rule. They can charge anywhere from $25 to $75 per hour. Who can afford a good massage three or four days a week? The solution is self-massage.

BENEFITS OF SELF-MASSAGE

1. While it is advisable to consult a massage therapist first regarding your needs and specific problems, self-massage can give you continuous benefits without extraneous expense.

2. Self-massage helps you learn about your own body—its aches and pains, tender points, strong and weak spots, and pain tolerance. The more you know about your body, the better able you are to take care of it.

3. Even if you need the help of a professional, one might not always be around on a training ride, during a bike race, or at the gym. To be able to work on yourself has obvious benefits of convenience and expedience.

4. Massage protects against injury. Jack Meagher, in his book *Sports Massage*, has demonstrated that massage will decrease the chances of injury by 20 percent.

5. Self-massage acts like biofeedback. Your hands are the biofeedback instrument that your brain monitors. Massage will tell you what state your body is in.

6. Massage is very relaxing. It reduces tension and anxiety and relieves stress. In short, massage feels good. Admittedly, it feels best when someone else massages you, but even working on yourself produces good results.

WHAT TO MASSAGE

There are certain areas of the body that are most abused by the bicycle. These are the points that should be attended to by massage:

1. LEGS. The quadriceps, or the upper thighs, need the most work of all the leg muscles. These muscles are the workhorse of the pedaling machine and build up the most lactic acid. After a strenuous workout, it is the quadriceps that feel it the most.

The area surrounding the knee is also stressed in cycling and can benefit from self-massage. The ligaments in this area become tight with

PHOTO BY MICHAEL SHERMER

Massage your calves by grasping the muscle with one hand and pulling toward the knee. Pressure should be applied with both the fingers and the palm of the hand. Pressing the muscle inward against the bone provides ample leverage.

Janice Simmons, my massage therapist for the 1984 season, demonstrates how to massage your upper leg. Always massage away from the heart and toward the knee. One technique is to massage the inner thigh with the right hand, then the outer thigh with the left hand, alternating back and forth.

Having a sore neck may not be remedied just by rubbing the large neck muscles beneath your collar. Muscular tension may begin where the muscle attaches to bone, in this case back behind the ear.

strained muscles or loose and "grisly" with overuse. For some, this area is extra-sensitive and massage seems to feel very good.

Finally, the gastrocnemius, or large calf muscle, is subject to stress, particularly when hill climbing or sprinting. The muscle should be worked on from the base of the back of the knee down to and including the Achilles tendon.

2. WRISTS AND HANDS. The hands and wrists take a beating from gripping the handlebars and absorbing road vibration for hours at a time. The most superficial nerve in the body runs through the little-finger side of the palm of the hand and controls the last two fingers of each hand. Many people experience numbness or paralysis of these fingers.

3. NECK AND UPPER SHOULDERS. Being hunched over a bicycle for hours is unnatural for human beings and can bring about stress and trauma to the neck and shoulders, which can be helped by massage.

4. THE FEET. Clamping the feet onto the pedals as they press down on a wooden or equally hard-surfaced shoe can bruise or damage the nerves and muscles on the balls of the feet. In addition, many acupressure points can be found on the bottom of the feet, which are reported to be beneficial in pain relief as well as to aid the healing process.

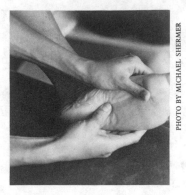

PHOTO BY MICHAEL SHERMER

PHOTO BY MICHAEL SHERMER

Doctor of Chiropractic Vicky Vodon shows how you can stretch your own neck by using both hands and rotating the head to the right as far as you can without pain, then repeating to the left. Do not attempt to crack your neck; *this should be done only by a doctor.*

General massaging of the bottom of the foot provides numerous benefits, but mainly general relaxation. It is easiest to massage toward the toes. For cyclists, the ball of the foot can become sore or bruised from pushing on a steel pedal through a hard-soled shoe.

HOW TO SELF-MASSAGE

There are almost as many types of massage therapies as there are massage therapists using them. Everyone has his own particular, individual method of doing massage. As you work on yourself, you may develop your own special technique that produces the best results for you.

SWEDISH STYLE

This is the type of massage you may have received from a friend who rubbed your back and shoulders. It feels good, is somewhat relaxing, but doesn't really help to alleviate true muscular and joint problems. It is done by applying just enough pressure to make you feel good without any discomfort at all. It should be done with both hands making long sweeping motions in the lengthwise direction of the muscles and, if possible, always toward the heart.

While this method is effective in promoting blood circulation and feels relaxing, the following methods are better for the serious athlete.

PETRISSAGE

Kathy Dynes, massage therapist and chiropractor, who has worked with both John Marino and myself in several ultra-marathon rides, recommends this type of massage, which she described as a kneading of the muscles. "You treat the muscle almost as if it were a loaf of bread. Cup your hands around the muscle and squeeze it, continuously, on and off, with both hands. The amount of pressure should be enough to really work the muscle so that it feels a little uncomfortable and possibly even a little painful."

Kathy then noted that you should not go beyond the pain threshold to the point where it is excruciating. "Go to where it hurts somewhat, but not beyond."

I had one massage therapist recommend a rating scale of pain from one to five, five hurting the most. He would massage deeper and harder to the point where I would rank it a three. This is the level at which he would hold the massage. If I rated the massage a four or five, he would adjust the massage accordingly.

Janice Simmons, a massage therapist from Huntington Beach who went on both my 1984 Seattle-to-San Diego ride and the 1984 Race Across AMerica, also uses the Petrissage approach. "There are two ways of tackling the muscle. You can work on the belly, or main mass of the muscle, or start at the ends of the muscle and work in." Janice explained that, when working from the ends in, you start with the origin or insertion of the muscle, that is, where it attaches to the bones of the body. If it were your quadriceps, for instance, you might start with the palms of your hands up just below your hips and push slowly down toward the muscle's insertion at the knee. "You should follow the path of the bone," Janice observed. "Most muscles run parallel to bones, so this is a good way to massage them."

For the other method, massaging the belly of the muscle, Janice recommends beginning in the middle and working outward on the muscle. She agreed with Kathy that a certain amount of pain is necessary for progress to be made. Remember the old adage "no pain, no gain!"

ACUPRESSURE

The third method is taken from the ancient Oriental practice of acupuncture. Acupressure works by pushing down on specific pressure points in the body to relieve muscle tension and pain. For instance, one of the classic pressure points is found between the thumb and forefinger, right behind the major tendon running through this area. Applying pressure here can help relieve headaches, cramps, and nausea.

Dr. Vicky Vodon, the director of the Chiropractic Health and Sports Care Center in Huntington Beach, California, is herself a specialist in chiropractic. Vicky strongly believes in acupressure and practices it daily

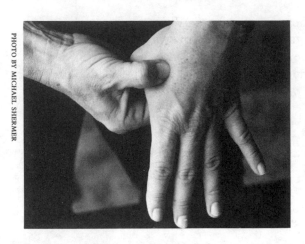

Vicky hits the pressure point between the thumb and forefinger, which attenuates pain, particularly headaches and stomach cramps. It is also recommended for menstrual cramps. Another twist is to apply ice to this area.

with most of her patients. "By leaning into a certain spot for a few seconds, I can make a tense, hard muscle become a soft, relaxed one."

Dr. Vodon has been working with me and my neck problems since the 1983 Race Across AMerica and has worked wonders. Since I have received acupressure from her, and massage therapy from Janice Simmons, I have yet to develop a neck problem, even in the three major events I competed in for 1984: the Spenco 500, the Seattle-to–San Diego, and the Race Across AMerica.

"Just search around for tender spots in your muscles," Dr. Vodon noted. "Then press a thumb or palm into that spot. Push hard enough so that it hurts a little, but then just feel the tension leave that muscle."

Kathy Dynes applies this method to all people, not just cyclists or athletes. "What happens is that you contract certain muscle groups so much that they stay contracted even when not being used. This is called *muscular tension.* To relieve this, just use acupressure on those certain spots, holding down until that muscle or your thumb gives up!"

Dr. Vodon agreed. "A lot of my patients have tension-related problems that do not stem from athletics, but normal everyday living. They need to practice self-massage on a daily basis."

Anyone who spends much time on the telephone will concur that neck problems can stem from hours of holding the neck at an awkward position—off to one side. The telephone devices that prop the telephone up so your neck is straight can help, but ideally a speakerphone or one with lightweight headphones will eliminate the problem.

Many people who work in stress-producing occupations, such as business executives, find that massage effectively relieves tension. A quick massage during the lunch hour or a longer, full-body massage after work can make you feel like a new person. When I was working for *Bicycle Dealer Showcase* magazine, crouched over a telephone Monday through Friday, eight to five, I had massages once a week from Kathy Dynes during my lunch hour. The benefits were incalculable. The afternoon after the massage was the best part of the whole week.

DOS AND DON'TS

1. Use massage oil or lotions for better motion over the muscles.

2. Shaved legs work best for massage, but it isn't critical, if you use good lotions or oils.

3. If possible, massage before and after every workout.

4. You can even massage your own back by lying on tennis balls and moving around, letting them stay in one place for a few seconds each.

5. Either massage the length of the muscle or massage it at a 90-degree angle.

6. Whenever possible, massage toward the heart. This allows the circulation to pump out more quickly the impurities in the system.

7. Don't massage a muscle or tendon that you think might be injured. If there is swelling or extreme pain, see your doctor or professional therapist.

8. Don't massage too deep in the style of rolfing (named after Ida Rolf), which is not massage but a tearing apart of the muscle groups.

9. Find a comfortable position on the floor, in a chair, on a couch, or on a bed and try to relax the body as much as possible.

10. To prevent fatigue in your hands, use your arms and body to apply pressure.

Massage is both an art and a science. It requires knowledge of anatomy and physiology of the muscular and circulatory system and also the ability to apply that knowledge to the healing of the human body, either someone else's or your own.

9
STRETCHING FOR EXCELLENCE

"The only exercise some people get is jumping at conclusions, running down their friends, sidestepping responsibility, and pushing their luck."

Arnold H. Glasow

"A generation ago most men who finished a day's work needed rest; now they need exercise."

General Features Corporation

The body is a delicately balanced, intricate machine. It consists of hundreds of bones, muscles, tendons, and ligaments, all functioning in synchrony like the cogs in a giant watch. When tuned, the body will operate perfectly, but when treated improperly, it won't perform to its maximum potential.

When you start your car in the morning, you wouldn't dream of putting it into gear and punching the accelerator to the floor. Yet many people who treat their cars with respect treat their bodies with contempt. They think nothing of moving from a sitting position after a day's work to a full run without warming up their own engines.

Today's society is locked into a sedentary lifestyle, and all of us must plan our days to include exercise. Very few occupations involve exercise as part of the job. A typical executive rushes over to the gym after work to try to get in his workout as quickly as possible before the night's activities begin. This is where many of the common sports injuries occur. Doctors call them "weekend athlete injuries."

The weekend athlete is the person who usually works out sporadically during the week and then goes all-out on the weekend. He usually does not take the time to stretch and warm up properly, thus inflicting injuries upon himself.

With the application of medicine to sports and the increase in knowledge of physiological processes, leading athletes, coaches, and sports medicine doctors are realizing the importance of warming up, stretching, and cooling down.

Anyone can learn to stretch, regardless of the sport, age, or amount of flexibility. Often we watch the incredibly limber gymnasts contorting themselves into human knots, and we groan in sympathetic pain. In stretching, though, all things are relative. If, in touching your toes, you feel the same amount of tautness and pain in your muscles at mid-calf as someone else does when touching the ground, those are equal stretches, relative to the body doing the stretch.

WHY SHOULD I STRETCH?

1. to relax the muscles

2. to keep muscles loose and supple

3. to stretch tendons and ligaments

4. to increase range of motion in all joints

5. to improve circulation

6. to help prevent muscle injuries such as tears and strains

7. to help prevent joint injuries by exceeding your range of motion

8. to heighten psychological awareness of the body's working parts

WHEN SHOULD I STRETCH?

1. before any physically taxing activity, and not necessarily just sports—for instance, working around the yard, walking, hiking, moving furniture, etc.

2. in the morning before the start of the day's activities

3. during breaks at work to relieve muscle tension in the neck and back

4. after sitting or standing for long periods of time

5. during an athletic event, if there is a lull in the action, to keep the muscles supple and loose

6. anytime you feel like it while doing activities such as watching television or listening to music

HOW SHOULD I STRETCH?

Stretching should be done slowly, without bouncing or jerky movements. Stretch to the point where you feel a slight tension in the muscle, then slowly increase the stretch until you feel a slight pain. Do not stretch until it hurts beyond reason. The slight pain is just an indication that the muscle is taut. Hold this slight stretch for 15–30 seconds, then slowly release it. Try it again and this time attempt to stretch a little beyond the previous point.

Proper breathing is very important in stretching. Your breathing should be slow, rhythmical, and under control. Exhale while you are going into a stretch; inhale while coming out of a stretch. Do not hold your breath during the stretch. Breathe consistently during the 15- to 30-second stretch.

Stretching is not an athletic contest. It isn't considered macho by any athletes to be able to stretch into various contorted positions. The key to successful stretching is to be relaxed. Don't worry about flexibility; if you stretch relaxed, flexibility will come. It's just one of the many positive results of regular stretching.

Therefore, stretching is the key ingredient in warming up and cooling down before any athletic activity, including cycling. Cycling differs from many sports because it rarely involves contact with others, and it isn't as stressful on the joints, tendons, and muscles. Most of the body is relaxed and comfortable while riding a bicycle, with the legs moving in a smooth, flowing motion.

Doing the pictured stretches can greatly improve your cycling. In warming up on the bike, it is best to begin pedaling in an easy gear with low revolutions per minute, working up to a high rpm, then shifting to a higher gear that will slow your rpms, and working up, once again, to another higher level of rpm. Continue to do this until you have reached a gear and rpm level that you are comfortable with.

It may seem at first to be a time-consuming nuisance to have to go through the routine each time you exercise. But once you get into the habit, it really becomes a part of the sport itself, and it feels wrong to begin without stretching.

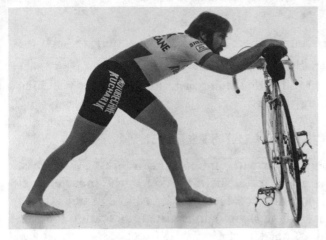

Single Calf Stretch: *Using your bicycle to hold yourself steady, stretch each calf separately, holding it for 30 seconds each leg. Keep the knee of the stretching leg locked as you lean forward.*

Double Calf Stretch: *After stretching each calf individually, stretch both together, again using the bicycle to hold yourself. Hold stretch for 30 seconds total. You may use a wall or chair to hold yourself, but a bicycle is handy on the highway.*

On-The-Bike Stretch: *You can even stretch while cycling. While coasting on flat ground or on a slight downgrade, if safety permits, lean forward with one leg straight and the other bent under the handlebars. This will stretch the calf of the straight leg and arch your lower back. Hold for 10 seconds if possible then switch legs to stretch the other side.*

Hamstring/Groin Stretch:
Keeping the leg to be stretched straight, reach and hold the foot with both hands for 30 seconds on each leg. The other leg is tucked behind the body.

Hamstring/Groin Stretch with Leg Tucked Inward: *In this stretch the opposite leg is tucked forward in front of the body and provides a slightly different stretch than the previous hamstring-groin stretch. Hold for 30 seconds on each leg.*

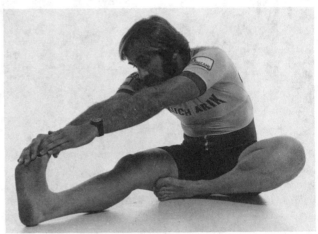

The Splits: *Deborah Shumway demonstrates the ultimate stretch for the inner thighs. Deborah is a nationally ranked cyclist who finished third in the inaugural Tour de France for women in 1984. She has won many races and titles in the United States.*

Side Bends: *Spread your legs and bend sideways from the waist—stretch, do not bounce. Switch sides and repeat, holding for a couple of seconds each side. Repeat 25 times.*

Assisted Hamstring/Groin Stretch: *Using a chair or table top, lean forward enough to where you feel the back of your thighs stretch pretty tight, hold for 30 seconds then switch legs. Since you will be bent over in this stretch, don't forget to breath!*

Stretch with a Friend: *Grab a friend's forearms and take turns stretching forward and back slowly. This stretch is good for the inner thighs, back, and hamstrings.*

PHOTO BY JIM CASSIMUS

Tricep Stretch: *Hold the elbow of one arm with the hand of your other arm. Slowly pull your elbow and hold for 20 seconds. Switch sides. This is excellent for stretching out the triceps and shoulders.*

PHOTO BY JIM CASSIMUS

Hip Stretch: *Thrust one leg behind and keep your weight on the forward leg. Feel the stretch through the hip and groin. Hold for 30 seconds and switch sides.*

PHOTO BY JIM CASSIMUS

Calf/Hamstring Stretch: *Shifting your weight from your back to your forward foot, gently flex your foot, bringing your toes off the ground. Hold for 15 seconds then lower the toes to the ground. Hold again. This stretches the entire leg, especially the calves and hamstrings.*

Hamstring/Groin Stretch: *This is how the stretch should look when you are limber enough to place your nose down to your knee. Hold this for 15 seconds or longer if possible. Switch sides. Most women can stretch further than men in this exercise.*

Quad Pulls: *Grab your foot and pull your heel toward your buttock until you feel the stretch in your quadriceps. Hold for 20 seconds then switch sides.*

Quad Stretch: *Grab your foot and bring it up toward your thigh. Hold each leg for 30 seconds. If you can hold the stretch without leaning aginst the wall, your balance will improve. This stretch is extremely important for cyclists because the quads are the main muscles that spin the cranks.*

Toe Touches: *This stretches primarily the hamstring as well as the quads. Hold for 20 seconds, do three times.*

Back Stretch: *With the left leg slightly bent, place the right foot over the knee and rest it on the thigh. Then gently swing or rock the right foot toward the ground. You will feel your lower back on the left side stretch and even crack. For the opposite stretch, reverse the leg positions.*

Hamstring Stretch: *With both feet together, lean forward as far as possible until you feel the stretch working. Hold for 10 seconds and repeat three times.*

Neck Stretch: *The best way to crack and stretch your neck is to rotate your head in a circular motion. Stretch the neck so that when your head is forward the chin is touching your chest, and when the head is back, it is slightly touching your back. Rotate the head in a clockwise motion many times, then switch to a counterclockwise motion.*

PART
III

THE ULTIMATE MACHINE

10
GEARING UP

"Let us rather run the risk of wearing out than rusting out."

Theodore Roosevelt

Most people learn about gearing systems through experience alone. All cyclists know that the shifter on the left side of the bike controls the front derailleur and the shifter on the right side controls the rear derailleur. A normal 12-speed bicycle has two chainrings connected to the pedals' crank arms, and a six-speed cluster or freewheel on the rear wheel. The front derailleur shifts the chain from the little chainring to the big chainring and back. The rear derailleur shifts the chain up and down the six cogs, from the lowest to the highest gear and back. Thus, you have 6 choices of gears in the rear and 2 choices in the front—a total of 12 gear alternatives.

The object of the drivetrain is to propel the bicycle forward under the power of the legs. On flat ground, this is relatively easy at low speeds, but as rolling hills and mountainous grades loom ahead on the highway, you must shift gears according to your strength level to negotiate the climb. The object of a gearing system is to allow you to maintain a fairly steady cadence. This can easily be calculated by counting the number of times one leg goes around in a complete circle in 10 seconds, then multiplying by six. Sixty revolutions per minute (rpm) is a slow to medium cadence. Eighty rpm is a medium cadence. One hundred rpm or more is a high

The front derailleur moves the chain between the two
chainrings via a shift lever on the left side of the bicycle.

The rear derailleur moves the chain up and down the
freewheel via a shift lever on the right side of the bicycle.

cadence. It is generally agreed that for good aerobic exercise one should
maintain a medium to high cadence, approximately 80–120 rpm. This
keeps the heart rate high and makes for a quality workout.

The gearing system becomes important in maintaining that steady
cadence on a rolling or hilly course. If you begin to climb a hill and your
cadence slows, shifting to a lower gear will restore your original cadence.
When you begin to descend the hill and your speed increases dramatically, you will need to shift to a higher gear in order to keep pedaling.

Pictured is a Regina six-speed freewheel with a gear range of 13, 15, 17, 18, 19, 21.

Once again, the object is to maintain a constant cadence.

Gears are classified by number of teeth. A "42" chainring has 42 teeth on it. A "14" cog is a gear in the freewheel that has 14 teeth on it. Cyclists typically refer to their gears in these terms. One might say, "I was climbing in my 42 × 21, but it was so steep that I had to shift to my 23." This means the cyclist was riding in the 42-tooth chainring on the front and the 21-tooth cog in the back. Since the hill was steep, he had to shift to a lower gear, in this case the 23-tooth cog, in order to keep a reasonable cadence.

The more teeth there are in the front chainrings, the bigger or higher the gear. In the rear, the opposite is true. The more teeth the cog has, the smaller or lower the gear, so the easiest gear to pedal in would be the smallest chainring and the largest cog. The most difficult gear to pedal in would be the opposite—the big chainring and the smallest cog. When a cyclist is relating how hard and fast he was riding, he might say: "I was in my 52 × 13 and really hammering!"

Gearing systems are not sequential in design, although many novices mistakenly believe this to be so. This would mean that, on a 12-speed bike, gears 1–6 refer to the position of the chain on the small chainring, and the gears just shift on the freewheel in the order 1-2-3-4-5-6.

Gears 6–12 would then be the position of the chain on the big chainring, and the gears simply shift down the freewheel 7-8-9-10-11-12. This couldn't be further from the truth.

With this gearing arrangement, shifting up through the gears from smallest to biggest requires 7 changes of the front derailleur and 12 changes of the rear derailleur. Obviously, this isn't as simple as most people believe.

My current gearing system is set up as follows:

Chainrings: 54 and 42
Freewheel: 13, 14, 15, 17, 19, 21

Actual ranking from 1 to 12, or smallest to biggest gear, looks like this:

1. 42 x 21	4. 54 x 21	7. 42 x 14	10. 54 x 15
2. 42 x 19	5. 42 x 15	8. 54 x 17	11. 54 x 14
3. 42 x 17	6. 54 x 19	9. 42 x 13	12. 54 x 13

What if your gearing system isn't arranged in this manner? How can you objectively evaluate your own gearing system to decide on an appropriate gear? A gear ratio chart can aid you. Table 1 plots number of teeth on the rear sprocket on the horizontal axis and number of teeth on the chainrings on the vertical axis. To find the number of gear inches, which will be the method of ranking the gears, correlate the chainring size with the cog size and read across the graph. For instance, a 42 chainring with a 21 cog is a 54-inch gear. From the explanation above, you would expect the 42×19 gear to be larger in inches. A quick check of the table shows it to be 59.7 inches—a larger gear.

Gear inches is a term that originated in the late 1800s when the "high-wheeler," or "ordinary" bicycle, was commonly used. Since the pedals were attached to the large front wheel and there was no chain or freewheel, the gear inches represented the diameter of that large wheel. An ordinary bike with a 54-inch gear had a front wheel that was 54 inches in diameter. In other words, the larger the wheel, the farther the bicycle would travel with each pedal stroke. The larger the wheel, the harder it would be to pedal up a hill. Thus a small gear or small wheel was needed for a hilly ride.

Translated into today's bicycles' chains and freewheels, the distance you travel with each pedal stroke will depend on the circumference of the wheel and on the gear inches. To calculate the circumference of the wheel, multiply its diameter by pi (3.1416). A 27-inch wheel has a circumference of 84.82 inches. Thus, on a 27-inch ordinary bicycle, one pedal stroke would net you a distance of 84.82 inches, or a little over 7 feet. To calculate how far you travel with each pedal stroke on a modern

The front chainrings usually come as a pair, though on mountain bikes there may be three, and on time trial bikes there may be only one. When the chain is in the larger chainring you travel farther per pedal stroke than if the chain were in the small chainring.

PHOTO BY MICHAEL SHERMER

bicycle, multiply the number of gear inches (from Table 1) by pi. If you are in the 42 × 21 gear, you would multiply 54 by 3.1416 = 169.65 inches, or 14.14 feet traveled.

The following table translates the gear ranking given above into distance traveled.

TABLE 2: DISTANCE TRAVELED BY GEARS

	Gear Teeth CR Cog	Gear Inches	Distance (Inches)	Distance (Feet)
1.	42 x 21	54	169.7	14.1
2.	42 x 19	59.7	187.6	15.6
3.	42 x 17	66.7	209.5	17.5
4.	54 x 21	69.4	218.1	18.2
5.	42 x 15	75.6	237.5	19.8
6.	54 x 19	76.7	240.9	20.1
7.	42 x 14	81	254.5	21.2
8.	54 x 17	85.8	269.5	22.5
9.	42 x 13	87.2	273.9	22.8
10.	54 x 15	97.2	305.4	25.5
11.	54 x 14	104.1	327.1	27.3
12.	54 x 13	112.1	352.5	29.4

As you can see, my biggest gear allows me to travel over 29 feet with each pedal stroke. The obvious conclusion, then, is that the higher the rpm, the greater the distance traveled each minute. An rpm of 60 nets me 1,764 feet traveled every minute. An rpm of 100 translates to 2,940 feet per minute. In a flat-out sprint at 140 rpm, I could cover 4,116 feet per minute, or nearly a mile. Of course, one cannot maintain 140 rpm in a 112-inch gear for any appreciable length of time as anaerobic threshold is passed quickly and the muscles go into oxygen debt, which can be recompensed only by termination of the extreme exercise.

The gear chart should be used to adjust your bicycle's gears. If you are going on a training ride, a race, or a tour that is extremely hilly, then you will need a gearing system that has low enough gear-inches to accommodate those climbs. Most of the adjusting can be done on the freewheel. Rarely do the chainrings get switched as it is not as simple a task as replacing the rear wheel with a different freewheel.

For the most part, the fitter you are, the less variation is required between gears. Most competitive cyclists can get by with a 52 $\times$ 42 chainring set up with a 13–21 freewheel structure. The 54-inch lowest gear can get a fit cyclist over almost any hill.

Some cyclists like to have a slightly larger chainring. Some move up to a 53 or even a 54, particularly if they like to push big gears. I prefer this method. Due to my ultra-marathon background, I favor pushing larger gears at a slower cadence. However, many sports physiologists feel that this puts excessive strain on the knees. Spinning high rpms is considered better for the knees.

Occasionally one finds a chainring smaller than a 42. Tourists who carry heavy packs and mountain bike racers frequently need a chainring as small as a 36 to reach a mountaintop. Some touring bikes even sport three chainrings to give extra gear options.

A three-chainring setup with a six-speed cluster would be an 18-speed. There are even 21-speed bikes that are fitted with a special 7-speed freewheel and three chainrings, but gear inches plotted for a 21-speed drivetrain from the gear ratio chart (Table 3) usually involves duplication of gears. For instance, a 52 $\times$ 28 is a 50.1-inch gear. A 42 $\times$ 22 is a 51.5-inch gear. The difference is so small that you could never distinguish between the two gears.

Experience and the use of the gear ratio chart on the following page will help you decide which system is best suited to your conditioning and cycling needs.

TABLE 3: GEAR RATIO CHART

Number of Teeth on Freewheel

	12	13	14	15	16	17	18	19	20	21	22	23	24	25	26	27	28
40	90.0	83.1	77.1	72.0	67.5	63.5	60.0	56.8	54.0	51.4	49.1	47.0	45.0	43.2	41.5	40.0	38.6
41	92.2	85.2	79.1	73.8	69.2	65.1	61.5	58.3	55.3	52.7	50.3	48.1	46.1	44.3	42.7	41.3	40.1
42	94.5	87.2	81.0	75.6	70.9	66.7	63.0	59.7	56.7	54.0	51.5	49.3	47.3	45.4	43.6	42.0	40.5
43	96.7	89.3	82.9	77.4	72.6	68.3	64.5	61.1	58.0	55.3	52.8	50.5	48.4	46.4	44.6	43.0	41.4
44	100.0	91.4	84.9	79.2	74.3	69.9	66.0	62.5	59.4	56.6	54.0	51.7	49.5	47.5	45.7	44.0	42.4
45	101.2	93.5	86.8	81.0	75.9	71.5	67.5	63.9	60.8	57.9	55.2	52.8	50.6	48.6	46.7	45.0	43.4
46	103.5	95.5	88.7	82.8	77.6	73.1	69.0	65.4	62.1	59.1	56.5	54.0	51.8	49.7	47.8	46.0	44.4
47	105.7	97.6	90.6	84.6	79.3	74.6	70.5	66.8	63.4	60.4	57.7	55.2	52.9	50.8	48.8	47.0	45.3
48	108.0	99.7	92.6	86.4	81.0	76.2	72.0	68.2	64.8	61.7	58.9	56.3	54.0	51.8	49.9	48.0	46.3
49	110.2	101.8	94.5	88.2	82.7	77.8	73.5	69.6	66.1	63.0	60.1	57.5	55.1	52.9	50.9	49.0	47.2
50	112.5	103.8	96.4	90.0	84.4	79.4	75.0	71.1	67.5	64.3	61.4	58.7	56.3	54.0	51.9	50.0	48.2
51	114.7	105.9	98.4	91.8	86.1	81.0	76.5	72.5	68.8	65.6	62.6	59.9	57.4	55.1	53.0	51.0	49.1
52	117.0	108.0	100.3	93.6	87.8	82.6	78.0	73.9	70.2	66.9	63.8	61.0	58.5	56.2	54.0	52.0	50.1
53	119.3	110.1	102.2	95.4	89.4	84.2	79.5	75.3	71.5	68.1	65.0	62.2	59.6	57.2	55.0	53.0	51.1
54	121.5	112.2	104.1	97.2	91.1	85.8	81.0	76.7	72.9	69.4	66.3	63.4	60.8	58.3	56.1	54.0	52.0
55	123.7	114.2	106.2	99.0	92.8	87.3	82.5	78.1	74.5	70.7	67.5	64.5	61.8	59.4	57.1	55.0	53.0
56	126.0	116.3	108.0	100.9	94.5	88.9	84.0	79.5	75.6	72.0	68.7	65.7	63.0	60.4	58.1	56.0	54.0

Number of Teeth on Chainrings

11
EQUIPMENT AND FITNESS ENHANCERS

"Machines don't break records; muscles do." **Lon Haldeman**

"My bike is my iron mistress." **John Howard**

"The only limitations are those self-imposed." **Michael Shermer**

"Fatigue is a disease, and I don't want it." **John Marino**

Before the start of the 1982 Great American Bike Race, *Bicycling* magazine published an interview of the four competitors who were about to embark on the first U.S. transcontinental bike race. In addition to our personal backgrounds, training methods, and strategies for the race, the author of the article headed each of our stories with the above quotations dug out from the interviews that he felt best represented us.

For all the talk in the bicycle industry regarding aerodynamic components, super-lightweight tubing, spokeless wheels, and computer-designed bicycle frames, Lon Haldeman's statement sheds some light on the relative importance of machinery and gadgets versus the rider himself. I would have to agree. If I had to put a figure on it, I would rank the cyclist himself as contributing 90 percent to the winning of a race. The bicycle and related equipment make up the other 10 percent. However, many times the difference between first and second place can be a mere 10 percent. In the 1984 Race Across AMerica the time difference between the first and last of the four official finishers was this exact figure—10 percent. Can the machine make a difference?

Unequivocally, the answer is yes. Not only the bicycle and its components, but also the various devices to help in training, can add up to higher standings in a race.

THE BICYCLE

Though an entire chapter, indeed an entire book, could be devoted to frame designs and racing geometry theories, suffice it to say that, in terms of a bicycle, the better the equipment, the better the performance. In cycling equipment, as in most merchandise, you get what you pay for. Of course, there are the so-called "you're-paying-for-the-name" brands in both bicycles and components. Though everyone seems to agree that Campagnolo components have always been the *crème de la crème* in bicycle equipment, the consensus also is that they are overpriced. In this case, while paying for the name may add a small percentage to the price at the retail level, most folks who are serious cyclists and racers seem to be willing to shell out the necessary cash. So revered are these components, in fact, that in Tullio Campagnolo's home country of Italy, where the manufacturing plant is located, it has become a colloquial expression to describe a shapely woman as "Elle est tout Campagnolo," meaning she is well equipped in every way that counts. The preference for the name is putting a high demand on the capacity of the factory to produce enough *gruppos* or groups of components.

With the recent growth of the sport of cycling, other quality component manufacturers have been cashing in on the "quality first" idea set forth by Tullio a long time ago. For instance, I have recently been test riding Shimano components, a Japanese manufacturer. So efficient is the S.I.S. shifting mechanism that I've calculated I save over 2,000 shifts in the RAAM.

As for the bicycles themselves, they all must bear stock components of the quality of Mavic, Campagnolo, Shimano, Sun Tour, Galli, or Maillard. So it comes down to the actual frame—the tubing, the brazing, the painting, and the final touches that make it a personal, handcrafted machine as opposed to an assembly-line production.

Paying $1,500–$2,000 does not guarantee a hand-built frame, perhaps even made by the original designer himself. A highly rated, respectable name in racing bicycles is Bianchi, named after Eduardo Bianchi, who originally hand-brazed and painted each and every frame that left his shop. He has long been dead, and Bianchi bicycles are now produced not only in Italy but in the Orient as well, where mass production can be done with less expensive labor costs. The top-of-the-line Bianchis are still high-quality bicycles, used by many professionals around the world, but sophisticated brazing machines and modern paint booths have replaced the one-man operations of decades past.

A word to the wise: test ride as many bicycles as possible before

PHOTO BY MICHAEL SHERMER

Proper equipment begins with the bicycle. If you are not happy with your machine, you are less inclined to ride it. The most comfortable and efficient bike I have ever ridden is the Carbon Fiber Peugeot. It is light and stiff and absorbs road vibration.

making your selection. Asking local experienced riders, or even professionals, what their choices are may bring you a slightly tainted view. Professionals are under contract to ride for bicycle companies and will naturally recommend the particular model they are advertising during that particular year. And a local rider who has racing experience but is an amateur and can't afford to plunk down $2,000 every few months for a new bike may have a narrow view, limited by finances rather than personal preference.

I was fortunate in having had two bike sponsors over the past six years who gave me a choice of different frames. My first major sponsorship came from Motobecane Bicycles, imported from France, which gave me a choice between the traditional steel frame and the innovative aluminum design by Vitus Tubing. Fortunately, I ignored the advice from pessimists who warned that the aluminum frame would collapse, shatter, or be so flexible that you couldn't even climb an easy hill on it. Instead I went with my subjective feeling after riding the aluminum Prolight, as it was called, and since then I have never gone back to steel. The Prolight was not only several pounds lighter, but also was infinitely more comfortable on ultra-marathon rides.

My current bike sponsor, Cycles Peugeot, made me almost the same offer. The company allowed me to choose between a steel frame and the new Carbon Fiber design. Once again my subjective feeling was that the Carbon Fiber frame had all the advantages of the aluminum frame—it was light and comfortable. In addition, however, it seemed a bit stiffer, and therefore more efficient, without sacrificing the comfort. After logging 25,000 miles on the Carbon Fiber Peugeot, I can conclude that it is even more comfortable than the Prolight. This would not be incongruous with the research findings on tennis rackets and golf clubs made out of the same material. Apparently the carbon material has a dampening effect on vibration, as picked up from a tennis ball by the racket, a miss-hit from the golf club, and highways that were designed for fat-tired cars traveling at 60 miles per hour, not skinny tire bicycles moving 20 miles per hour. Particularly in long-distance riding, road vibration can take its toll on the body after hours and even days of constant abuse.

A recent road test article in *Bicycling Magazine* rated the Peugeot Carbon Fiber bicycle quite high. Not only did it pass all of the standard frame stiffness tests, it was extremely comfortable to ride, over any distances.

Jonathan Boyer, the first American rider to break into the elite European racing circles, including the Tour de France, now rides the aluminum Vitus frames with Mavic components. Boyer tells me that he will never go back to steel frames. This statement is made by a man who rode hand-crafted Confente frames for years. Mario Confente, before his death, was known as one of the finest frame builders in the world. For Boyer, and many others in the brutal world of professional racing in Europe, every advantage counts, even if it is just a pound or two less of weight going up a hill.

John Howard, Ironman Triathlon champion and Great American Bike Race competitor, prefers, on the other hand, steel frames. He even has his own brand of bicycle: The John Howard bike. John once announced at a bike clinic he and I were running that Ironmen ride steel frames and sissies ride aluminum. He stated this after I had just given my positive findings of riding aluminum frames. I wonder if Jonathan Boyer would agree?

Lon Haldeman feels that having a bicycle that fits perfectly is so important that he rides handbuilt frames called RRB Cycles. RRB is Racing Ron Boi, a close friend and support crew member of Lon's on all of his rides. The bikes are perfectly suited to Lon's large body structure and powerful legs. Lon apparently feels that it is important enough that he even turned down the opportunity to earn $25,000 in the 1983 Race

Across AMerica. Raleigh Bicycles offered him $25,000 if he won the race on a Raleigh.

Correct bike size is of great importance. A 27-inch bike is not the size you want unless you are six and a half feet tall. Many people mistake the wheel size for the frame size. Most 10- and 12-speed bicycles have 27-inch wheels. The greatest variation in bike size lies in the frame, which may be as small as 17 inches to as large as 25 inches as measured by the distance from the middle of the bottom bracket to the middle of the top tube where it joins the seat tube. There are many sophisticated and impressive formulas for calculating the exact size bike you should use. These usually involve inseam length in relation to torso length and many other measurements. A fast and simple test is to straddle the top tube of a bike with both feet flat on the ground. The top tube should be between an inch and two inches from the groin area. If contact is made, the frame is too big. If it is three inches or more below the groin, the frame is too small.

TRAINING AIDS

Beyond the bicycle, cycling machines and gadgets are mostly oriented toward improving your training. Rollers, stationary bikes, wind trainers, bike computers, training logs, portable cassette players, and weight-training stations are all touted as devices to make you go faster.

ROLLERS

Rollers are training device that essentially make your bicycle stationary for indoor use. They are designed so that the bicycle can be balanced on them while you are pedaling. One roller goes under the front wheel, and two rollers go under the rear wheel. To ride rollers requires an act of balancing that takes a bit of practice. One short twitch of the front wheel will send you flying to the floor. Once mastered, however, rollers can provide an easy and effective method for training during inclement weather or at night.

Most rollers are built so that even in your highest gear your rpms will remain relatively high with very little effort. I use the Kreitler roller system, and I can easily hold my cadence at 100+ rpm when riding in my 54 × 13 gear. This is great training for spinning, balance, and holding the bicycle in a straight line.

To simulate riding on the highway, though, requires an adaptation to the rollers called a *wind system*. For the Kreitler roller system you can purchase a turbo wind device that is driven by the turning of the rollers. The circular blades cut through the air, causing friction and thus drag on the rollers. This produces a much more difficult workout as you must pedal harder to maintain the same rpms. In addition, the housing around the blades is directed toward the cyclist, creating a wind that is equivalent to what you would feel when riding on the highway at 20 miles per hour.

Riding in a high gear at a fairly high cadence of 100+ rpm with the wind system on the rollers requires a tremendous output of energy, thus giving you a high-quality workout. With the Kreitler wind system, there is even an adjustable "door" to vary the amount of air that is sucked into the turbo blades, thus allowing you to vary the amount of drag, or the intensity of the workout.

WIND TRAINERS

Wind trainers are different from rollers in that most of them require the front wheel of the bicycle to be removed and locked into place in the trainer. The wheel is held in place by a vertical post that has a quick release skewer, while the rear wheel of the bike rests on a roller. Connected to the roller are two turbo wind drums with blades that produce friction as they cut through the air. The friction then produces drag on the roller, making for a more difficult training session.

PHOTO BY MICHAEL SHERMER

All roller systems have an adjustable front roller. The front tire of the bicycle should sit directly on top of the roller or slightly behind it. An easy way to measure this is to line up the valve stem at the bottom and adjust the front roller accordingly.

On wind trainers, such as the original one invented by Richard Bryan and manufactured by Skid-Lid Manufacturing of San Diego, the faster your cadence, the more difficult it becomes to pedal. Therefore, a high output of energy is required to maintain a high rpm.

The advantage of the wind trainer over rollers is that you have to work harder for the same number of rpms. The disadvantage is that the front wheel is locked in place so that no balance is required, which means you can't train your ability to ride in a straight line. The wind trainer does, however, allow you to stand up out of the saddle and practice riding up hills in this fashion. To stand up on the pedals on rollers is next to impossible at any reasonable speed.

Al Kreitler Custom Rollers with the wind system teach proper riding balance and give a formidable workout. The wind system has an adjustable mechanism for increasing or decreasing the roller resistance.

PHOTO BY MICHAEL SHERMER

STATIONARY BIKES

Stationary bikes are constructed with a large wheel or drum that rotates under the power of the spinning pedals. Friction is applied to the wheel with rubber brakes or a nylon band that surrounds the circumference of the wheel. There is usually a knob that allows you to control the amount of pressure, thus varying the intensity of the workout.

Stationary bikes have the advantage of not requiring any time or effort to set them up. With rollers and wind trainers you have to adapt your own bike. In the case of the wind trainer, you must remove the front wheel, which means you can't use a bike computer, as most of these computers operate by means of a rotating magnet attached to the front wheel. Virtually all stationary bikes have a speedometer and an odometer to measure miles per hour and miles traveled.

Another advantage is that stationary bikes tend to be a bit more stable to allow you to ride out of the saddle without much sway. I have witnessed Lon Haldeman ride a Monarch stationary bike for hours at a time, alternately sitting and standing up out of the saddle. While standing up, he sometimes even rides with no hands on the bars to stabilize himself and just uses one hand holding on to a beam in the ceiling. It appears that this riding method builds up even stronger leg muscles as it isolates those muscle groups to concentrate on only one movement.

With any indoor equipment, you may be handicapped by the inability to move along, with constantly changing scenery to keep you interested. When you are on the road the wind cools you off, and the time passes by quickly as you accelerate down hills, fly around hairpin corners, and enjoy the local geography. Riding indoors is, to say the least, limiting in scope.

Riding indoors, however, can actually be enjoyable and productive. For instance, I use the time not only to get a quality workout but also to listen to lecture tapes, watch videotapes of television documentaries, or even just let my mind vegetate on a diet of "Star Trek" and "Twilight Zone" reruns. If you set it up right, you can even have your telephone next to the bike and make your calls while you ride. This becomes more difficult, of course, when you are riding strenuously.

BIKE COMPUTERS

A reliable bike computer is a must for accurate feedback on exactly how you're progressing. As you become better conditioned, the differences on a day-to-day basis will become smaller, with your average miles per hour differing only by 10ths. For this reason, your computer should be able to calculate average miles per hour to one or two decimal places. Other functions that are important are current miles per hour, miles traveled on the current ride, and elapsed time. Other, less critical measurements that some computers make are such things as cadence, gear inches, and cumulative miles traveled (over days, weeks, months, or even years if your computer lasts that long). One of the biggest problems with most of the bike computers is reliability. It is not at all unusual for a computer to go blank when it is hot or cold or while you are riding on a very bumpy road. Rarely have I ridden 300 miles without some malfunction that rendered the computer useless.

TRAINING LOG

The training log or training chart in Appendix VI at the end of the book will suffice for logging miles ridden in the course of weeks, months, and the year. To record other information, however, any notebook will do. Get into the habit of logging on a continual basis your food intake, weight, miles ridden, time elapsed, average miles per hour, and anything else you think is pertinent. You might even want to set up a subjective rating scale that reflects how you feel on a day-to-basis. A scale of 1–10 might work, with the 10 being reserved for those truly exceptional days when you drop the local champion on a ride and the 1 being reserved for the days when you just turn around and go back home after 15 minutes!

MUSIC

For me, listening to music on the bike is the best training aid for intermediate to long rides. Since I often find myself riding alone, boredom can be a major problem, and music is a cure. A Sony Walkman or a similar portable cassette player will suffice. Since the headphones can interfere with normal helmet wear, I recommend the Sony headphones that just fit inside your ear. They are more comfortable and also give you better sound.

Many states are trying to pass laws prohibiting cyclists from using portable stereos when riding. The argument is that cyclists cannot hear oncoming traffic and therefore are more accident prone. The purpose of such laws is to protect the cyclist, since it is hardly likely that a bicycle is going to harm a car much. I have used stereos now for many years of riding, both in training and in the Race Across AMerica, and I have never, over the course of probably 50,000 miles, had any trouble hearing the sounds of the environment around me. In addition, I know many riders who use music, and I have never known them to have any problems.

As long as no one else is likely to be injured because of my personal

A computer can really enhance the value of a training ride by allowing you to determine the standards you need to beat as your fitness level progresses. Pictured is the Solar Powered Cat Eye computer.

choice, I would prefer that this decision be left to me. This issue is not unlike the helmet issue. I feel that anyone who doesn't wear a helmet is making a big mistake. In fact, I think that not wearing a helmet is outright foolish and may be influenced by the machismo attitude of narrow-minded bikies. However, I would defend their right not to wear one if they so choose.

The value of listening to tapes on a portable stereo goes beyond the mere enjoyment of music. Since the average American spends as much time per year in a car (500 hours) as a college student spends in the classroom in a year, listening to lecture tapes or motivational tapes can be quite productive. In the last five years of cycling and driving my car I have taken courses in archeology, astronomy, U.S. history, ancient history, the Middle Ages, modern history, and philosophy. Not only does it add to intellectual growth, but it actually keeps you on the bike longer in order to finish a lecture!

PHYSIOLOGICAL TESTING

In the long run, a visit to a sports testing laboratory could be very beneficial. Body fat, blood, VO_2 uptake, lung capacity, and residual lung capacity testing on a yearly basis will give you an indication of your condition. Many health and fitness clubs offer sports testing, with some being more legitimate than others. Consult an athlete or a doctor who is familiar with them in your local area for a recommendation.

A good stereo system playing fast-rhythm music can make the hours seem much shorter. The best earphones for cycling have no headpiece— they plug comfortably into your ears. Pictured is the Sony Walkman.

The more information you collect on your body, the better able you are to judge your fitness level and therefore how to alter your training program to suit your specific needs.

Beyond the equipment considered to be ancillary to the sport of cycling, such as rowing machines, Nordic ski machines, jump ropes, and the like, the aids you choose to improve your training should be kept in perspective. Since muscles, not machines, break records, it should be kept in mind that training aids do not take the place of training; they merely enhance it.

12
DON'T FORGET

Do you remember the old expression, "For want of a nail the shoe is lost, for want of a shoe the horse is lost, for want of a horse the rider is lost"? The rider in this case is not on horseback, but a bicycle outing can be quite analogous to taking a trip on horseback. If your mode of transportation fails, the trip is over.

Forgetting any item, particularly an important one, can spell disaster for the entire trip. I recall an incident in the early days of my training for the Race Across AMerica, before I had accumulated a list of cycling essentials.

The mid-June sun was already blazing down on Los Angeles. Temperatures soared into the 90s, with 102 predicted as the high for the day.

I'd had a hectic week of business transactions and endless phone calls, and that morning I was anxious to embark on my 200-mile training ride and forget the world of contracts and finances. I dashed out of the house, intending to grab a snack somewhere along the highway—I didn't have the time or the patience to eat breakfast or to pack food in my jersey. Of course, I thought I could fill my water bottle somewhere along the road, so I wouldn't need to mount extras on my bike.

Forty-five miles down the road toward San Diego—a stretch famous for no services for tens of miles in any direction—came the telltale hissing from the rear wheel. I dismounted my Peugeot and reached for my spare inner tube. None! In my rush to leave the house I'd forgotten to pack one.

Ah, but I had a patch kit. I ripped open the well-worn box like a child on Christmas morning. I had only one patch left. The tube of glue, however, looked strangely like my tube of toothpaste at home—squeezed flat and nearly empty.

I applied the patch, but the nail I'd picked up left a gaping hole in the tire as well as the inner tube. When I pumped up the tube it bulged through the tire's puncture.

It burst about a mile later, leaving me stranded in the middle of Camp Pendleton Marine Corps Base without a tube, a patch kit, food, or water. Not wanting to destroy my expensive alloy rim by riding on it without a tire, I hitchhiked into nearby Oceanside. I ended up paying full retail price for a tire and tube, although I had dozens at home. When the owner of the cycling shop casually asked me what I did for a living, I mumbled something vague. How could I admit that I was a professional cyclist?

With the growing popularity of bicycle racing, long-distance cycling, touring, and triathlons, more people than ever are taking serious long-distance rides of 30, 50, 100, and even 150 miles in a day. I can remember just five years ago riding down the coast highway and rarely seeing another cyclist, especially one that was fully equipped with a good bike, cleated shoes, and a helmet. But today, with the excitement of national television exposure for Olympic road and track racing, triathlons, and ultra-marathon cycling, the roads are nearly congested with serious but somewhat novice cyclists.

To avoid a repeat performance of my Camp Pendleton fiasco, I now use the following checklists for my rides. Using this method, I have ridden up to 300 miles in a day without any bags attached to my bike and without a "sag wagon," or following support vehicle.

ESSENTIAL ITEMS FOR ANY RIDE

Spare tube or sew-up tire and rim glue or rim tape if using sew-ups

Patch kit—complete

Water bottle—filled

Tools: spoke wrench, tire irons, Allen wrenches or open-end wrenches, screwdriver

Helmet, preferably hardshell

Money

Personal items—medication, ointments, etc.

ITEMS FOR SPECIAL RIDING CONDITIONS

HOT WEATHER

Sunglasses

Sunscreen or sunblock

2 or more water bottles (one mounted on the handlebars or stored in the back of your jersey)

E.R.G., or an electrolyte replacement drink

Scarf or handkerchief to protect the back of your neck from the heat

COLD WEATHER

Leg warmers

Arm warmers

Wool jersey

Wool warm-up jacket

Shoe covers to keep feet warm

Long-fingered gloves or glove liners

Bike cap under helmet

Windbreaker

Handkerchief or scarf for neck or nose

NIGHT RIDING

Bike lights—front and rear

Reflective tape on bike, clothes, and helmet

Reflective vest

Small flashlight for map review, tire patching, etc.

RAIN RIDING

Booties or waterproof shoe covers

Fenders on bike, if available

All clothes of wool, which stays warm even when wet

Eye protection—clear or tinted goggles

Extra socks

50–100-MILE RIDE

2 water bottles

Food in jersey pockets or in handlebar/frame bag

Change of clothes if it is an overnight trip

Bike computer, if desired

100–150-MILE RIDE OR BEYOND

3 water bottles, unless there are plenty of services along the course or you have the newly designed longer water bottles

Extra money and/or credit cards

Moist towelettes to clean up with during a break or when finished

Maps of the course

Night riding equipment if necessary

Extra food—as much as you can carry in case stores are closed

A granola bar or an apple to save through the entire trip in case you "bonk."

Seat pad (Spenco)

Extra socks

Padded gloves (Spenco)

OPTIONAL PERSONAL ITEMS

Chapstick

Insect repellent

Leg oil for cold weather cycling

Hand lotion

Vaseline

Soap or shampoo

Vitamins

Portable tape player and tapes

Camera and film

Extra spokes

First-aid kit

Brake/gear cable

Sandals or tennis shoes for walking around on a break

Comb or brush

Swiss Army knife

Aspirin or other painkiller

Your destination may determine what extra supplies you should carry along. Many times I will make a one-way ride to a friend's house, spend the night, and ride back the next day. This calls for a change of clothes, another pair of shoes, a toothbrush, a razor, etc.

When a training ride is well planned it's surprising how circumstances seem to synchronize perfectly. Preparation in advance will dispel any undue anxiety, allowing you to concentrate on your cycling.

PREPARATION FOR ULTRA-MARATHON CYCLING

Preparation for an ultra-marathon cycling event is an entirely different ball game than a single day ride or race, or even a multi-day stage race where riders compete in events but have rest and sleep periods in between. The word *marathon* is defined as a long-distance race, a contest of endurance. *Ultra* refers to the surpassing of a specific limit or range, exceeding what is common, moderate, or proper.

The term *ultra-marathon cycling* then, simply means riding in the shortest time possible over a distance considered to be beyond human limits. The exact distance and elapsed time will progressively change as cyclists become more proficient in this sport, so the mileage will increase, the time required will decrease, and what is today's ultra-marathon race could be tomorrow's warm-up ride. The characteristics of the event, such as terrain, weather conditions, and distance, together with the age and physical condition of the competitor, must be taken into consideration when a race is planned. An ultra-marathon ride for a 70-year-old is different from that for a 25-year-old. The ultra-marathon cycling distances for the physically disabled may differ from those for the nondisabled.

The sport of ultra-marathon cycling has grown so much in the past 10 years that an entire book could be devoted just to this form of cycling. In fact, there is such a book, entitled *The Ultra-Marathon Cycling Association Manual*, written by John Marino, Lon Haldeman, and myself and edited by Robert Hustwit. The book is sanctioned by the Ultra-Marathon Cycling Association (UMCA), the governing body for the sport. This body was formed in 1980 by John Marino and myself as a matter of necessity since the other governing bodies in the sport of cycling had little or no interest in pursuing the advancement of this faction. Lon, John, and myself were three of the four riders to participate in the original Great American Bike Race in 1982. Robert Hustwit is the executive director of the UMCA and the race director of the Race Across AMerica. The book is available from the offices of Ultra-Marathon Cycling, Inc., 3022 Hesperian, #215, Santa Ana, CA 92706. It covers everything involved with the sport, including UMCA rules and regulations, current records, UMCA–sanctioned events, and detailed instructions on preparing for an ultra-marathon event. These preparations include arrangements for support crews, support vehicles, eating and nutrition, night riding, sleeping, conservation and dissipation of body heat, and problems encountered with rain, traffic, equipment, and training.

The following list is reasonably complete for an ultra-marathon event of 3–10 days. This is the type and amount of equipment I would take on a ride such as the Seattle–to–San Diego Challenge, the Miami–to–Maine race, or the Race Across AMerica. A shorter long-distance ride such as the Spenco 500 would not necessarily require all of the equipment listed here, but you wouldn't want to nullify all of the training and preparation undertaken for such an event by neglecting to take along a part, an article of clothing, or some medical supply. In the Spenco race, for instance, it was so hot during the day, promising to remain so throughout the evening, that taking a woolen jacket seemed inappropriate. I threw it into the support car anyway, just in case. Sure enough, between the hours of 3:00 and 5:00 A.M. the air was moist and quite cool, and donning my woolen warm-up suit saved me from freezing.

The day to day routine of an ultra-marathon event is discussed at length in the chapters in Part IV, "The Highway Education." Basically a rider has two to three vehicles with six to eight support crew members. The vehicles include a motor home, a van, and/or a small car. The motor home needs to be equipped with bathroom facilities, electrical outlets, a water pump, a stove or microwave, and a refrigerator/freezer unit. While almost all eating should be done on the bicycle, the value of the motor home is in preparing hot foods and cold drinks and shakes. A microwave oven and blender can be carried along and plugged into the electrical outlets.

BICYCLE EQUIPMENT

As with anything in life, you get what you pay for. The better the equipment, the better off you are. Comfort is the key to the ultra-marathon event, so perhaps the stiff racing frame geometry is not the best choice of bike, but this is an individual preference and you should experiment long before the event. Two months is a reasonable lead time during which to test your bike and accustom yourself to it completely. Your bike will become part of you. It is merely an extension of your body on the highway. You will love and hate that bike. But one thing is certain: if you don't like it from the start, you will despise it 1,000 miles down the road!

2 complete bikes

Spare components

4–6 pairs of wheels

30 tires

Wheel covers for storing spare wheels

Chains

10–20 water bottles

Handlebar padding

2–4 saddles

Saddle covers or padding (Spenco)

Mechanic's tools

Extra decals for the bike and support vehicles (Remember your sponsors; they need the exposure.)

FOOD-RELATED SUPPLIES

The food itself is an individual choice that will vary greatly, depending on your needs. The supplies, however, are fairly universal and should include the following items:

Cooler

Paper towels

Plastic bags

Bucket

Knives, forks, and spoons (both plastic and metal)

Rubber bands

Napkins

Water bottles

Styrofoam or plastic cups

Trash bags

Ice

Pots and pans

Other cooking utensils—spatula, cutting knife, etc.

Blender

Microwave oven

Ice crusher

Cutting board

Spices

Food staples

ULTRA-MARATHON RIDE CHECKLIST

You should prepare a list that includes all of the essential items listed earlier in this chapter as well as any other personal or special-condition items you'll need. Carefully review your list before leaving for an extensive ride, tour, or competition.

Two pairs of cleated cycling shoes—three or four pairs would be better. (You may have to cut, alter, or experiment with a pair or two to find something comfortable. For example, during the 1984 RAAM I had to slit the sides of my Bata/Power triathlon cycling shoes because my feet had swollen abnormally. Even though these shoes fit perfectly all year long, ultra-marathon cycling does unusual things to your body.)

6 pairs of thin cycling socks (best for the heat)

6 pairs of thick socks (best for the cold and wet)

2 pairs of leg warmers (If it rains, you can switch to a dry pair after.)

2 pairs of arm warmers

6 pairs of cycling shorts with chamois or foam lining

4 skin suits (tight jersey/pants combination made out of lycra)

6 pairs of short-fingered gloves (Padded gloves are a necessity; Spenco gloves are a good choice.)

2 pairs of long-fingered gloves for cold and wet weather

6 jerseys—wool, nylon, etc.

2 pairs of warm-up outfits

2 hardshell helmets (Bell V-1 Pro)

6 caps

2 or 3 pairs of sunglasses

2 pairs clear or lightly tinted goggles for night riding

Contacts or prescription glasses if you wear them (have extras)

Suntan or sunblock lotion (Block is best for true protection.)

Chapstick or lip balm

Insect repellent (especially helpful to the support crew)

Leg oil for cold weather cycling

Massage oil for a rubdown

Hand lotion

Vaseline

Chamois fat to apply to the chamois lining in shorts to keep it soft

Schlock sock—for males only (If your shorts don't fit properly, the constant rubbing of the shorts on the genitalia can cause chafing and rawness, so a soft material "sock" or protective device can be slipped into the pants.)

Rubbing alcohol

Soap and shampoo

Vitamins

Bottled water (In many places in the United States the water from the tap is not drinkable.)

Binoculars for checking out the competition, reading street signs, etc.

Flashlights for reading maps at night, etc.

Cash (Not all gas stations and restaurants accept credit cards.)

Credit cards

Reflective vest for night riding

Lights and reflectors for the bike (In most states it is illegal for a cyclist to ride at night without lights on the bike.)

Portable tape player

Portable tape recorder for the crew to make tapes for you to listen to

Frame bag (Kucharik) to store the tape player or other items while riding

Notebook paper

Calculator

Pens and pencils

Sleeping bags for crew or yourself, especially to sleep in a van or station wagon

Food cup container: handlebar-mounted water bottle cage

Food cups (Plastic cups work best.)

CB radios in each vehicle

3-4 complete sets of maps—one for each vehicle, plus an extra

3 alarm clocks

2 cameras

Film

Hair dryer (great for drying clothes, especially chamois shorts)

Rain gear

Rain gear for the motorcyclist (if you have one)

Gloves for the motorcyclist

Helmet for the motorcyclist

Street clothes for after the event—a suit if you win!

13
TO COMFORT ON A BIKE

"The single biggest reason people quit riding their bikes is pain. Everyone wants to be comfortable on a bike."

Dr. Wayman Spence
Founder, Spenco Medical Corporation

On April 19, 1984, one of the greatest bicycle competitions ever staged in the United States began in Waco, Texas. It was the Spenco 500, a 500-mile race through the magnificent hill country deep in the heart of Texas. It pitted man and machine against temperatures of 95 degrees, winds of 40 miles per hour, and a continuous series of steep hills and gradual climbs. The conditions took their toll. Of the 330 brave souls who entered, only 79 finished. All men are afraid in competition. The coward lets his fear overcome his will to start a race and give it his best shot. In this respect, 330 people won the race.

The Spenco 500 was also a historical event in the evolution of bicycle racing. It was the first time that road racers and ultra-marathon riders were thrown together on the same battlefield in a race over a distance that compromised between a 100-mile road race and a 3,000-mile ultra-marathon race.

The rules were lax. Almost anything was allowed. Drafting, combined teams, relay teams, support teams, open feeding, aid stations, and many

A member of my support team for the Spenco 500, Christa Morones has crewed for me on every ultra-marathon race I have done with the exception of the first Seattle-to-San Diego ride. She has accumulated 19,500 miles of traveling in a support vehicle.

other advantages were permitted. It was like taking touring, racing, and ultra-marathoning rules and throwing them all into one rule book!

Though John Howard and I were picked as prerace favorites, both of us knew there were plenty of potential dark horses who would give cause for consternation. The question of the day was: Would the road racers be able to maintain a blisteringly fast pace for 500 miles, or would the ultra-marathoners catch them down the road as they dropped out exhausted?

The race started at a very fast pace, like any road race offering plenty of prize money—in this case $10,000 for first place. With a tailwind for the first 47 miles, it was a top-gear, 53-x-12 for the first two hours. A break immediately formed. It read like a script: the lead break contained Howard; neoprofessionals Steve Speaks, Charlie Holbrook; and a handful of other road racers. A second break chasing them was made up of myself, Michael Secrest, Pete Penseyres, and the other RAAM riders. Howard's team worked like Swiss clocks, echeloning in a synchronized pace line. We scrambled to catch the leaders, though too frantic to maintain order and discipline. The gap between the front line of riders and the second widened to 5 minutes, then 10. By the 75-mile mark the leaders were 20 minutes ahead of the second group. At 100 miles the gap was nearly 45 minutes.

The fierce tailwinds switched to strong headwinds with reports registering them at 30–35 miles per hour. The heat and the trying conditions soon began to affect the riders, who fell prey to the hardships and began dropping out of the race one by one. Howard's group dwindled to six. By nightfall I was alone with a seemingly insurmountable gap to close. The nighttime was my only hope. Listening to fast-rhythm music, I rode solo for the next 15 hours, bridging that gap to within 10 minutes at the 275-mile mark.

Cutting through the wind by yourself, however, costs dearly, and by morning I was greatly fatigued. By the next afternoon the gap was reopened to 30 minutes with the race nearly over. Howard's group shattered, but not in the manner I had expected. These road racers had the endurance to push that final 100 miles with Steve Speaks and Charlie Holbrook taking first and second well ahead of Howard in fourth place.

Though I had given the race my best effort, seventh place did not feel very satisfying. If only I could have bridged that gap. Unbeknownst to me, however, I had. The next morning at breakfast I was approached by Charlie Holbrook, who explained to me the prejudice most road racers display toward ultra-marathoners. Many of the racers feel that long-distance cyclists are basically tourists who can endure long periods without sleep and who certainly are not serious athletes. During recent years this attitude has created a schism between road racers and marathon riders that has grown quite wide. The Spenco 500 was the race that may have changed this situation.

I was quite moved when Charlie apologized for any negative remarks he may have made in the past about the Race Across AMerica and long-distance cyclists. He admitted how unbelievably tough it had been to cover 500 miles and couldn't imagine going another 2,500. After recovering from the shock, I expressed my own surprise at the incredible speed he and Speaks had maintained for 500 miles. I truly expected them to capitulate by sunrise. We shook hands in what I hope was a first step in bridging the gap between these two forms of cycling.

Finally, I would like to add this: Of the many rewards in cycling—the trophies, prize money, sponsors, travel, publicity—none is as significant as earning the respect of one's peers. In this light, seventh place had a different meaning for me.

The Spenco 500 was also a testing ground for the comfort of the bicycle. I had 28 hours, 45 minutes to think about how to be comfortable on a bike. As we wound through the hills and valleys on our way to Comfort, Texas, and back, I realized that everyone in this race, from the

most experienced ultra-distance and road racing cyclist to the Sunday
tourist, had the same problem of comfort to deal with. Perhaps those
with more training miles would hurt less; however, it is simply a matter
of degree.

TECHNIQUES FOR RIDING COMFORTABLY

Having fun on a bicycle is directly related to how comfortable you are.
Many major body areas—the feet, knees, rear, hands, neck, arms, and
back—are susceptible to discomfort while riding. There may be others
more specifically, of course, but these spots are typically troublesome for
cyclists.

FEET

Two typical problems with the feet are arch problems and "hot foot."
Arch problems probably stem from wearing tennis shoes instead of
cycling shoes. Proper cycling shoes, whether cleated racing shoes or
uncleated touring shoes, have stiff soles to support the arch and provide
pedaling efficiency as you need not push through a thick cushion as in a
tennis shoe. For racing, cleated shoes are a must as they hold the foot on
the pedal and allow you to pull up as well as push down on the pedals.
This is much more efficient and can help relieve some of the pressure
since you are not always pushing down. Some people have arch support
problems anyway, in which case an orthotic may help.

The advantage to touring shoes is that you may walk normally in them
when you aren't cycling. A cleat can interfere with walking.

"Hot foot" may be caused by riding in the heat, by shoes that are too
tight, or by feet not built to push a solid hard sole. For some, the solution
is to use a comfortable touring shoe with a semisoft sole, such as the Bata
Biker. For those who wish to continue to use a cleated shoe, an insole can
be inserted to provide some cushion while not detracting from efficiency.

One final foot problem is swelling. If you have this problem, you can
use shoes that are a half size larger or slit the sides with a razor blade
where the little toe presses the shoe to relieve pressure.

KNEES

The angle at which your foot rests on the pedal can cause knee problems.
If the foot is turned in or out too much, it may cause the knee to follow

through its circular motion at an odd angle and put stress on the tendons on either side of the patella, or kneecap. Most cleated shoes have adjustable cleats. Try different angles until you determine your most comfortable position, then lock it down.

Knee problems related to poor seat positioning can easily be corrected. As a general rule, if there is pain behind the knee, then the seat is too high. If the pain is on top or on the side of the knee, then the seat is probably too low. To set up your seat height correctly, set yourself on the bike seat with both feet on the pedals. You will need someone to hold the bike for you or lean against the wall. With your pedals in the 6 o'clock and 12 o'clock positions (straight up and down), there should be approximately a 10- to 15-degree bend in the knee. Never should your leg be perfectly straight. Once this is set up, take the bike for a ride. When you pedal, your hips should not be rocking back and forth. If they do, it means you are reaching for the pedals and the seat needs to be lowered.

Regardless of your current seat height, when raising or lowering the seat, it should be done gradually over a period of about two weeks, in order to allow your knees to adjust to the new torque and angle.

Knee problems may also be caused by incorrect saddle position. Your saddle can be adjusted forward and backward as well as up and down, and there is a general rule for that as well. Putting yourself up on the bike with feet in the pedals again, rotate the pedals to the 3 o'clock and 9 o'clock positions, parallel to the ground. With the forward knee, take a plumb line or a piece of string with a nut or bolt tied to the end of it and, holding the string on the side of the leg, positioned in the middle of the kneecap, let it drop a straight line down somewhere near the axle of the pedal. Ideally the string should fall directly through the middle of the pedal axle. If it falls behind the axle, move your seat forward. If it lies in front of the axle, move your seat back. The angle at which the knee makes the pedal revolution can affect efficiency and comfort.

REAR

Do not be deceived by any bike expert on the subject of the rear. No one is exempt from the possibility of saddle sores. Obviously, the more you ride, the more you will become accustomed to sitting on the saddle. Your skin will develop a toughness that will help protect it. Of course, the more you ride, the greater the likelihood of your developing saddle sores. Precautions must be taken.

The saddle itself can help prevent soreness. There are many different types on the market, such as those made of leather, plastic, synthetic materials, and combinations of leather, plastic, and padding. Regardless of what type you select, make sure you break it in and adjust to it before making any further decisions as to another selection. Usually, leather saddles need to be softened and broken in, which takes time and many miles of riding. A simpler solution is a good-quality saddle pad like the Spenco Saddle Pad. While there are many on the market, what you should look for is a pad that evenly distributes road vibrations throughout the seat and away from the pressure points in your rear. Many of the seat covers and pads, such as those made of sheepskin, may seem comfortable at first, but the material, once sat upon, will not retain its original shape. Instead, it makes indentations where you have been sitting and within a short period of time becomes useless.

Cycling shorts can also contribute to comfort. They are generally better than running or tennis shorts as they are made specifically for the pedaling motion and will not "creep" up on you or cause chafing as other shorts might. Also, your cycling shorts should be washed after each wearing as the bacteria that accumulate from sweat and dirt can cause saddle sores to develop much sooner than need be. In the Race Across AMerica and other long-distance rides I always change my shorts daily and wash thoroughly to prevent sores from starting.

HANDS

As with knee problems, positioning on the bike can help eliminate hand problems. The tilt of your saddle can determine the amount of pressure your hands will exert on the handlebars.

The most common hand problem is numbness of the fingers caused by pressure on the superficial nerve that lies close to the surface under the skin of the palms. This numbness is called *palmar palsy*, and it can be very annoying and even end a cyclist's career permanently if the condition grows serious.

As a rule, the angle of the seat should be parallel to the top tube. If you are having hand problems, tilt the nose of the saddle slightly upward. This will force you to sit farther back on the seat, relieving some of the pressure on the hands. Try this several times at different angles until you get a comfortable balance in pressure. However, if the saddle nose is tilted too high, this can cause extra pressure in the groin area, possibly causing numbness and thus defeating your original purpose.

I also strongly recommend a good pair of cycling gloves. The leather covering will help prevent chafing, blisters, and the like. If they are padded properly, gloves can protect that superficial nerve in the palm and therefore prevent numbness. Like the seat pad, the glove padding should distribute the road vibration evenly throughout the glove surface and away from the pressure point on the palms. The elastomer found in the Spenco gloves and saddle pads fulfills this need.

It is also good practice to shift the hands around the bars frequently so that pressure can't build up at any one point. You can ride with your hands on top of the bars, on the brake hoods, in the curve of the drops, or on the bottom of the drops. Shifting every 30 seconds or so will help relieve pressure.

NECK

The stem length also requires positioning on the bike. This can greatly affect the angle at which your neck bends forward. Place yourself on the bike with both feet on the pedals and your hands in the drops and look straight down toward the axle of the front wheel. You should not be able to see it; it should be concealed by the handlebars. If the axle is in front of the handlebars, you need a longer stem. If the axle is behind the handlebars, you need a shorter stem.

A new stem may not be necessary, however. First try adjusting your seat backward or forward until that front axle disappears. But keep in mind the plumb experiment performed earlier for proper knee positioning.

Stiffness of the neck can be relieved when riding by exercising to loosen the muscles. When stopped at a signal, let your head drop onto your chest, then rotate it around in circles, and you will feel the tension disappear. Repeat this in the opposite direction. You might even try rubbing your neck with your hands to relieve a little tension. If you have serious problems with your neck, however, consult a doctor or chiropractor for a professional opinion.

ARMS

The main problem related to arms is fatigue. Fatigue in this case also radiates into the shoulders and upper back. The cause of this problem is twofold: incorrect positioning on the bike and lack of strength.

As with the other areas of the body, position on the bike can greatly enhance or hinder the ability of your torso to support itself while riding.

If the stem is too long, you are stretched out too far, making it uncomfortable for your arms and forcing you to lock your elbows. Locked elbows result in the vibration from the highway traveling directly through the bike, into your hands and arms, and finally into the shoulders and back, which must absorb the shock.

If the stem is too short, it forces the body into an upright position that is more suited to a 3-speed touring bike than to a 10-speed racer. This position causes you to bunch up your shoulders and draw the arms in toward the body, which can lead to tension and tightness in the upper back, the shoulders, and the arms.

The correct stem length, as determined by the process described in the "neck" section, should benefit you. The correct position for the arms requires them to bend approximately 45–90 degrees at the elbow. This makes the elbow a "shock absorber" for the rest of the body. Your arms should be relaxed, not stiff and tight. The bicycle moves forward by the pedaling action of your legs, not by gripping the handle bars with tensed arms. As the great Eddy Merckx once responded to a reporter who commented on the small size of his arms, "It doesn't take much strength to steer a bike!"

In addition to being bent at the elbow, the arms should be positioned parallel to the top tube of the bike. The arms should not bow out from the body, for this is not only more tiring but also less efficient aerodynamically, as the arms can catch wind and slow you down.

This position may seem awkward at first if you are not accustomed to it. However, a few weeks of practice should remedy arm fatigue.

Fatigue can also be caused by lack of strength. Many cyclists have seriously unbalanced bodies with huge, magnificent legs and skinny, weak arms. Though Merckx was correct in his observation that it doesn't take much to steer a bicycle, a certain amount of strength is valuable when climbing hills by standing out of the saddle and when sprinting, touring or riding long distances, and during ultra-marathon racing. Here, weightlifting and sports such as swimming can help build strength that may be called upon in cycling. Chapter 9, on weight training, describes some upper-body exercises that can strengthen the torso for cycling.

I have found that swimming helps a great deal with upper-body development while at the same time providing aeorbic training. Using the four basic swimming strokes—freestyle, backstroke, breaststroke, and butterfly—builds considerable strength and forces the lungs to work. Swimming can also be a great novelty for those who ride so much that cycling occasionally becomes a chore.

There are two basic riding positions on a bicycle—sitting and standing out of the saddle—plus infinite variations on them. When climbing hills, both are recommended, depending on your body type and relative strength. Most good climbers suggest alternating sitting and standing to use slightly different muscles. Even on flat ground, getting out of the saddle occasionally relieves stiffness and potential pain in the rear.

BACK

Much of the advice given in the above section on the arms and shoulders applies to the back. In particular, stem length and tension on the upper back and shoulders are related to back problems. The lower back, however, involves different muscles. If you have lower-back problems related directly to cycling, the solution may not be too difficult. On the other hand, if like most people your lower back pain exists regardless of activities on the bike, the prognosis may not be as optimistic or as simple.

I can sympathize with anyone suffering from back pain. It can range from a dull, irritating ache to a crippling pain that interferes with normal daily activities. For three years of my life I was plagued by what began as a sharp specific pain in the lower left side of my back. That pain became a dull ache covering my entire lower back. The pain changed from an occasional annoyance to a constant, ever-present frustration. It progressed from an irritating pain to a crippling agony and forced me to digest 10–20 painkilling tablets a day. Trips to new physicians, experts in the field of spinal disorders, failed to cure the problem. I went from one doctor to the next, trying over a dozen in three years.

This may sound like a familiar scenario. Many people find themselves in similar predicaments because the knowledge and information gathered to date on spinal disorders lacks depth and completeness with regard to etiology and cure. For myself, diagnosis ranged from scoliosis and arthritis to blood disorders and a spinal tumor. The latter theory was the correct diagnosis. The prognosis ranged from 100-percent recovery to a life without movement. One doctor told me to give up athletics and develop my mind. Another had me wear a body cast that held me rigid from neck to waist for a full year.

Since the only sport I could participate in was archery, I had a lot of fun startling the teacher by having a friend shoot arrows at my chest. The arrows bounced off my chest harmlessly when they hit the cast, which was hidden by a shirt!

The solution in my case was surgery to remove the previously unseen tumor. It had, over the course of three years, grown large enough to be detected by special X-ray techniques. Its removal was also the cure for the pain.

Not everyone is as lucky as I was. My fellow ultra-marathon cycling competitor and friend John Marino has suffered constantly throughout his career in cycling ever since a weightlifting accident terminated his career as a professional baseball player. The only sport that would allow John to compete without such excruciating pain was cycling. Though

John has tried chiropractors, fasting, hanging upside down, massage, and many other cures, he still occasionally suffers from the pain.

Back problems, then, are not simply diagnosed and cured, even by experts in the field. I wouldn't pretend that by simply changing your stem length or seat height you can make the pain disappear. The lower back, in particular, doesn't respond readily to such simple cures. I know that John has tried literally hundreds of different combinations of positions on the bike, some of which work better than others but none of which completely solve the problem.

One advantage that may apply here as well as to other areas of discomfort is a bike adjusted to your specifications by an expert. A device called the Fit Kit can take numerous measurements from your body and graph them on a chart in order to calculate exactly how long your stem should be, how high your seat should be, how far forward the seat should be, what size cranks you should use, and what size bike frame is best for you.

Ideally, you may even want to have a bike custom-made for your body. Expert frame builders will consider inseam length, arm length, torso length, overall height and weight, and style of riding when they design your frame. Even the frame geometry, or the angles of the tubing, can make a difference in the comfort of the bike for your body. Only an expert should be consulted, however. The Fit Kit is very expensive and is likely to be found only in a pro shop. Your local pro shop can probably refer you to a professional frame builder who would be able to construct a customized bike for you.

Finally, for all the rules and generalizations regarding positioning on a bicycle in relation to comfort, only you can decide on the most comfortable position for your body. All bodies are different, and no single position will be correct for all people. You can use these guidelines to help, but ultimately your comfort can be determined only by you, the cyclist.

As a rule, cycling allows you to build your body into an ideal condition. The process can be compared to the evolutionary process of natural selection. The animals you now see in their natural environments evolved to suit that environment. Though Charles Darwin wasn't referring to strength in his theory of survival of the fittest, strength does seem to be the factor that makes champions in cycling. Cyclists that are good hill climbers are small and lean with small upper bodies. Cyclists that are good sprinters in flat criteriums and on velodrome tracks tend to be big and bulky with large arms and shoulders. Ultra-marathon cycling, being such a new sport, has yet to evolve the ideal body. Time will tell.

PART
IV

THE
HIGHWAY
EDUCATION

14
A NEW WORLD RECORD
THE FIRST SEATTLE-TO-SAN DIEGO CHALLENGE

"I don't regret anything in my life. I remember the hard work all those years: going to school in the early morning, taking the train to the courts for six hours of practice, then taking the train home, arriving late in the evening, finishing up with homework. It has gotten results. But even if it hadn't, even if I wasn't able to become a champion, I would still know that I gave it my best shot. I tried. I got on the train and tried."

Bjorn Borg

The first Seattle-to-San Diego taught me a lesson on what ultra-marathon cycling was all about. Previous to this ride the longest I had ever ridden was 200 miles. I had no concept of riding well into the night, sleeping for a few hours, then starting all over again the next morning. I had never experienced having to eat on the bicycle and deal with stomach disorders while riding.

I learned the joys and hardships that come with an ultra-marathon ride. It was misery most of the time, but there was just enough satisfaction to motivate me to try again, which I did and I haven't stopped since.

I learned that within me lay another person that I didn't even know existed. Had it not been for the inspiration of John Marino and the hurt I felt for Maureen Hannon, paralyzed in an accident months prior to the ride, I would never have found that person.

September 15, 1980, the scheduled launch date of my first Seattle–to–San Diego bicycle world record attempt, lay one week away as I flipped open the June 30 issue of *Time* magazine and focused on the quote above in an article about one of the greatest athletes of all time, Bjorn Borg. Having won the coveted Wimbledon tennis trophy five consecutive times, Borg was easily deserving of such a title and finds himself ranked with Eddy Merckx (five-time winner, Tour de France) and Muhammad Ali (three-time heavyweight champion of the world) in my book of exemplary individual athletes. This quote consistently returned to the forefront of my mind as I asked myself over and over why I was attempting such a feat.

The statistics were clear enough. According to the maps, San Diego lay approximately 1,500 miles south of Seattle, following a coastline route. My goal was to establish a world record by completing the distance within the span of a week. A quick calculation revealed that this meant riding over 200 miles a day for seven straight days. Since no one before me had ever raced down the length of the United States on a bike, any time would have been a record. However, there would be no point in establishing a time that could easily be shattered, and since only a handful of people in the world have ever ridden 200 miles per day for seven consecutive days, I made this my goal. Eight days would be a record but not a personal triumph.

As my day of reckoning got closer, there were few preparations I could make that had not already been taken care of. I had trained rigorously for months, whipping my body into a condition unparalleled in my life. I had all the modern equipment available to aid me. On my Italian handcrafted Bianchi 12-speed bicycle, I had a Pacer 2000 bicycle computer, grab-on handlebar grips, a cassette tape player, and a food cup for on-the-bike consumption.

I had arranged for a motor home, motorcycle, and mechanic's van to accompany me every moment of the trip. I had five sets of wheels, nearly two dozen tires, and enough spare parts to build a second bike, as well as accessories such as lights, rain gear, helmets, gloves, six sets of bicycle clothing, arm warmers, leg warmers, warm-up outfits, and so on.

Most important, however, was my support crew, which consisted of individuals who not only were experts in their respective fields but also were dedicated enough to want a record as much as I did. I carefully picked the greatest team ever assembled for such an adventure. The all-star cast included the following:

JOHN MARINO, CREW CAPTAIN. At the time of this trip, John was the transcontinental record holder with a time of 12 days, 3 hours, 41 minutes. John had done the transcontinental ride three times, so there was little that could happen on my trip that would come as a surprise. In addition to being a superb athlete and crew leader, John was my mentor and confidant and was at least 50 percent of the reason for the motivation behind this record attempt.

KATHY DYNES, MASSAGE THERAPIST. Kathy was the massage therapist for Marino on the 1980 Los Angeles to New York trip and pulled some nearly miraculous stunts to allow him a speedy trip across the United States. Having worked on my body twice a week for three months before this event, she knew every muscle, tendon, and joint that would be well used for the week.

PHOTO BY PETER ROSTEN

June 16, 1980, John Marino departs Santa Monica on his record-breaking solo transcontinental ride. This was my inspiration for first attempting the Seattle–to–San Diego course as I rode with John the first 125 miles into Palm Springs. I am the second from the right.

On the way to San Jose, the first Shermer support team (left to right): Joanne Penseyres, Michael Ruvo, George Oakley, Kathy Dynes, Dan Cunningham, and crew captain John Marino.

PHOTO BY MICHAEL SHERMER

DAN CUNNINGHAM, BICYCLE MECHANIC. This was to be Dan's third role as crew member on a world record ride. He had already served as the mechanic on a tandem record ride from Los Angeles to New York as well as on John Marino's 1980 ride, and I knew there was nothing that would pose an insurmountable problem for him.

JOANNE PENSEYRES, NUTRITIONIST. Her husband Pete was one of the Tandem Transamerica riders, and she cooked and cleaned and massaged four tired riders for nearly 11 straight days. I estimated that cooking for just one cyclist would seem a joy by comparison.

MICHAEL RUVO, PRESS AGENT/PHOTOGRAPHER. Michael, like me, was new at this game. Not only had he never been on a bicycle trip; he had, for all intents and purposes, never been on a bike. He was, however, one of the best press agents around, having been trained by the renowned entertainer and agent Mario Machado. An adventurous sort, Michael was willing to give it a try.

GEORGE OAKLEY, DRIVER AND FRIEND. George's job was to do anything and everything that needed doing and wasn't being done. A longtime friend, George was devoted to my cause, and I knew I could trust him in the face of any trying odds or obstacles. He didn't let me down.

DECIDING TO RACE

What, in heaven's name, would lead me to believe that I could successfully tackle a task that others before me had spent years training for? The fact of the matter is that a year before I couldn't tell the difference between a bicycle derailleur and a railroad derailleur, and never in my life had I ridden farther than 25 miles.

Landing a job as the managing editor of *Bicycle Dealer Showcase* magazine, the voice of the bicycle trade industry, led me to an interview with John Marino. He was charming, captivating, and compelling, and three weeks later I had my first century under my belt. Within six months I had logged a double-century, deciding at the end of that 16-hour day that marathon cycling took a lot of guts, a little insanity, and definitely was not for me.

Attitudes change, however, and two significant events over the next two months changed the course of my destiny forever. On May 1, 1980, my girlfriend, Maureen Hannon, was in a tragic automobile accident, incurring a broken back that left her paralyzed from the waist down. Devastated by this blow to an individual I was so close to, I quit riding for over a month.

The second event happened on June 16 when I decided it was time to come out of my shell and join John Marino on the first leg of his transcontinental record ride. At the 125-mile mark I decided that it was time to get off my can and do something to help Maureen. After all, my legs worked fine, so why should I let them go to waste? John was on his way to a new record for the breadth of the United States. I would set one for the length, cycling from Seattle to San Diego.

I contacted the Cure Paralysis Foundation and for the next three months devoted 100 percent of my life energies to the cause of helping Maureen, raising money for the charity, and establishing a new world record.

Doubt loomed as September 15 approached. Could I really do it? All the indicators pointed to a successful trip. Body Accounting, a sports testing center in Irvine, California, told me my aerobic fitness level was equivalent to figures taken on the men's national team. My body fat was under 10 percent. Programmed conditioning through advice from John left my body in as good condition as possible for the trip.

A cytotoxic blood examination by Physician Laboratories in Manhattan Beach, California, gave me a scientific analysis of which foods my body could process efficiently and which foods were toxic, or poison to my cells. Dairy products were eliminated, along with beef, grains, and certain nuts. Alacer Corporation supplied me with enough vitamins and mineral supplements to fuel the whole U.S. Olympic team. I was lacking nothing.

To prepare my mind, I attended several sessions of hypnosis with Gina Kuras, a professional hypnotherapist. She helped me train my mind to deal with pain, fatigue, and, most importantly, boredom. I knew that spending 18 hours a day on a bike for 7 consecutive days could lead to some serious psychological problems. She even made me a cassette tape to play during the trip. Gina was there in more than just spirit.

As I stared blankly at the wall mirror the night before I was to leave for Seattle, I knew that I had to do it. There were no excuses. Though an unproven athlete and an unheard of cyclist, I had done everything humanly possible to prepare myself for the trek. Win or lose, record or no record, victory or defeat, I was going to give it my best shot.

AN ILL-FATED BEGINNING

Ironically, the trip began with trouble—not at the start in Seattle, but on the journey from Los Angeles to Seattle. The motor home broke down three times on Interstate 5 with two clogged fuel lines and one flat tire. Naturally, the breakdown occurred 100 miles from nowhere, so the repairs had to be self-administered.

After spending two hours to find the part of the fuel line that was

PHOTO BY MICHAEL RUVO

When you are first starting off in this sport you take anything you can get your hands on. In this case, the bargain I received on this well-used motor home was not worth the savings; I spent more than $1,000 in repairs.

Prerace interviews are important to publicize the sport of cycling and to satisfy sponsors who cover the enormous expenses involved with long-distance cycling.

PHOTO BY CHRISTA MORONES

clogged, John Marino dreamed up a solution for cleaning it—blowing it out with a bicycle pump. We dismantled our Silca floor pump to accommodate a fuel line instead of a Presta valve. Within minutes we had the motor home back on the road again.

Since the fuel line clogged at an inconvenient place, the flat tire naturally occurred at an inconvenient hour—midnight in northern California. Since there was no spare tire, Chuck's Towing service was happy to drive the 100-mile round-trip in the early morning for only $190.

We safely reached Seattle—late and considerably frazzled. However, the warm reception from Josh Lehman, the city bicycle coordinator of Seattle, brought my anxiety level down. Considering the task that now lay only one day away, I was doing OK.

DAY ONE

At precisely 7:00 A.M. on September 15, 1980, I reached down and touched the pressure-sensitive start button on my Pacer 2000 bicycle computer, and the race was on.

Conditions were ideal—clear, sunny skies accented with 75-degree temperatures. I was escorted out of the city by Angel Rodriguez and his girlfriend Carla on their custom-built tandem. Cycling on the interstate was illegal in Washington, so I had to take surface streets from Seattle to Portland. Navigational problems arose instantly, as the turns and jogs are many and the signs either unclear or nonexistent. At least half a dozen errors were made, resulting in a great deal of lost time and energy.

The lulls set in at around 2:00 P.M., after I had covered about 125 miles. My body was detoxifying, forcing the poisons out of the muscles and joints and into the bloodstream for elimination. I had experienced this before on long rides, and I was now worried because in the past my standard recovery period was two to three hours—time I could not now afford to lose. Kathy then performed her first miracle. While massaging my abdomen, she dug her thumb into a pressure point under my rib cage, and within 10 minutes I was back in the saddle feeling great.

I passed the first milestone at around 6:30 P.M. After crossing a bridge over the Columbia River, I saw the "Welcome to Oregon" sign. I was now only a short distance from Portland, my destination for the day.

Reaching Portland at 11:00 that night, I pushed through and past the great city and ended the day on the southern outskirts in an abandoned gas station, having ridden 203 miles for that day.

DAY TWO

The research on sleep patterns shows that we sleep in 90-minute cycles—
from a light sleep to a deep sleep, through dream sleep, and back up to
a light sleep, totaling 90 minutes. With this in mind, I scheduled myself
for three 90-minute sequences per night, dropping off at midnight and
arising at 4:30 A.M.

By 5:00 A.M., I was cruising down Interstate 5 with a brisk, cool
tailwind, maintaining a steady average of 18–19 miles per hour. Breaks
were kept at a minimum—10–15 minutes every 4–5 hours, though as the
days progressed, so did the length of the breaks.

I hooked up a Kucharik frame bag to house a tape recorder so that I
could occupy my mind with some good tunes.

In addition to the music, the crew was constantly dreaming up pranks
and gimmicks to raise a chuckle or two in a face full of pain and fatigue.
I found my water bottles, for instance, were decorated with pictures of
nudes from *Playboy*, accented with cleverly chosen quotes from *Mad*
magazine.

Later on in the day, I was notified that Kathy would be standing with
a paper plate on her chest, and as I rode by I was to take careful aim with
my water bottle and strike a bull's-eye. I missed the plate. In fact, I
missed Kathy entirely but succeeded in nailing Marino square in the
face!

The day ended on an up note—a 2,000-foot mountainous up note. But
the swift descent brought me to a rest stop six miles north of Grants Pass,
where we met George's wife Vicky and her friend Jean, who had driven
up from Medford to greet us. As this was something I was looking
forward to most of the afternoon and evening, I went to sleep peacefully
after riding 210 miles for the day.

DAY THREE

Though I didn't know it at the time, day three was the beginning of the
end for my knees. The hills and mountain passes began immediately that
morning and didn't subside until the sixth day.

I rose once again at 4:30 A.M. The temperature had dropped to a chilly
36 degrees as I pedaled up the second of the four major passes into
Grants Pass. Bundled up in two sets of warm-ups, in addition to a jacket
or two, I reached the top of the summit completely drenched in sweat
and peeling clothes off as fast as possible. The quick descent on the other

side, however, convinced me that it was better to be warm and sweaty than cold and icy.

Grants Pass was my connection for Highway 199, the mountainous pass to the California coast. Midway across the pass, I conquered Oregon and crossed the border into my home state. Shortly past the "You Are Now Leaving Oregon" sign, Kathy marked the passage into California with a "Welcome to Washington" sign, good for a few more laughs.

We reached Crescent City and the Pacific Ocean that afternoon and finished up a few miles south of Eureka late that night. The terrain was extremely hilly with narrow windy roads, providing me with some stiff competition against the logging trucks whose only objective was to get from point A to point B as quickly as possible, regardless of safety. I provided little resistance for them on the shoulder of the roads, minding my own business and finishing at 191 miles for the day.

DAY FOUR

This was to be my worst day. The hills were unending, the weather cold and rainy, and my knees were throbbing in pain. Looking back, regardless of what physical condition an athlete is in, I don't believe that knees are meant to go 500,000 pedal revolutions in one week.

The rain provided its own form of misery. Wearing glasses is a problem that I thought I could overcome by wearing expensive ski goggles. They leaked. John offered me his plastic goggles, which were not meant to go over glasses. They leaked. This left one option: I rode without glasses and squinted to keep out the rain for a good five or six hours.

By 11:00 the rain had subsided, and I found some fresh inspiration in the form of a couple of female cyclists pedaling down the coast with the same destination of San Diego but with a more sensible time frame as a goal—one month. They seemed intrigued by my record attempt and inquired if "I knew that guy who rode from LA to New York."

"You mean John Marino?" I queried slyly.

"Yeah, do you know him?"

"Sure, he's driving the motor home," I replied smugly.

Well, what followed can best be described as a couple of star-struck teenagers stammering over themselves to get the first glimpse of "those magnificent legs!"

Inspired by participating in a world record ride, I pushed on, finally ending the day after covering 172 miles.

DAY FIVE

By this time my knees were in so much pain that I was riding with one hand, while the other administered on-the-bike self-massage therapy. My breaks grew longer as I practiced the fine art of procrastination, which of course decreased my average considerably. I was behind schedule. At the pace I was going, with the long breaks I was taking, there was no way I'd make it to San Diego on Monday.

Worried, my crew made me a motivational tape led by John, who basically told me that if I didn't get my butt moving I would never make it in a respectable time and I could never be considered a world champion.

This tactic worked. I didn't get off the bicycle for about six straight hours and completely lost sight of the motor home. "Good," I vengefully thought to myself. "I'm doing so well that they can't even keep up with me. We'll see who won't make it to San Diego on Monday!"

Unfortunately, it wasn't my tenacity that separated me from my crew. The second flat tire, resulting in a $200 towing and repair bill, left me at the Golden Gate Bridge, chatting with one of the founding fathers of mountain bike racing, Gary Fisher, who escorted me through the city. Finally we were united and, after a TV press conference, pushed on to San Jose. The way to San Jose is the El Camino Real, and on Friday night this becomes the cruising strip for any teenager who can beg, borrow, or steal a car. The reception I received was terrific. We bedded down around midnight, at 190 miles for the day.

DAY SIX

The sixth day turned out to be blissfully uneventful. I picked up a remarkably stiff tailwind, pushing my cruising average up to 24 mph. I knew this would be my day.

It is amazing how a tailwind can cure all aches and pains, especially the mental ones. I felt the best I had ever felt in my life. The previous five days of "conditioning" had culminated in a peak of physical stamina. I stayed on the bike all day, taking minimal breaks to change a music tape or get a quick massage. By early evening I had ridden nearly 200 miles, so I knew that I would achieve the record on Monday—it was just a matter of what time I would arrive in San Diego.

The crew had calculated that a sub-seven-day record was possible but that I would have to give up all sleep and arrive in San Diego at around

5:00 A.M. Since one of the main purposes of the trip was to raise publicity for the Cure Paralysis Foundation, I decided at that point to sleep and go in during the day. I set a new personal record for the most miles ridden in 24 hours when I completed 237 miles for the day.

DAY SEVEN

By now I was in familiar territory. We passed through Santa Barbara and were heading down Highways 101 and 1, roads I was quite familiar with, having driven them dozens of times in the past.

The world of bicycling can be small, and this day provided a classic example of a small coincidence in a large world. The week before my trip I was chatting with Phil Wood of Phil Wood Hubs, who, located in San Jose, told me about a unicyclist he had run into who was taking the same route that I was, from Seattle down to Santa Barbara. Phil thought there was a possibility we might meet somewhere along the way and, calculating his rate of speed as compared to mine, figured we would meet somewhere near Santa Barbara Sunday morning. Well, lo and behold, at approximately 10:00 that Sunday morning I approached what appeared to be a very wobbly bicyclist. Upon closer examination I found it was the unicyclist.

There is more than one way
to bicycle down the coast!

PHOTO BY MICHAEL RUVO

We exchanged stories as we rode side by side, and I clocked his top speed to be 11 mph. When asked about his reason for the trip, he replied, "I just wanted to clear my head and find myself before I go off to college." I couldn't think of a better way to do it!

We stopped in Long Beach and visited Maureen at the hospital, a joyous meeting with hugs, in spite of my less-than-inviting state. A sound night's sleep brought me to the seventh-day-plus time and to the final push into San Diego.

The last 100 miles were the most satisfying of the trip. I felt excellent; I was familiar with the terrain; and, most importantly, I knew that I

PHOTO BY MICHAEL RUVO

The agony of victory—the road construction in the background triggered my hands-free fall at the finish line in front of San Diego City Hall. The only injury was a slightly bruised ego.

My sister Karen showered my with champagne after the fall. The moment of finishing an ultra-marathon ride helps justify the pain and fatigue of the many days before.

PHOTO BY MICHAEL RUVO

would be able to get a full night's sleep without getting up at some indecent hour.

As the city drew nearer, I was accompanied by Kevin Montgomery, of Skid-Lid helmets, and a friend on his tandem, who along with Dan escorted me along the most expedient route to the city hall. As we approached, I noticed a great deal of street construction around the city hall, blocking my prearranged course to the building steps. We detoured around the block, and as I came down the back street the crowd turned around and began to cheer.

I raised my hands above my head in the traditional victory salute, and as I did so I passed into a shadow where, unbeknown to me, lay a large pothole awaiting my front wheel. Naturally, they met, and as they did so I dropped my hands in a desperate attempt to save face in front of television, newspapers, family, and friends. To no avail. Within seconds, rider and bike were flying end over end into a surprised and startled crowd! I came up with a slightly bruised ego, but at this point it didn't matter. It was all over.

The total distance for the trip was 1,515 miles for an elapsed time of 7 days, 8 hours, 28 minutes—a new world record.

15
THE LONGEST DAY
THE HAWAII IRONMAN TRIATHLON

"When a man has quietly made up his mind that there is nothing he cannot endure, his fears leave him."

Grove Patterson

The lesson to be learned from the Ironman is to never attempt an event when you are completely unprepared for one-third of it. I could swim and bike alright, but I had never run more than 13 miles in one stretch. I learned a painful lesson that to be a triathlete you have to be proficient in all three sports.

I also learned how a champion prepares for his victory. I stayed with John Howard in Hawaii that year—the year he won—and observed what it takes to be a champion. When I left Hawaii I knew I would never go back again, triathlons are not for me. But I came away with an image of professionalism that I could apply to my own specialty—ultra-marathon cycling. I began that year to strive to be the best long distance cyclist in the world.

The light was ebbing, and darkness flooded the sky as my tired legs and blistered feet pounded out the final miles down the Hawaiian highway. As I watched the sun break the horizon's smooth crest and slip beneath the ocean, I wondered how many millions upon millions of trips the sun had made across the sky. The day's temperature ranged from 95 to 100 degrees, with the humidity reaching a high of 85 percent. The scorching highway, surrounded by a desert lava wasteland of small, barely rooted shrubs, reached an unforgivable 156 degrees. A typical day for the Kona side of the large island of Hawaii.

February 14, 1981, was not typical for the 333 athletes who came to test their limits of endurance. In the course of the day, these men and women swam 2.4 miles in the rough open surf off the Kailua-Kona coast, then biked 112 miles across the open desert, and finished with a full 26.2-mile marathon run on a searing lava-bed highway. After 26 hours and 20 minutes, 299 individuals knew there was nothing left that they could not endure.

These three events that made up the triathlon were conceived to be back to back to back, with only enough time to change clothes in between. Indeed, to win the event and be known throughout the world as the "Ironman" leaves no room for error.

A rigid, time-consuming training schedule is now the only way to compete successfully with the top triathletes. I have been carefully following the progress of George Yates, an individual who has been chasing that all-elusive Ironman title for many years. Each year George has increased his finishing position, and each year he has intensified the seriousness of his training program. This direct correlation between effort and results netted him a 33rd-place finish in 1981, a 12th-place finish in 1982, and a 7th-place finish in 1983. George trained in at least two of the events every day, many times practicing for all three. For the swimming, this included trips to the rather chilly Pacific Ocean off the coast of southern California.

There is no secret to training. As a successful businessman once said, "The dictionary is the only place where success comes before work." Like most of the athletes who finished in the top 20 or so, George made a commitment to excellence in performance that could be reached only through dedicated hard work.

In the 1981 triathlon, as in all endurance events of this caliber, hundreds of people who knew they couldn't win in the traditional sense were competing to be winners for themselves. Even finishing was a formidable task.

A blind man, guided by a paddleboarder in the ocean, sitting on the back of a tandem for the bike ride, and led by a friend through the run, completed his goal in 16 hours. Walt Stack, 73 years young, finished last, but finished—in 26 hours and 20 minutes. Many of the 10,000 spectators and 900 volunteers stayed to watch him cross the finish line.

As for me, I figured that after establishing the world record for riding the West Coast of the United States for the first time in 1980, the

Though forced to walk the last few miles of the marathon, I managed to run the final 100 yards to the finish line in Kona, Hawaii.

triathlon would be no problem. I was wrong. After the first hour and 20 minutes into the contest I was 189 places behind the leader as I left the ocean and mounted my bike. I had my moment of glory when I passed 150 cyclists before the 85-mile mark. With a brisk tailwind on the first half of the ride I averaged 22 miles per hour for those 56 miles.

My downfall came later as many of those 150 people, being seasoned runners, passed me as I took more than four hours to run the marathon. Never having run more than 13 miles in my life, I found that each passing mile brought new and interesting stresses to my body. When I hit the 26-mile mark I wondered who had added the extra two-tenths of a mile that makes up a full marathon. No matter; I was feeling no pain, just numbness.

During such a long and stressful day, I saw numerous incidents and events that added color to an otherwise grueling and monotonous task. I passed one fellow on a bike whose left crank had come completely out of the bottom bracket and left him pedaling with just his right leg. The first woman out of the water searched frantically around the changing room for her temporarily lost cycling shoe. At the changing room prior to the last leg, about 25 of the competitors, knowing they had no chance of winning, busied themselves with massages, told ocean and bike stories, and wondered about their placing in the race at this point.

The beginning of the triathlon is humorous to watch. At the sound of a cannon, thousands of people simultaneously dive into a narrow strip of ocean. With a plethora of thrashing arms and legs, it seemed like a frenzied shark-feeding.

Speaking of sharks, many of the competitors questioned the likelihood that a shark would find its way to a delightfully muscular meal. None was sighted. However, a few dolphins joined the lead swimmers, possibly wondering what business this other mammal had in the Kona Sea.

The February 1982 triathlon provided one of the most dramatic finishes in the history of any marathon sport. In the women's division the lean, slightly built Julie Moss found herself in the lead midway through the marathon run. Later she was to comment that at that point she was surprised to find herself in that position and had "only come to finish." As the miles and hours waned, so did Julie's energy, and by mile 20 her body began to show signs of extreme fatigue. It was nightfall by then, and her run had slowed to a trot, aid stations had become walk-through rest areas, and 8-minute miles became 10-, 12-, then 15-minute miles. She was soon to hit what cyclists call the "bonk" and runners call "hitting the wall." Time and energy were almost gone.

On the horizon was Kathleen McCartney, whose body seemed to grow stronger with each passing mile. Not knowing how far in front Julie Moss was, Kathleen pushed onward, expecting a very respectable second place. She had no idea that the gap was closing with each stride across the lava pavement.

With two miles to go, Julie hit the wall and her body quit. She collapsed in a heap, with spectators crowding around, unable to help for fear of disqualifying her. Her mind did not give up, however, and through the inner will that drives all winners, she struggled to her feet after four unsuccessful attempts on legs that looked and acted like a newborn colt's. Julie started again with a walk, which soon became a trot, bringing hope and tears to the many well wishers along the roadside.

Now aware of the closing McCartney, Julie cried out, "How far back is she? I've got to know." Kathleen's stride became quicker. Like the horse nearing the barn, she sensed an end to this misery and a dim hope that she could possibly catch the leader.

The end was near, and all Julie Moss had to do was hang on. If she could just maintain this pace for the final mile, victory would be hers. With less than 100 yards to go, however, a second collapse came, and with it the moans and cries of a now partisan crowd. "Get up, Julie, you're almost there," came the support. "Just a few hundred more feet."

Within two minutes Julie was unbelievably back on her feet, waddling down the street, with the Bud Light Triathlon finish line banner now within sight. With each step came agony, driving home the thought that victory would be so sweet when it finally came. Meanwhile, an undaunted Kathleen McCartney drove on.

With 15 feet to go, staring at the white finish line through blurred eyes, Julie broke into a final run for the gold, collapsing for a third time, three feet from victory. Now crawling on her hands and knees, eyes focused only on the end, she was too delirious to see Kathleen sprint past unceremoniously, oblivious to Julie and the crowd surrounding her.

"How far behind the winner did I finish?" Kathleen queried.

"You just won," came the news, and for a few moments the shock set in.

"Oh, my God," cried Kathleen. "I had no idea."

The crowd was divided. They had a winner, but the woman to be crowned was on her back, unconscious, with her sweat-stained hair draped across the finish line. The most respectable second place in the history of marathon sports. Julie Moss had discovered the psych in cycling. She reached beyond the known limits of human endurance and left her fears behind forever.

16
EXPLORING THE LIMITS
THE 1981 SEATTLE-TO-SAN DIEGO CHALLENGE

"A hero is no braver than anyone else; he is only brave five minutes longer."

Ralph Waldo Emerson

I went into the 1981 Seattle-to-San Diego ride with the vision I took from Hawaii—treat every race as a professional would. I went into this ride 100 percent more prepared than I was for the previous West Coast trek, which was more of a tour.

I learned to prepare myself by making lists of all items I would need on the trip. It is so easy to forget small items that seem insignificant but 1,000 miles down the highway they become critical. I also learned that if you look, act, and talk like a professional does, you eventually begin to perform like one as well. I shaved my legs, sacrificed tasty junk food for quality nutrition, and devoted more and more time to one purpose—*cycling*.

Exploring the limits of human endurance began for me in 1981 when a powerful cyclist from San Francisco shattered my record of 7 days, 8 hours for the Seattle-to-San Diego ride established in 1980.

Doug Steward took a shorter inland route and toppled the record by covering the course in 4 days, 22 hours and knocked the wind out of my sails. No sooner had the ink dried on the news releases than a health enthusiast from Irvine, California, Clint Worthington, completed the same route in 4 days, 18 hours. I owe a great deal of my current success to these two gentlemen.

154

"Enough is enough," I thought to myself. My conquerors averaged 275 and 288 miles per day, respectively. That makes the 1980 trip look like a Sunday fun ride. I would have to be the first in cycling history to average over 300 miles per day.

Marino and I sat down and plotted it out: a new course, less sleep, shorter breaks, all meals eaten on the bike, a 24-hour first day without sleep, and a nonstop blitz at the end. It could be done. I had my goal.

To cover that many miles in a day requires a nearly flawless orchestration of rider, support crew, and equipment. I left nothing to chance. I acquired the finest equipment and clothes, a support crew of professionals whom I knew to be well suited for a trip of this nature. I even took my chances on a tire that had served me well in 1980. My front tire, a Pneudan tubular, had gone the distance without a flat. With my four-leaf clover in hand, I had my mechanic and crew captain Dan Cunningham mount it a second time—"just to see how long it would last."

DAY ONE

At 12:01 A.M., Sunday, August 23, 1981, Seattle City Hall played the same role it had one year ago—the granite starting block. For good luck, Angel Rodriguez of R & E Cycles accompanied me nearly halfway through Washington on his Rodriguez tandem, with his girlfriend Carla as the stoker.

PHOTO BY LARRY BARBER

The handoff: Christa passes a food cup on Interstate 5. Later techniques, like passing from a moving vehicle, proved to be more efficient and provided less opportunity for mistakes—like dropping the cup.

To break the record, I knew I would need a first day well in excess of 300 miles. Covering the first 100 miles in 5 hours and 3 minutes, I was quite encouraged. I reached the 200-mile mark in Portland by 11:00 A.M. and was headed for a triple-century when a headwind beat me into a 13-mile-per-hour average for the entire afternoon. I finally hit 300 miles along with darkness and light rain, forcing me to don the rain gear and go against the elements. But Lady Luck was with me that year, as the rain and winds quickly subsided, and at midnight my bike computer read 340 miles—a personal high.

DAY TWO

Psychologists say that 4½ hours of sleep is sufficient for survival. When I arose at 4:30 A.M. survival was at the forefront of my mind. I knew this would be a tough day since I vividly remembered the hills that lay ahead. What I wasn't able to fathom was how I would feel after a 340-mile ride the day before. After five consecutive 1,000-foot ascents averaging a dismal 8 miles per hour, headwinds and frustration occasionally got the better of me as I took short breaks for both physical and mental relief.

As my home state of California drew closer, the nine-mile, seven-percent grade on Interstate 5 loomed large in my mind. I had to hit this before darkness fell so I could take full advantage of the screaming downhill across the border. Neither climb nor descent was a disappointment. It took exactly one hour to get up the mountain and nine minutes to get down!

Crossing my home state border naturally required a crew celebration, including party streamers, singing, a bicycle license plate spelling MIKE, and Christa Morones donning my cycling gear, skin suit, false beard and chest hair, sunglasses, and helmet—so much a replication of me, in fact, that in pictures seen later, it was difficult to tell who was who.

In spite of the fun and frivolities, this was my slowest, toughest day, ending in the cold, dark mountains 30 miles north of Redding at 11:00 P.M., 265 miles for the day.

DAY THREE

By now the excitement of the trip had worn off. I was oblivious to the ever-present camera crews. Even a beautiful sunrise in the scenic mountains of northern California did little to dissipate the fatigue, pain, and stiffness I was experiencing after 605 miles in just two days.

Rest breaks should be run like Indy 500 pit stops, compressing as many activities into as short a time period as possible. Here Kathy Dynes massages one foot as the other is being cooled by ice. Christa is reviewing the route with me as I consume cookies and drink a Hansen's fruit juice drink. Meanwhile, the bike has been looked over and vehicles gassed and cleaned.

After the last 250 miles of constant hills, I was looking forward to some fast, flat highway. At the 700-mile mark, I was halfway home and approaching the state capital—Sacramento.

The closest thing to a disaster on the trip occurred 50 miles north of the capital city, when motor home, mechanic's van, film crew, and rider were all completely separated from each other and lost. Since we had all discussed the possibility of meeting on the steps of the state capitol to see Governor Jerry Brown, I pressed onward in hopes the others would do the same. Undaunted by heat, traffic, and medfly quarantine warnings, I arrived at the capitol steps to find the entire crew, as delighted to see me as I was them.

We pushed on to Stockton, for a 285-mile day, bedding down at 2:00 A.M. It would be my final hours of sleep as the most precious commodity of all was running out—time.

DAY FOUR

After a three-hour nap I began what John Marino calls "the blitz." For me this was a 500-mile, nonstop race to San Diego. I saw the first Los Angeles sign, indicating that there were 339 miles left, and I knew I was within striking distance of the record—but it would be close.

By midday, temperatures had risen to above 100 degrees, and after more than 500 miles of flat highway I was begging for a bump. Interstate

5 would grant me no relief. I now had to call on the reserves from within—the mental discipline to keep the cranks spinning.

The key to enduring pain and fatigue is to detach the mind from the problem at hand and let the body adapt. Yogis can walk on nails without pain by utilizing meditation and detaching their minds from the pain. Music from Dan Fogelberg and the Moody Blues via a portable cassette player helped me detach myself from the pain.

It was now in excess of 110-degree heat, and the key to riding in such heat is a good skin suit, which was custom-made for me by Kucharik Bicycle Clothing; lots of cold Hansen's juices; and a crew to dump buckets of water over my head. I survived the heat, suffered a mild sunburn accompanied by heat blisters on my thighs, and reached the "grapevine" north of Los Angeles with 200 miles left to ride.

The grapevine is a nine-mile, seven-percent grade heavily trafficked with hundreds of four-axle trucks on a tight schedule of delivery. A cyclist at midnight is not of primary concern. This could have been a psychological crisis had I not had a surprise visit from John Marino, who pulled alongside and wanted to know if I happened to be riding to San Diego and if he could join me!

At the 24-hour mark of the blitz, I shelved my special cytotoxic diet of fruit, chicken, fish, and pasta for a sugar-coated donut. What could it hurt? As it so happens, a half-hour sugar high, followed by the bonk, left me flat on my back on a bus-stop bench, trying to get my body moving. A six-minute nap, a cup of tea, and the final sunrise of the ride got me moving to San Diego with no looking back. Now it was just a question of avoiding aggressive motorists, keeping well fed and watered, and gutting out the last of 14 century rides.

By now riders were picking me up along the way to escort me the final miles. With adrenaline flowing as I closed in on the finish, I was feeling no pain. The final mile found one thought on my mind—don't crash at the finish line.

I made my last left turn to the city hall in San Diego and was greeted by a police escort, barricaded side streets, and a very warm and large welcoming committee. I stayed upright across the finish line, hands above the head—4 days, 14 hours, 15 minutes since I left Seattle.

Dan Cunningham immediately peeled off the front tire—it had gone the entire distance again! Charlene Shank of the United States Cycling Federation quickly calculated the statistics—1,386 miles, 301.3 miles per day average, with the final stretch from Stockton to San Diego covering 501 miles in 32 hours.

PHOTO BY CHRISTA MORONES

Crew captain Dan Cunningham gives me a victory pat on the back after first crowning me with the tire that made the distance of both Seattle–to–San Diego rides, a total of 2,800 miles. USCF official John Butterfield records the official time of 4 days, 14 hours, and 15 minutes.

PHOTO BY CHRISTA MORONES

A moment of glory, but only an overture to what was to come the following summer— the Great American Bike Race.

17
REACHING
THE LIMITS
THE GREAT
AMERICAN BIKE RACE

endure \ in-'d(y)u(ə)r \: 1. to continue in the same state 2. to remain firm under suffering or misfortune without yielding

Webster's New Collegiate Dictionary

In the 1982 Great American Bike Race I received the surprise of my life. I discovered that you can ride 48 straight hours without sleep. Unfortunately this was an example of negative discovery. I found out by sleeping while my competitor, Lon Haldeman, rode through the first and second nights without sleep. What a shock that was— to go to bed one hour behind the leader and wake up four hours behind!

Another thing I learned about was one of sleep deprivation's by-products: hallucinations. My mind did things that I had never experienced before. In addition to seeing things that simply were not in my visual field, there were psychic experiences as well. I went through Springfield, Illinois, recognizing every street and building, though I have never been there in my life.

I also learned about nutrition. I discovered that too much sugar is destructive while too careful of a health food diet does not provide enough calories. I had never before in my life eaten over 10,000 calories a day and still lost weight!

At 10:06 A.M. PDT, on Wednesday, August 4, 1982, the longest, most demanding bicycle race in history began. The 1982 Bud Light Great

American Bike Race was to put the world's four top ultra-marathon cyclists in a 3,000-mile competition to determine once and for all who was the best. Geographically, it would be a race from the pier in Santa Monica, California, to the Empire State Building in New York, New York. Psychologically, it was a battle of wills to see who could suffer without yielding the longest. Who could endure the most pain? Who could sleep the least?

Tuned and trained to a peak of physical and psychological preparedness, Lon Haldeman, John Howard, John Marino, and I launched the inaugural Great American Bike Race from the pier and, in addition to hundreds of well-wishers, left behind tension, nervousness, years of planning and training, and the knot in the pit of the stomach that comes with the anxiety experienced before a major event in one's life.

The race really began in 1978 after John Marino first crossed the country by bicycle. In an interview in 1979, when I first met John, I asked him what his plans for the future were. "I've got a dream," John explained. "Someday I'd like to organize the Great American Bike Race and get three or four cyclists to race across the country."

The years went by as ultra-marathon cycling records traded hands. John Marino set a new record in 1980. Lon Haldeman destroyed that time, and on this August 4 race day he remained the man to be beaten. John Howard was crowned the Cyclist of the Decade ('70s) and became the Ironman of the triathlon in Hawaii in 1981. Meanwhile, the Seattle–to–San Diego course was traversed four times within one year

PHOTO BY BRUCE MARTIN

Jim Lampley and Diana Nyad review the course and logistics of the race for the cameras as the four riders await the 10:00 A.M. start.

John Howard, Lon Haldeman, John Marino, and I stand poised and ready for the start of the first and longest ultra-marathon bicycle race in history.

with my time of 4 days, 14 hours being the fastest for the year and qualifying me to participate in this, the first transcontinental race.

One morning over breakfast in Cleveland, Ohio, at the April 1981 Bikeamerica Exposition, John Marino, John Howard, and I decided we would have the ultimate showdown the following year. Four months later, after Lon's record crossing, Marino invited Haldeman to make it a foursome.

These four—a unique gathering of backgrounds, talents, skills, and personalities—rode out of Los Angeles together, until San Timeteo Canyon Road, approaching the 75-mile mark at Beaumont, California. At this point, the race, which had been neutral as we crawled our way through city traffic, began with the desert and over 100-degree unforgiving heat. Having never challenged this 3,000-mile course, neither John Howard nor I had any particular strategy. Marino's philosophy, as explained by a sign in his motor home, was "Remember the tortoise and the hare."

Lon, whose demeanor was quiet and unassuming before the race, had a strategy that became obvious from the beginning. He set out with an incredibly grueling pace that left all of us, including the "hare," John Howard, in the dust. As fast as Lon pulled out in front, Marino fell behind with numerous bike problems, including flat tires and a crank that fell off.

Although the order of the race was to change numerous times

PHOTO BY BRUCE MARTIN

A portable cassette player mounted in a Kucharik frame bag with lightweight headphones makes the hours go by quicker and the pace pick up when listening to fast-beat music. A white skin suit was designed by John Kucharik for the purpose of reflecting the desert sun off the body.

throughout the next few days, the order that prevailed in the desert on day one—Haldeman, Howard, Shermer, Marino—was to be the finishing order.

The second part of Lon's strategy came with sunrise on day two as Haldeman chose to skip sleep while the rest of us got off our bikes for several hours.

Marino's problems continued, and the excessive 115-degree heat left Howard out on the side of the road at the Arizona border, where I passed him to move into second place near midnight. At 3:00 A.M. I was 90 minutes behind Lon and planned on sleeping only 3 hours. It would turn out to be one of the longer sleep periods of the race. Since Lon would surely sleep 4–5 hours, I figured I would catch him in the morning. However, I was to awake to the news that I was now 4½ hours behind— Lon had ridden throughout the night.

Unlike the Seattle-to-San Diego challenge, which can be catalogued in day-to-day mileage and times, the Great American Bike Race produced a new element no one expected except Lon—sleep deprivation.

As the days passed, second, third, and fourth places exchanged hands, but Lon Haldeman stood steadfastly in front, seemingly tireless. Howard caught me in Flagstaff, Arizona, and together we rode for a few hours, discussing strategies by which to catch Lon. Again at 3:00 A.M. I bedded

John Howard lost valuable time the first two days, as his training didn't prepare him for the heat of the desert or the blistering pace that Haldeman set the first 700 miles.

PHOTO BY BRUCE MARTIN

PHOTO BY BRUCE MARTIN

Massage therapist B. J. Anderson and chiropractor Dr. Bill McKean attempt to put some life back into my body at the Arizona/New Mexico border.

down for three hours, trying to pace myself, hoping Lon would eventually break. This was a tactical error. Lon once again deprived himself of sleep, and Howard continued on into the night, knowing that with each sleeping minute he was pulling farther away from me.

By the fourth day we had passed the continental divide and were approaching the Great Plains states of Texas, Oklahoma, and Kansas. Having never crossed the continental divide, I mistakenly expected a dramatic dropoff in the geography and was hoping for a fairly steep descent that would last 50 miles. What I discovered was that in the southern United States the continental divide is very subtle. If a sign hadn't been posted on the side of the road, I never would have been aware that I had just crossed the divide.

As we passed through the plains, hundreds of thousands of acres of corn were spread out as far as the eye could see. Silos strategically placed every 10 miles marked the progress of the race and served as goals along the way for me. I would time myself between silos to see if I could improve my speed. After over 1,000 miles, however, speed was no longer a factor. It was now just a matter of staying on the bike as long as possible. Since Lon seemed to be averaging approximately 1 mile per hour faster, in the course of a 21-hour riding day, that would amount to a 210-mile spread over a 10-day crossing. I would now have to make my move. I would need to go without sleep for nearly 6 consecutive days.

Being a psychologist, I knew what the consequences of this decision would be. In classic sleep deprivation experiments, after only two days of sleeplessness, subjects begin to lose fine motor control in manual dexterity tasks, and their thinking slows. After three days of sleep deprivation, hallucinations begin, and subjects begin to lose touch with reality. By day four hallucinations run rampant, and there is a definite loss of touch with reality with the subject unaware of his location or his reason for being there.

It was interesting, yet distressing, to watch these symptoms unfold before my eyes. While descending the nine-mile drop into Albuquerque, New Mexico, I "saw" John Marino running alongside me. Approaching Indianapolis, Indiana, I hallucinated that trees were creatures and monsters leaning over the road to attack me. In Athens, Ohio, I visualized blotches of pavement as every type of animal imaginable— dogs, lions, giraffes, and snakes.

I wasn't the only one suffering these mental effects. As an article in *Bicycling* magazine reported: "Three days into the race John Howard was overcome by the noonday sun, a huge searing ball of fire that broiled his back. Suddenly he slammed on the brakes and screamed, 'Look out for the brick wall!' Aghast, his crew members leaned out the support car window. They knew there were no brick walls on Highway 89."

I never knew what the expression "loss of touch with reality" meant until I reached Decatur, Illinois. Riding along the two-lane highway, my crew captain, Dan Cunningham, pulled alongside in the mechanic's van and inquired if I needed anything to eat. "Who are you?" I queried. "Where am I, California?" Composed but inwardly shaken, Dan carefully explained that they were my support crew for this race to New York and that I was in Illinois. "Oh, all right," I responded as I continued to pedal down the road.

What makes this experience especially interesting is that I was aware the entire time of my hallucinations and distortions of reality. Even

*Riding through Jefferson
City, Missouri, my hands
became extremely fatigued
and partially paralyzed, so I
had the handlebars wrapped
in an additional layer of
foam and tape.*

PHOTO BY BRUCE MARTIN

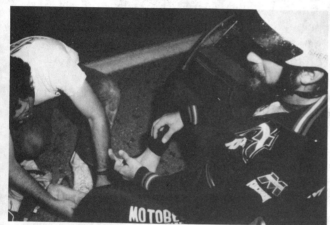

*Crew captain and mechanic
Dan Cunningham also did
whatever needed to be
done—in this case dressing
me!*

PHOTO BY BRUCE MARTIN

having someone explain to me the reality of the situation, or even knowing in my own mind that the creatures were not real and that John Marino was not really running along next to me, didn't change the effects of the physical stress and sleep deprivation. The psychological side effects were in force whether or not I was aware of them.

This leads me to believe that these hallucinations and distortions of reality are chemically based. If psychologically determined, then my awareness of them should have enabled me to change them.

Psychologists specializing in sleep and dreams now know that sleeping is tied in with a chemical in the brain called *serotonin*, and dreaming is connected with a chemical called *noradrenaline*. An increase in serotonin induces sleep. An increase in noradrenaline induces dreaming. It is my feeling from my personal experiences that these hallucinations were induced by noradrenaline. My brain was experiencing the dream state, even in the semiawake state.

A RACE WITHIN A RACE

At the Illinois border Lon Haldeman had accumulated an insurmountable lead. He had put nearly 175 miles between himself and John Howard, and had built up a 195-mile lead over me. John Marino was suffering excruciating saddle boils, located so that, no matter how he sat on the saddle or how many different saddles he tried, pain wracked his body. John's pace dropped dramatically. More importantly, his time off the bike increased—a sign of the end.

For me, the thought of trying to chase down Lon became increasingly depressing. I knew what 200 miles meant—over 12 hours of riding time. Even with five days of little or no sleep I was unable to close the gap to within striking distance.

My final hopes were dashed coming out of Athens, Ohio, descending a hill at nearly 30 miles per hour. I fell sound asleep and made direct contact with the guardrail separating the road from the cliff below. While only a few bruises and scrapes were incurred, the crew determined it was time for sleep. It was, indeed, a rude awakening.

With first place virtually locked up by Lon and out of my reach, I focused my thoughts, attentions, and energies on reeling in John Howard, who was within striking distance. He had narrowly escaped from my clutches in Springfield, Illinois, where I was closing in while he was sleeping. The police escort that accompanied each of us through the entire state of Illinois informed me that he had just spoken to another officer who was with John and that Howard was sound asleep in downtown Springfield. Now only 15 miles out of town, I picked up the pace. As I was nearing the city limits, however, Howard's crew informed him of my approach, and he immediately got back on the bike and went flying down the highway. My crew then plastered an old magazine picture of Howard on the rear window of the motor home and wrote beneath it: "John Howard: Wanted dead or alive."

By concentrating on catching Howard I was able to gain some ground on Haldeman, but the distance was so great that it would now take an act of God to stop him, and at that time I felt that perhaps this was the only way he could be stopped! The distance between Howard and myself fluctuated the rest of the way to New York as John maintained dim hopes of Lon slowing or collapsing.

DIET

It was calculated after the race that each of us consumed over 10,000 calories a day in order to maintain the pace of crossing the country in 10 days. Marino and I have been known to choose carefully planned, scientific diets, programmed to meet every need. A cytotoxic blood test provided us with a list of foods that we were allergic to. The test analyzes the cellular reaction of red and white blood cells to 150 different food substances. For instance, my red blood cells show an extreme allergic reaction to dairy products. The cells actually clumped together, causing a phenomenon known as *sledging*, in which single-cell-width capillaries are clogged by clumped red blood cells, thus inhibiting an efficient blood flow during exercise.

For the first three days I adhered to a reasonably strict fruit and vegetable diet until my body became so acidic that I began to develop white cold sores on my tongue. The reports filtered up from the Marino camp that he was suffering the same affliction. I also felt weak and unable to pedal at my normal strength level. I then switched to the Haldeman diet. After all, at this point he was over 100 miles ahead, so I figured it couldn't hurt to try a new diet.

The Haldeman diet is the All-American junk-food-junkie diet. It's also known as the "seefood" diet. You eat whatever you see. Lon eats hamburgers and fries, pizza, milk shakes, ice cream cones, and everything else that is presented to him.

This turned out to be one of the better strategic moves I made during the race. I felt stronger, the tongue sores disappeared, and I was able to spend more time in the saddle. In fact, when I first tried a chocolate milk

PHOTO BY BRUCE MARTIN

In ultra-marathon cycling, eating is done on the bike for increased time efficiency. Here a chocolate shake is consumed. Ice cream and shakes seem to be the favorites of most long-distance riders.

shake, it energized me more than anything I had tried thus far. I began to drink them as often as possible. This wasn't easy on the crew, who didn't always have the right ingredients in the limited motor home kitchen, and malt shops are not common in many of the desolate areas of the United States that the course took us through.

I recall an incident in West Virginia when I had been craving a chocolate shake all day. As dusk fell and the shadows stretched before me, the crew finally delivered—an extra-large chocolate shake, carefully prepared from a family-owned hamburger shop, the best kind. They passed it to me as I crested a long climb so I placed it in my handlebar water bottle cage, waiting until I got to the bottom of the long, bumpy hill that stretched before me. Traveling at over 35 miles per hour, I was soon wearing the shake from the waist down!

RECORDS WERE MADE TO BE BROKEN

At the beginning of the race, many wondered if it would be possible to break Haldeman's 1981 transcontinental record of 10 days, 23 hours. After all, he had very good weather conditions that year.

A social psychological process known as *social facilitation* occurs whereby competitors generally perform better against another competitor than against themselves or the clock. The Great American Bike Race supported that theory. At the halfway mark, Haldeman, Howard, and I were all on pace to beat the old record. Lon, in fact, was on an 8-day, 23-hour pace until the Midwestern headwinds and rain slowed him down.

Five days of continuous headwinds took their toll on our speed and daily mileages. More importantly, however, the winds were psychologically devastating. To be told you are traveling at only 12 miles per hour on level ground or, worse, on a slight descent becomes difficult to deal with day after day. To look down at the rear cluster and reaffirm that you are riding in a much easier gear than you would ever use on such flat terrain is very discouraging.

After four days of this I finally cracked. Disgusted at my dismally slow 13 miles per hour, I did a 180-degree turnabout and went flying down the highway at well over 25 miles per hour in the wrong direction! My crew was screaming frantically at me, but I only had a smile and this to say: "I've finally got my tailwind!" The thought of having to cover any more ground than was necessary beyond the 3,000 miles already slated brought me back to the cold reality of 13 miles per hour with my head tucked low on the handlebars and my legs straining against the wind.

Though our speed was diminished, the three of us were still on pace to break all previous transcontinental records. This included the four-man, two-tandem record of 10 days, 21 hours set by Pete Penseyres/Rob Templin and Bruce Hall/Brooks McKinney in 1979. If I couldn't win the race, I could at least try to beat their mark—the fastest crossing ever. Competition was pushing us beyond what we would be capable of if it were a solo attempt against the clock.

THE DOCTOR'S REPORT

Due to the exceedingly stressful nature of this event, the race had recruited a medical doctor whose specialty is sports medicine. Dr. Don Baxter went along for the ride, checking the riders daily for injuries, fatigue, proper nutrition, and overall state of mind. An excerpt from his official race report approximately 2,000 miles into the race read as follows:

> The temperature during the early morning hours dipped to a chilling 46 degrees, and Shermer, as well as the other riders, preferred to sleep to avoid the cold but were unable to do so if they were ever to catch Haldeman.
>
> The lack of sleep is taking its toll on Shermer. Many parts of his body are growing numb, including his feet and palms, and Shermer had difficulty walking when he was off the bicycle. Even tasks such as talking became a tremendous burden. Shermer found himself dozing off while on the road. His seat and knees still hurt, but his one driving concern was to pass Howard.
>
> The strain on Marino's knee was not improving, but he had gotten used to the pain and did not complain. Marino's lower back strain was causing him severe discomfort, and he often rode slouched over the front handlebars as far as he could to relieve the agony. Marino's biggest handicap was now emotional. He hadn't seen Shermer for days and seemed to lack the incentive to win but still maintained the unbelievable drive to finish the race. His face was now dark red, making his eyes seem more puffy than they actually were. He started to hallucinate and saw multiple images.
>
> Howard claimed to be feeling tired but looked quite healthy considering his lack of sleep. His appetite was ravenous, and when food was offered to him from the support vehicle he would grab at it with animal-like lunges. Howard was ingesting substantial quantities of meats, starches, and was now drinking abundant fluids.

Although Haldeman looked tired, he claimed to feel fine and supported this statement by maintaining a 15-mile-per-hour pace over any terrain he crossed. His palms grew numb, and he considered switching his hand brake from the left side of the handlebar to the right to help ease the pain but abandoned this idea for fear of forgetting which side the hand brake was on in the event of an emergency and possibly risking a severe accident. Haldeman was extremely well hydrated. He continued to drink his mixture of milk, instant breakfast, and honey and ate cheeseburgers and pizzas.

NEW YORK, NEW YORK

With less than 300 miles to go before reaching the Empire State Building, the news flashed back to me and the crew as we passed through West Virginia that Lon Haldeman had just won the race. Too weary to raise his hands in the traditional victory salute, Lon rolled across the finish line into a throng of people with an incredible time of 9 days, 20 hours, and 2 minutes. He was the winner of the first transcontinental bike race. Jim Lampley, the commentator from the race's start to its end for ABC's "Wide World of Sports," began to cry. Standing with Lon, live and on national television, Lampley stated that this was the most emotionally moving athletic event he had ever witnessed. Lon was presented with a trophy and the keys to his hotel room, where he quickly disappeared to make up many hours of lost sleep.

Fifteen hours later, in a semihypnotic state, John Howard crossed over the bridge onto Manhattan Island. "He appeared to be dozing off," the race official Robert Hustwit reported. "His crew members shouted at him. Then Howard woke up and, apparently not realizing where he was, took off in a sprint for the finish line, missing the appropriate turns and accelerating to over 30 miles per hour." John later explained that he thought he was in a road race with a pack of riders and it was the final sprint for the finish.

Howard then made his way through the clogged streets of Manhattan and finished with a time of 10 days, 10 hours, and 59 minutes. He went to the hotel and was not heard from again for two days.

Early the next morning I experienced a sunrise over the matchless skyline of Manhattan. I had just faced the final psychological obstacle. Reaching New Jersey, it seemed as if I should be finished. After all, New York is right next to New Jersey. When I was informed that I still had 90 miles to go at midnight, it was difficult to get motivated. I was nearing a state of severe depression. I just wanted to be done.

The Empire State Building, and the physical representation of what I had been visualizing for over 10 days, now came into sight. I was finally in New York. Crossing the George Washington Bridge, I was surprised to encounter one final obstacle: the streets of Manhattan, potholed and torn up, filled with broken glass, stripped-down cars, and derelicts staggering around after a long Saturday night.

At last I made my final turn and crossed the white finish line to be greeted by a large crowd of people, including my parents, who had flown out from Los Angeles, and a hug from a very emotional Diana Nyad, who not too many years ago had actually swum around this island! With a

My first transcontinental crossing of 10 days, 19 hours, and 54 minutes broke the previous transcontinental record and felt like the thrill of victory.

PHOTO BY BRUCE MARTIN

Diana Nyad interviews me and winner, Lon Haldeman with the Empire State Building in the background.

PHOTO BY BRUCE MARTIN

time of 10 days, 19 hours, 54 minutes, I achieved my goal of breaking all transcontinental records set before this race. The greatest moment of my life was a short one, for I, too, was ready for some sleep saturation.

The fourth and final finisher, Marino, came across the line in 12 days, 7 hours, and 37 minutes. Lon and I drove out to escort him through Manhattan since John was arriving on a weeknight during rush hour—a harrowing task to say the least. A large crowd of people was on hand to greet John, including his mother, who had also flown out from Los Angeles.

To this day, and to the extent that the sport of ultra-marathon cycling has been explored, I think it would be safe to say that we had extended the known limits of human endurance.

Larry Kamm, producer of ABC's "Wide World of Sports" program on our race, who was moving from cyclist to cyclist along the route for the entire trip, noted the following:

"In my 20 years as a sports television producer, I have never witnessed such an intense, emotional event. In an era of six-figure baseball players and seven-figure football players, who strike for not making enough money, you have these four men who pushed themselves to the limits for a cheap trophy and a hug from Miss Bud Light."

18
THE AGONY
OF VICTORY
THE
MIAMI-TO-MAINE
CHALLENGE

"You are not beaten until you admit it."

General George S. Patton, Jr.

The hardest lesson of this trip to learn was that when the humidity is nearing 100 percent, pouring water on your head and clothing does not keep you cool because the usual heat evaporation process that works so well in the deserts of California and Arizona fails miserably in Florida.

I did find, however, that I could come back from a seemingly insurmountable sickness and reach my goal that I had set for myself. The other form of sickness I had never experienced was depression. It was just so boring in Florida and Georgia and South Carolina that I became completely unmotivated and was faced with thoughts of wanting to abandon the record attempt. But I learned that if you endure pain, mental or physical, long enough, it eventually goes away. The depression disappeared and I made it to my destination.

It seems accepted practice in ultra-marathon cycling that, upon the completion of a cross-country race, cyclists announce that they will never again attempt such an agonizing feat. Nearing the end of the 1982 Great American Bike Race, I swore to myself and my support crew that I'd had enough of "ultra-painful" cycling and that I would let less sane individuals tackle the sport.

174

However, by the time I rolled up to the Empire State Building, thrilled by finishing third in the world's longest bike race, by breaking all previous transcontinental records, and by talking with ABC Sports commentator Diana Nyad, my resolve began to waver. By the end of the day I decided to participate again in 1983, this time to win. By the end of the week I had added a second goal for that year—an East Coast cycling record.

After all, no one had ever set a record for the East Coast of the United States, as I had the Seattle–to–San Diego West Coast race, so I would pioneer a record that others could challenge. At the same time, this would prepare me for winning the 1983 Race Across AMerica against the seemingly indomitable Lon Haldeman and a field of 10 others.

Miami and Portland, Maine, were chosen as the cities farthest removed from each other that could provide adequate press coverage. I was told that the trade winds, unlike the West Coast winds, tend to blow from south to north, so Miami City Hall was chosen as the starting point. This was the first mistake. As it happened, Miami City Hall isn't in the city of Miami. This I discovered two hours before the scheduled launch time of noon, Sunday, June 12. The most official-looking building we could find, and the place the Automobile Club recommended, was the courthouse in downtown Miami. The Ultra-Marathon Cycling Association judge, Michael Coles, approved this as the starting point, and at 12 o'clock sharp I began.

Unfortunately, everyone else interested in the race *did* know where the Miami City Hall was—a couple of miles south of the courthouse. Two television camera crews, several major-newspaper correspondents, a couple of radio station representatives, and over 50 cyclists from the local club were lined up there to see me off! Meanwhile, feeling a bit abandoned, I shoved off in total obscurity. The temperature was 95 degrees, with 98-percent humidity.

HEAT EXHAUSTION

Being a native southern Californian, acclimatized to dry desert heat, the extreme humidity was the beginning of my problems on the first day. At the 125-mile mark, I was struck down with heat exhaustion. In spite of the white lycra skin suit cut for me by Kucharik Bicycle Clothing, nausea led to vomiting, but I was determined to reach my goal of 400 miles for the first day, so I immediately resumed the journey. Soon nausea and vomiting again left me immobilized in the air-conditioned, high-tech motor home supplied by the sponsor of the trip, the Original Great American Chocolate Chip Cookie Company. What was to be a 15-minute break stretched into 90 minutes as cramps, shivering, and finally bodily convulsions resulted from extreme dehydration.

Finally back on the bike, I was force-fed yogurt and chocolate shakes in an attempt to keep some calories down. My goal for the day was lost, but as darkness fell, my mileage rate increased and I rode through the night, passing the hundreds of cities that dot the 400-mile Florida coastline. By midnight I was able to eat more appropriate foods and was back on the special diet designed by my nutritionist and sister, Karen Hiner. She designed a program that would allow me to maintain endurance and stay awake, while it also rebuilt muscle tissue. It seemed to be working.

DEPRESSION

Sometime during the afternoon of the second day, Florida became Georgia, though the scenery certainly didn't reflect the change. For the most part, the terrain could best be described as flat and boring. In spite of the heat problems, I had covered 370 miles in the first 24 hours, but I was still two hours behind my planned schedule. With no record to beat, it may seem that it should have been easy to ride relaxed, without the pressure of the clock bearing down on me, but personal goals and self-applied pressure can produce great anxiety. I was feeling it here.

My crew had given me the usual toilet paper banner to break through at the Georgia border, but I was feeling a form of depression I had never experienced before. There were no ABC Sports camera crews to talk to. There were no other competitors to race against. The southern coastal geography was mundane, and I still had 1,500 miles to cover—no light glimmered at the end of the tunnel. Existential questions crept into my thoughts: "Why am I doing this? What is the purpose of this trip? Why would anyone want to suffer this much for so little glory at the end?" By the end of the day these thoughts had become obsessions, filling my mind.

I couldn't quit. Once a ride of this scope had begun there was no way I could let down my crew, my sponsors, or myself. Yet riding the bike was the furthest thing from my mind, and even the idea of riding in the Race Across AMerica seemed absurd. Fortunately, it was a short depression, ending on the third evening when Michael Coles, owner of the Original Great American Chocolate Chip Cookie Company and a top ultra-marathon cyclist himself, rode with me. As the holder of the southern transcontinental record from Savannah to San Diego, he completely understood what I was going through as he mounted his bike and rode with me. A veritable ball of energy, Michael raised my spirits and gave me a boost that lasted a thousand miles. We talked, listened to music, sang, and pedaled through the night. He earned the nickname "Caffeine Coles" that night, as I refused an offer of coffee for staying awake, replying, "No thanks, I don't need coffee tonight. I've got Coles!"

When Coles returned to the motor home he left me with a special tape to listen to—90 minutes of upbeat music such as the "Theme from Rocky," "Eye of the Tiger," "Ride Like the Wind," and "Chariots of Fire." We dubbed it *the* tape." Music can really energize the brain, particularly when the brain is trying to survive on an hour of sleep a day!

By Raleigh, North Carolina, I was back on schedule. My goal was to average over 300 miles a day and to cover the 1,840 miles in six days by reaching city hall in Portland by 2:00 P.M. on the following Saturday. I was feeling stronger, but riding into Virginia meant encountering hills— a break in the monotony but a strain on the knees. Spenco gloves had saved my hands from fatigue and numbness. My feet were feeling better than they had on any previous trip, thanks to the innovatively designed shoe by Bata/Power with a white reflecting sole, padded tongue, and hundreds of small ventilating holes, which all contributed greatly to my comfort. Even the usually troublesome point of pain, the rear end, was in perfect condition as I was successfully testing a newly designed saddle from Persons Saddles, based on the old Cool-Gear model but with alloy rails, plastic shell, and a thickness of padding and leather covering altered to my specifications.

With each passing state border or major town, the light was becoming brighter at the end of the tunnel. Passing through the Civil War areas of Gettysburg and Harrisburg made me feel I was certainly in the North now. Pedaling on through the Pennsylvania towns of Hershey, Lebanon, and Allentown—the same route we took in the Great American Bike Race—left me with a feeling of getting close to the finish. Unbelievably, however, I made the same wrong turn near Reading, Pennsylvania, that I had made in last year's race. The hills were also becoming more numerous now, with ever sharpening grades.

COURSE CHANGES

Turning north out of Allentown, Pennsylvania, I took Highway 209 in New York, recommended by the Automobile Association of America. Though the route consultant insisted it was an ideal road for cyclists, this

was the worst road I have ever ridden on in the United States. It turned
out to be an 18-wheeler racecourse, a sort of Indy 500 for semis. What
little shoulder there was was littered with retread tire strips, muffler
parts, glass, and potholes. Len Vreeland, my mechanic from Allentown,
and Jeff Davis from Campagnolo, both familiar with the area, rerouted
me on a longer but much safer and certainly more scenic route through
upstate New Jersey.

TOUGH TERRAIN

When I encountered the hills a bike change became necessary. I switched
from a brand-new Campagnolo-equipped Motobecane Team Champion
to my old standby, the Vitus Aluminum Prolight. Weighing in at 18
pounds, it relieved much of the load of climbing the treacherously steep
grades of Highway 23 in Massachusetts. I have to admit that I was quite
surprised at not only the steepness of these grades, at 12–14 percent, but
the number of them. After 100 miles of hills, the 21-tooth cog gave way
to a 23. After 200 miles, the 23 became a 25.

Several more wrong turns, coupled with five broken spokes through
the Appalachian Mountains, forced my average mileage rate down, and
the prospects of making 300 miles a day seemed further removed. In
Hillsdale, New York, I passed through miles of some unidentifiable field
of crops that, although green, rolling, and scenic, also produced an
allergic reaction in me. I rubbed my eyes to relieve the unrelenting itch,
which forced them to swell nearly shut. My contact lenses had to be
removed, and I was forced to the side of the road for nearly an hour. It
was here, with less than 16 hours to go to my 2 o'clock goal, that the bad
news was delivered to me. The mileage calculations I had made before
the race were incorrect. The course was not 1,840 miles, as I had
originally thought, but 1,906 miles! To make over 300 miles per day I
would really have to hustle, and a sub-six-day record was out of the
question.

I pushed onward through the hills, my rate slowing due to the terrain,
fatigue, and sleep deprivation. To achieve my goal would mean a sleepless
blitz all the way to Portland. Having slept only six hours since the
journey's start, I wasn't excited by the prospect.

By midnight my eyelids felt like lead. At 1:00 A.M. I was forced into
alertness by a sign on Highway 66 warning that the road was obstructed
with flood debris for the next seven miles and that cars should proceed
only at their own risk. Dodging boulders, holes, tree branches, and dust,

I climbed a 15-percent grade, then descended an equally steep hill, having to stop halfway down due to cramps in my hands from braking so hard. It was on this stretch that I got the only flat tire of the trip. The Wolber Competition tires were nearly flawless.

BREAKDOWN

At 2:00 A.M. I stopped for a five-minute break. It was here, nearing Holyoke, Massachusetts, that the motor home broke down. The small motor home, nicknamed "tool box," had serious brake problems and would have to go ahead to Portland to be fixed. Personality conflicts, plus the stress of sleeplessness, heat, and confined space, caused a quarrel between a couple of the crew members. People were screaming while I was pleading that I wanted to continue in order to reach my goal. It was dark, we were lost once again, and I couldn't move on without a vehicle for lighting and support. Finally we got organized, and after nearly 45 minutes of wasted time I pushed on, accompanied by three of the original seven crew members in the large motor home, which we had christened "the ark."

Undaunted, I pedaled with a new strength and alertness that arose from anger. Nothing can physically arouse you more than a good emotional outburst!

I managed to avoid all hallucinations this trip, and with the final sunrise over Fitchburg, Massachusetts, a dot on the map for so many months, I was almost finished. Mark Rierden of the Fitchburg Cycling Club was kind enough to shake the sleep from his eyes and escort us through the town.

I then greeted the Connecticut border with a bacon and scrambled egg sandwich and reached the last border of the race, Maine, wishing it were all over. With 50 miles to go, I was extremely fatigued. My emotional alertness from the night before had waned, and I was falling asleep on the bike. I had heard every music tape several times and was trying to find a way to stay awake for a few more hours.

Like the cavalry coming out of the east, the Portland Bicycle Exchange Club arrived with about 20 cyclists to escort me all the way to the city hall. My speed increased, I forgot the various aches and pains, and the city limit sign was suddenly upon me.

Fortunately, Portland does have a city hall, where I was greeted by a wonderful crowd of cyclists, city officials, and curious onlookers. The record was pronounced by the UMCA judge to be 6 days, 1 hour, 55 minutes over a course of 1,906 miles for an average of 315 miles per day. I had made my mark and established a new world record!

Now quite alert, I was swamped with balloons and roses sent by Michael Coles's wife, Donna, from Atlanta, Georgia. The crew members put aside their differences just long enough to celebrate a task they had made possible for me to complete.

This was one of the toughest rides of my career. I have never suffered so many obstacles, both physical and mental. I have never slept so little, or pushed so hard, for so long. Like all records it will eventually be broken but it will require determination and self-sacrifice.

19
THE VICTORY OF DEFEAT
THE 1983 RACE ACROSS AMERICA

"Never stop being ambitious. You have but one life, live it to the fullest glory and be willing to pay any price."

General George S. Patton, Jr.

The first lesson I learned this trip was that it is much more exciting to be at the front of the race rather than somewhere in the middle. I pushed Lon and was only an hour behind after 1,000 miles. I've been at the back and I've been at the front and I can tell you from experience that the front is better.

Unfortunately I also learned what can happen when I don't pace myself. One of the consequences of being toward the front of the race was pushing myself beyond my limits and incurring an injury that would force me out of the race. I then had to deal with a new word in my vocabulary: *quitting*. From this experience, however, I learned that there is pride in knowing you have done your best and that winning doesn't necessarily mean crossing the finish line first.

The 1983 version of the world's longest bicycle race began sharply at 9:00 A.M., Wednesday, August 3, on a cool, overcast morning at the Santa Monica Pier. I had stood there exactly one year before with three other men in the inaugural Great American Bike Race. I felt just as nervous as I had then. At least this time there were 11 others suffering the same prerace anxieties. The normal physiological reactions to anxiety—yawn-

The start of the 1983 Race Across AMerica, 9:00 A.M. at the Santa Monica Pier. The ABC Sports camera crew blocks traffic as Dr. Bob Beeson (left) and I lead the 11-man, 1-woman field off the pier. It was overcast and cool, but temperatures soon soared into the hundreds as we progressed into the desert.

When the green flag drops, the foolin' around stops.

**RACE BEGINS
AUGUST 3, 1983
SANTA MONICA, CA**

'83™

MAP COURTESY OF RACE ACROSS AMERICA

The route for the 1983 race was to go farther north, through the small town of Harvard, Illinois, Lon's hometown. This was a tribute to the man who won the first Great American Bike Race. The course was considerably longer (250 miles) and much hillier than the first transcontinental route.

ing and the need for a rest room—were apparent in all 12 of us, 11 men and one woman.

ABC Sports was back, with Jim Lampley and Diana Nyad being joined by a newcomer to the staff—Olympic gold medalist and professional cyclist Eric Heiden. With much of the same staff manning the cameras and trucks for ABC, I felt a little more at ease knowing that 2,000 miles out in the middle of nowhere I would at least see some familiar faces.

The race began slowly through the downtown traffic lights of Los Angeles. It wasn't long, however, before both the pace and the temperature skyrocketed, with riders breaking away from the pack and temperatures soaring into the 100s as the Mojave Desert became a reality.

Predictably, Bernie Hansen, Bob Beeson, and Mike Secrest, the race's "speedsters," shot out into an early lead with a half dozen of the original 12 scrambling to hang on to their positions behind them. Lon Haldeman and I rode at a comfortable pace for the first 50 miles, talking and lamenting the fact that we were about to put ourselves through this agony again. After a few hours, Lon took off with the aim of leading the race, with me trailing a short distance behind. Within the hour Lon was to pass first-place cyclist Mike Secrest, and he never looked back. Four hours after the race's start would be the last time Lon saw any of the competitors across the breadth of the country.

The heat began to take its toll on me and others, and at one point I was as far back as ninth place. I continued to pace myself, pouring water on my head, neck, and back to bring my body temperature down. I began to pass riders one by one. John Silker, Bernie Hansen, and Bill Debrau were all suffering from overheating and were riding sluggishly through the desert town of Victorville, California, as I passed them to move up to fifth place.

Pete Penseyres was next, but I didn't realize I had passed him until I saw his wife Joanne, who informed me he was back in the motor home in Victorville with a violently upset stomach. Beeson, Secrest, and Haldeman remained ahead.

I won't easily forget riding into Las Vegas, Nevada, in the middle of the night. After riding for more than 15 hours without once getting off the bike, after climbing seven- and eight-percent grades for as long as 20 miles at a stretch, and after baking under the desert sun, I was finally rewarded at the top of the final climb with miles and miles of city lights sprawling out before my eyes. However, the clear desert air makes the lights appear much closer than they really are. When I crested that hill I began the long 15 miles that still separated me from the city's heart— the famous Las Vegas strip. After looking at featureless desert landscape all day, I found the hotel lights and casino sounds very attractive. I had a strong urge to check into the Hilton for a good night's rest! It would be another 10 days before I would be able to enjoy a shower and a full night's sleep in a bed.

During that stretch down to the gambling capital of the United States, I caught and passed Bob Beeson—but not without a fight. The massively built blond from Indianapolis challenged my speed time and time again, winding it up to 30 miles an hour, then backing off, winding it up again, then backing off again. Thanks to early-season speed training, I was able to hold my own, and I eventually won out as Beeson took a break, giving me a solid 90-minute lead before he got back on the bike. Secrest was next.

While parts of the 1982 Great American Bike Race course were quite scenic, the majority of that more southerly route was uniform and drab compared to the majesty of the Rocky Mountain route we carved our way through in 1983. Following Las Vegas, we cut through the Virgin River Gorge on Interstate 15, the most expensive 15 miles of highway in the United States. We were rewarded for crossing the relentless hills by magnificent overlooks into canyons created by a glacial age occurring over 100,000 years ago.

Rocky Mountain high—Colorado. I was soon to pass Secrest and move to within nearly an hour of Haldeman.

PHOTO BY JIM CASSIMUS

Paralleling Zion National Park through Utah, I finally overtook Michael Secrest the second night of the race. Rolling through miles of unpaved road, Secrest had slowed while I gritted my teeth and caught him. Another series of interval sprints ensued, winding it up to full speed, backing off, winding it up, backing it off, until I finally pulled ahead. For the next 12 hours Secrest and I were to catch and pass each other several times until we reached Grand Junction, Colorado, where the massive mountain grades begin.

At that point a report had filtered up to me that Secrest had told the ABC "Wide World of Sports" commentators Diana Nyad and Eric Heiden that he would show Haldeman and me how "real hill climbing" was done and that he would destroy us by Loveland Pass.

With the adrenaline flowing I rolled over the 10,000-foot Vail Pass and reached the 12,000-foot Loveland Pass with Secrest nowhere to be seen and Haldeman a mere one hour and 16 minutes ahead. A wedding taking place at the top of the Continental Divide provided me with a rather large collection of onlookers as I hit Loveland Pass and started the descent. The people who weren't aware of the Race Across AMerica passing through must have thought the bride and groom had spared no expense for their wedding by having ABC Sports film the occasion!

The 12-mile stretch twisting downhill into the small cities surrounding Denver brought me to within an hour of Haldeman. It was the closest I would ever come to first place.

There was no joy in Mudville as I finally reached Harvard, Illinois, now behind Haldeman by six hours and riding with a very stiff neck. I am consulted by Bob Hustwit to my right and the Mayor of Harvard in front of me.

We passed through the rest of Colorado, Nebraska, Iowa, and Illinois with little change in the positions of any of the riders. The camera crews don't accompany us as frequently, as the scenery leaves much to be desired in comparison with the western United States. The Great Plain states are the most difficult for me to negotiate mentally, due mainly to boredom and the immensity of the distance covered, with another 2,000 miles ahead. My body was tired and sore, my spirits were waxing and waning, and the competitive drive to win was being drained by endless days without seeing another competitor.

Many of the original 12 had dropped out before Loveland Pass. Ron Heyer left the race in Green River, Utah. The last time he was sighted he was lying under a bridge, trying to catch some needed sleep. The only woman, Kitty Goursolle, was forced out of the race when her support vehicle was destroyed in an accident. Bernie Hanson developed severe knee pains and dropped out in Utah.

Pete Penseyres, who was in last place after experiencing heat exhaustion on the first day, was now moving up the ranks.

By the time I reached Illinois my nearest threat was Secrest, who was 90 miles behind, with Haldeman fluctuating between two and four hours ahead of me. The race for first was exciting. Haldeman had a vehicle following me, giving him reports on my sleep patterns, speed, and number of rest stops. I, of course, reciprocated. The ABC camera crews were shuttling back and forth, waiting for significant events to develop.

Unfortunately, I encountered disaster in Harvard, Illinois—ironically enough, Lon's hometown. In the course of one hour I developed severe neck cramps and spasms, forcing my head downward until my chin was touching my chest. My crew massaged my stiff muscles, but theirs were untrained hands. I began the trip with a professional massage therapist, but he left the race in Omaha, Nebraska, due to fatigue. He had the unmitigated gall to explain to me, after I had just ridden 2,000 miles nonstop on a bicycle, that he, riding in an air-conditioned motor home, was tired!

For the next 200 miles I suffered through headwinds and rain until I reached Champaign, Illinois, where I was able to find a chiropractor to treat me. He told me that he thought the injury was fatigue-related, which made sense when I told him what we were doing.

I lost hours from the injury, but worse, I was losing my speed. Normally in the Race Across AMerica, when riding down a flat stretch of highway with no major winds, you can maintain a speed of 15–17 miles per hour. When you include sleep and rest breaks, the overall average drops to a paltry 12–13 miles per hour. After the neck problem developed, my on-the-bike average had dropped to 12 miles per hour, and I was stopping more frequently.

To make up for the lost speed, I tried to continue with even less sleep, which resulted in one of the most bizarre psychotic-like hallucinations I have ever experienced. In the middle of the night on the seventh day of the race I took a 45-minute sleep break. Normally humans sleep in 90-minute cycles that range from a light sleep, to a deeper sleep, to dreaming, and back up to a light sleep.

When I awoke after only 45 minutes, I must have been in the middle of a very elaborate dream—for the next hour or so I was thoroughly convinced that my entire crew were aliens from another planet and that they were out to kill me by running me over on my bike. So clever were these aliens that they even looked, dressed, and spoke like my crew and kept insisting that I get on the bike and continue down the highway. I was not about to let them talk me into such a death-defying action, so I kept making excuses to go back into the motor home—going to the bathroom, finding another musical tape, and coming up with a variety of other rationalizations.

I even began to quiz individual crew members on personal items in their lives that I knew no alien would know about. When they were able to answer them correctly I was even more amazed at how clever these aliens were and the extent they had gone to in order to dispose of me!

The problem was finally solved when the crew bedded me down for 90 minutes and I awoke rested and ready to ride—clear of mind. To this day, however, I remember how vivid that hallucination was. I even use the story in my psychology class when discussing paranoid schizophrenia to make the students realize how real these hallucinations are for the individual who suffers from them. It may seem quite impossible for someone to believe some of the absurd paranoid delusions the victim describes, but I can confirm that they are as real as this book you are holding and the words you are reading.

At this point, with my speed diminishing and rest breaks becoming more frequent, Secrest and Beeson passed me. Miraculously, Pete Penseyres had moved from last place to fourth place over the past seven days, and he was looking quite fresh. We rode together for several miles, talking about all that had transpired over the last week. It was like seeing an old friend. Unable to maintain the pace, however, I dropped back and waited for the next cyclist to close the gap and catch me. It was not to happen.

Over the next day and a half my neck got stiffer by the hour and my speed dropped to a dismal 8–10 miles per hour. A three-hour rest in Indianapolis helped, but 10 miles from the Ohio border the first thoughts of withdrawing entered my mind.

I had never seriously considered abandoning any athletic endeavor I had attempted in the past, so this was a very anxious time for me. Would I feel like a quitter? Would I lose self-respect? My physical distress caused mental agony.

Almost two hours later I finally covered the mere 10 miles to the Ohio border. There were only 500 miles to go, which in a race that is 3,200 miles long amounts to nearing the finish line. It might as well have been 5,000 miles to the finish. Riding with one hand on the handlebars and the other holding my head up, I feared permanent damage and danger to my life in the upcoming mountainous descents through the Appalachians. After 2,700 miles I officially withdrew from the race.

I did not experience the feelings of being a quitter, nor did I lose self-respect. During the television program on ABC Sports, Diana Nyad commented that doubt may one day whisper in my ear that I should never have quit. To this day I have not heard that whisper. There comes a point when bravery turns into foolishness and a game of sports becomes a game of death. There is no sport and no event worth that risk. I would be back to fight again next year.

The surprise sleeper was Pete Penseyres, who eventually caught and passed Secrest and Beeson and took a solid second place. John Silker, Lon's friend from Woodstock, Illinois, took a very respectable fifth place and Gary DelNiro from Kansas City finished sixth after struggling through the toughest race of his life.

20
THREE'S A CHARM
THE 1984 SEATTLE-TO-SAN DIEGO CHALLENGE

"We cannot do everything at once, but we can do something at once."

Calvin Coolidge

This would be the last time I would ever do this ride. Three's a charm but it is also enough. I figured that having logged as many miles as possible before the RAAM could only lead to a better performance in that race. What I didn't realize was that one can be overtrained. Riding 1,325 miles as hard as possible without stopping only eight weeks before a 3,000-mile race across the country is not a healthy thing to do.

I felt good about the record and know that it will take a monumental effort to break, but I was sorry I did so at the expense of my performance in the RAAM. The biggest lesson here is that there are limitations to the human body. There are only so many miles in a body in a year. You must choose them wisely.

As I made final preparations for my third attempt at breaking the Seattle–to–San Diego record on Saturday morning, June 23, 1984, I reflected on my first run down the western United States coastline four years earlier. The first time I made the ride there was no record to beat. There were no previous guidelines from which to determine the quality of the first record set. So for me, at that point in my young cycling career, 7 days, 8 hours, and 28 minutes was acceptable and met with my goal of

Richard Clayton, the record holder for the Seattle-to-San Diego course, in 1982, established the pace I would have to set in order to beat his mark of 4 days, 2 hours, and 23 minutes. Here Richard is presented with a certificate of achievement from the Ultra-Marathon Cycling Association by John Marino, Lon Haldeman, and me, the associations's founders.

completing the trip in one week.

Acceptable compared to what, however? With 20/20 hindsight, I look back at how truly slow that ride was in comparison with today's standards. My average for the 1980 ride was a meager 206 miles per day. My average in the Great American Bike Race was 285 miles per day. On the East Coast the figure climbed above the 300 mark to 315 per day. Competition breeds quality through a natural selection process; those who want to survive in the jungle of professional sports do so by only one means—success.

For the Seattle–to–San Diego challenge, the survivors before the 1984 race were:

1980	Michael Shermer	7 days, 8 hours, 28 minutes
1981	Doug Steward	4 days, 22 hours
1981	Clint Worthington	4 days, 18 hours
1981	Michael Shermer	4 days, 14 hours, 15 minutes
1982	Richard Clayton	4 days, 2 hours, 23 minutes

I once read in a magazine interview of the great Eddy Merckx that he would never consider challenging the hour record after he himself had broken it, unless someone else came along and broke his record. He felt that it was unnecessary for anyone to prove himself in a single event more than once. If someone were the best in an event, he saw no reason for that person to invest energy and time in being better than himself. Unfortunately for the cycling world, it was after Merckx retired that Francesco Moser broke Merckx's hour record. With today's advanced technology and improved aerodynamics, it would have been interesting to see how much better Merckx might have done with a new mark to beat.

With this in mind I had no interest in challenging the Seattle–to–San Diego record more than once, unless someone else bested my mark. As you can see from the list above, I have had several opportunities!

There was more to doing the Seattle–to–San Diego ride than just recapturing my record for the third time. Many people questioned whether the four-day barrier could be broken. There was the "triple crown" of ultra-marathon cycling that I wanted to be the first to hold: East Coast, West Coast, and transcontinental records simultaneously. Since I still held the East Coast Miami-to-Maine record, and the 1984 Race Across AMerica was coming up in August, if I could recapture my West Coast record and win the RAAM with a world record time, the triple crown would be mine.

Finally, my motivation for training for the Race Across AMerica by riding endless centuries and double-centuries day after day was waning. Ultra-marathon cycling takes a lot out of your body, mind, and spirit, and I thought this would be a great 1,325-mile training ride a mere eight weeks before the big race across the country.

One of the most difficult aspects of endurance cycling is the isolation one experiences when riding for days on end. It is not only boring; for an individual who is gregarious it can be almost devastating. The boredom of ultra-marathon rides is greatly alleviated when people come out to ride along with you.

In the RAAM we put a 15-minute limit on cyclists joining competitors. The purpose of the rule is that the RAAM is a race of individuals, not teams. Though drafting is prohibited, even having someone ride alongside you is psychologically beneficial. It makes the time go by faster, distracts the mind from pain and fatigue, and usually increases your speed. Without the rule a smart competitor would have a support crew filled with racers to pace him across the country.

No such rule applies to solo record attempts, so I arranged the start of

PHOTO BY ANGEL RODRIGUEZ

Though drafting isn't allowed in ultra-marathon cycling, I rode the first 100 miles with cyclists from the Seattle-to-Portland double-century ride and a fellow long-distance rider to my left, Gary Verrill. I covered the first century in 4 hours and 25 minutes.

this year's West Coast ride to coincide with the annual running of the Seattle–to–Portland double-century. With a turnout of several thousand riders, I would have plenty of company for the first 100 miles. After Centralia, I was to leave the Seattle–to–Portland route to follow a shorter course into Portland along the interstate.

The race began promptly at 6:00 A.M., with most of the Seattle-to-Portland riders leaving at 5:00 A.M. The timing was perfect, because for the next 4½ hours I was passing riders and picking up wheel-suckers until I had a train nearly 50 cyclists long!

This naturally caused my average speed to increase, and I covered the first 100 miles in a personal record of 4 hours and 35 minutes—without drafting! That is an average of nearly 23 miles per hour, a speed that is a bit fast with which to begin a 1,325-mile race against the clock.

The effects were felt down the road as I became dehydrated, then gulped copious amounts of liquids in an attempt to "pay back" the system and found myself throwing up on the side of the road. The time gained on this fast first century was lost in the time spent off the bike in the back of the motor home.

To recover, I got back on the bike, rode at a rather leisurely pace, and took in small amounts of water by sucking on ice cubes. This quenched the feeling of desperate thirst one experiences when dehydrated, without bloating the stomach and causing regurgitation. By nightfall I was well past Portland and my speed was restored to normal.

I continued to ride throughout the night without once getting off the bike for more than a minute.

I had set a goal of riding well over 400 miles in the first 24 hours, but due to the illness I knew that would be impossible. If I could approach 400 miles the first day, I would be able to make up the lost time in southern California where it is flat and the riding is fast. The first day ended after 382 miles and a desperate feeling that I would be playing catch-up the rest of the trip.

Geographically, the terrain can be divided into three parts: flat, hilly, and flat. For the first 400 miles there is nothing more than gradual ascents and descents as Interstate 5 rolls through the midland valleys of Washington and Oregon. Valleys don't exist without surrounding mountains, however. Heading south, you pass the spectacular volcanic ranges highlighted by Mt. St. Helens in southern Washington, Mt. Hood east of Portland, and Mt. Shasta in northern California. It makes for quite a sight, as you can see them for hours when riding on a bike at 20 miles per hour.

As you approach the California border the Siskiou Mountains stand in your way like an Iron Curtain barricade blocking passage into another land. You climb pass after pass, hour after hour, anticipating the grand 10-mile descent at the California border. When it finally comes, though, you can't help looking farther up the road and seeing more climbs and even steeper grades. It makes you wonder why the engineers that designed the road didn't just leave it at the top of the range, instead of roller-coasting up and down.

By the afternoon I finally reached Mt. Shasta, and by the evening of the second day I was winding my way around and past Lake Shasta. This was a very frustrating day. Mt. Shasta is so big that it takes hours to see much progress as the grades are long and the winds are typically headwinds. Normally, this would be rewarded with the breathtaking sight of Lake Shasta that I had experienced on both trips in the past. This year I was so far ahead of previous years' rides that I reached the lake at night and missed all the scenery. That would seem to be a positive note except that I needed to be even farther ahead to be on schedule.

I continued to play the role of being behind, with all the anxieties of worrying about whether all this effort would be for naught. I dreaded the possibility that all the time, energy, and money that had been invested by my sponsors, my crew, and myself, would be washed away because I failed to recapture the record by a matter of hours or minutes. What would be the point? There is certainly no value in the novelty as I had done it twice before. I dug deeper within myself to try to increase my speed and gain back the lost ground.

With the exception of the mountain range that surrounds the Los Angeles basin, the stretch from Redding to San Diego down Interstate 5 in California is extremely flat and relatively fast. There is typically either no wind or a slight tailwind, and the trucks blowing past create a slight push from behind. If there would be any opportunity to make up lost time, it was now.

The price to pay for flat terrain in long-distance cycling is boredom, and the San Joaquin Valley in central California takes first place in this category. There is absolutely nothing for as far as the eye can see, which makes the mental game of marking progress by the passing of landmarks very difficult. The only source of feedback is the clock and occasional mileage markers of major cities down the road. It is difficult to be motivated, however, when the next major city is Los Angeles, and it's 369 miles away!

I took my third and final sleep break of 90 minutes in a hotel room in Stockton, California, where I was able to get the only shower of the trip. There were 500 miles left to go from this point. Though I had made up much of the time lost on the first day and was right on pace to match the record time Richard Clayton had recorded in 1982, I was still in a position to get all the way into San Diego and miss the record by minutes.

I was no longer bored. I had a new project to think about—calculating the miles left to go, divided by how much time was left, and comparing that figure with my current speed. This simple task shouldn't have seemed difficult for one who teaches a section on statistics in his psychology classes. But try doing any calculations on only four hours of sleep in four days and your mind loses its acumen. I was doing math problems until I couldn't stand math any longer. The most frustrating thing was that I kept coming up with the same answer—it would be close, one way or the other.

I finally reached the last major climb—the grapevine, as it is called in Los Angeles. It is the range that divides Los Angeles from the fertile farmland to the north. It is also the range that traps the air pollution for which Los Angeles is famed. In the middle of summer, in the heat of the day, it can get as hot as 110 degrees on the climb. It was June 26 at noon when I reached the mountain. It was unbearably hot, and my body was aching. The lactic acid in my legs created excruciating pain from the mere touch of the fingers.

My massage therapist, Janice Simmons, worked wonders on my thighs as I rested for 10 minutes before attempting the ascent. The only way to relieve the pain induced by lactic acid is to remove it through deep tissue massage. With the slightest touch producing agonizing pain, this would seem impossible. Janice found the solution. She took large blocks of ice and rubbed them up and down on both legs, essentially anesthetizing the muscles through freezing. She then kneaded the muscles like raw dough and sent me on my way to climb the 10-mile grade much more efficiently.

I crested the mountain and started the descent into the Los Angeles basin when the entire trip was nearly ended. The motor home became separated from me for several hours, and the crew lost track of my location. Meanwhile, the van, which had only a minimum of supplies on board, got a flat tire, and much to everyone's surprise and dismay, there was no spare! We were faced with the choice of abandoning the race or my going on alone.

This was no choice for me. My last major ride was the 1983 Race Across AMerica, which I had to terminate early due to a neck injury. There was no way I was not going to make it to San Diego. My crew captain, Michael Coles, emptied his pockets of all his money and gave it to me, my sister Tina stuffed the rest of the available food into my jersey, and I continued on to San Diego, alone and a bit apprehensive.

Fortunately, I knew the route through the megalopolis of the City of Angels and coursed through the outlying cities and suburbs as if it were a normal training ride. My greatest fear was that the support vehicles would be unable to find me, and when nightfall came I had no lights— they had been left in the motor home. If they didn't find me by the time I reached Newport Beach, the race would be over with less than 100 miles to go.

As the sun dipped under the western horizon and the temperature dropped along the coast highway, I was not only having trouble seeing; I was getting hypothermia. When you are this tired, your body's resistance to extreme temperatures and stress is lowered. Add to this wet clothes and a cold sea breeze, and the riding can be most uncomfortable.

Since my home is in the Los Angeles area, I was stopping every few miles to call people I knew to see if they could come out to rescue me. Unfortunately, this was one of those summer weekends when it seemed that everyone was out of town. I finally reached my parents and Bob Hustwit, the executive director of the Race Across AMerica, and gave them my location and speed and hoped they would find me.

Within the hour there was an almost humorous meeting of my parents,

Hustwit, the van with a now fixed flat tire, and the motor home, which finally found me. As nightfall deepened, the cavalry came to the rescue and the ride continued.

Fifty miles north of San Diego, cyclists, including me, are routed through the state park and Camp Pendleton Marine Corps base. The state park, however, is just the old coast highway used before Interstate 5 was built. There are no streetlights, and there is one stretch of about four miles that narrows into a bike path. Cars obviously cannot follow, so I was reduced to seeing by the dim light of a cheap lighting system. It was midnight, dark and cold, and the sleep deprivation of the last four days was taking its toll. I was quite literally falling asleep on the bike!

I can honestly say that if Michael Coles hadn't ridden with me through that path, I never would have made it. My strongest urge was to curl up right on the path and sleep for a couple of days. Michael kept up a nonstop monologue for 20 minutes, trying to make me laugh, talk, react—anything but sleep. As I came out of the Marine base and entered Oceanside, San Diego seemed only a stone's throw away.

While there was still some doubt as to the breaking of the record, it looked as if I would reach city hall before the 8:00 A.M. cutoff time. As I passed through the coastal cities of Leucadia, Cardiff by the Sea,

Two of my strongest supporters: Mary Harrod, who is my partner is Shermer Cycles of America; and my father, Richard.

PHOTO BY PATRICK MAHER

Team Shermer support crew, (left to right): Janice Simmons, massage therapist; Tina Shermer, driver; me; Christa Morones, assistant crew captain; Michael Coles, crew captain; Karen Hiner, nutritionist; and Dan Cunningham, who has been a crew captain on previous rides.

Encinitas, and La Jolla, it looked as if there might even be a chance of arriving before 6:00 A.M. and breaking the four-day barrier. I breathed a sigh of relief from knowing that my efforts would pay off in a new record. One question remained: Could I break the four-day barrier?

The final hour of that ride was without a doubt the fastest riding I have ever done at the end of an ultra-marathon race. I maintained an average of 23–28 miles per hour, and the closer I got, the faster I pedaled.

The sun was now coming up over the eastern horizon, as I had seen it do three times before. If I could make city hall before it actually broke the line of the horizon, I would achieve my goal.

As I made the final turn onto B Street in downtown San Diego and rolled up to the city hall steps for the third and last time in my career, I felt a sense of satisfaction that comes from knowing you will never again have to do something that you both love and hate. As I looked over my shoulder toward the east, the sun finally broke through. I asked Michael the official time of the race.

"5:49 A.M.," he replied. "Three days, 23 hours, 49 minutes." I broke the four-day mark by a mere 11 minutes!

Two coasts and two records had been conquered. Only one challenge remained in the triple crown of ultra-marathon cycling—the transcontinental. It was now just a matter of time.

21
ORDEAL AND TRIUMPH
THE 1984
RACE ACROSS AMERICA

"Battle is the most magnificent competition in which a human being can indulge. It brings out all that is best; it removes all that is base. All men are afraid in battle. The coward is the one who lets his fear overcome his sense of duty."

General George S. Patton, Jr.

As this book goes to press an unfortunate series of circumstances have arisen to throw a dark shadow on the 1984 RAAM. With the airing of the race on ABC's "Wide World of Sports" February 17, it became apparent that Lon Haldeman, the 1982 and 1983 winner, violated a strict rule of the race that says support crew members cannot ride with their cyclist. The purpose of the rule is to prevent a rider from having cyclists pace him across the entire United States, thus giving him a psychological advantage and possible drafting advantage over other cyclists. Since the RAAM is an individual event, such pacing is prohibited.

In this race Lon was having difficulty seeing—he had double vision. His wife, Susan Notorangelo, who had just dropped out of the race as a competitor herself, drove up to be with her husband. Though the rules strictly prohibited her from joining the crew and helping Lon, she did so in spite of a verbal recapitulation of the rule to her by the race director Bob Hustwit. The violation of the rule was "flagrant," in the words of Diana Nyad, the ABC commentator who was on the scene.

After hours of long distance phone conversations and days of emotional stress, the race organizers and Lon Haldeman have come to the conclusion that Lon will be allowed to withdraw his position from the 1984 race. The record will forever show that the standings of this event are as follows:

1. Pete Penseyres

2. Michael Secrest

3. Jim Elliot

4. Michael Shermer

I learned from the 1984 Race Across AMerica that this race is so difficult that, for the express purpose of being prepared for this one race, it requires the dedication of year-round training. There are only so many miles in your legs in one year and a certain period of time is required to recover. Attempting more than one ultra-marathon record ride in one year may detract from later performances.

I also learned that no one is invincible, or above reproach. The Race Across AMerica has arrived as a real race. To win is the ultimate victory in this sport.

The 1984 version of the world's longest and toughest endurance contest was for me both an ordeal and, in the end, a triumph. In the previous two races of 1982 and 1983 I found mere participation rewarding enough to balance the pain of spending 22 hours a day in the saddle. But 1984 was to be different. My goal in entering the race was to win—not just to do my best, but to be the best. I recall a comment I heard while watching the Olympics: "The glory is not in the triumph but in the trying." However, after two grueling transcontinental bike races, three trips down the Pacific Coast from Seattle to San Diego, a ride up the East Coast from Miami to Maine, and a somewhat frustrating seventh-place finish in the Spenco 500 race in Texas, I was ready for the major win of my career. After the original Great American Bike Race in 1982 I had set the goal of holding the East Coast, West Coast, and transcontinental records at the same time. I had found plenty of glory in trying. I was ready for the triumph.

I had geared my entire year toward what I call this "triple crown" of ultra-marathon cycling. In the winter I raced in the RAAM training races of 200, 300, 400, and 600 kilometers. In April I participated in the 520-mile Spenco 500 race in Texas, and in June recaptured my Seattle-to-San Diego record. Between events I rested and built myself up to

Ultra-marathon cycling is growing in popularity. We expect more than 10,000 people to jam the Huntington Beach Pier in 1985 as did more than 5,000 people pictured here for the start of the 1984 race.

As the Race Across AMerica grows, so does its following, especially if your hometowm is the start of the race. This race is so tough that one needs every advantage, physically and psychologically, that is available.

a peak for the next race. On paper the schedule appeared to be an ideal training plan to win the Race Across AMerica. In retrospect, racing the clock for 1,300 miles at full intensity a mere eight weeks before the RAAM may have been my ultimate downfall.

As the race began, I felt both mentally and physically ready to do battle with my foes. Indeed, battle is what it felt like this year, not only against the usual enemies of wind, rain, heat, cold, hills, boredom, fatigue, sleep deprivation, and a bruised and battered body, but against the additional foe of a much improved field of competition. I equate the race to a battle due to my off-season studies of the infamous General George "Blood and Guts" Patton, who, it seems to me, would have been well suited psychologically for such an undertaking as the RAAM. His quote opening this chapter exemplifies the spirit of the Race Across AMerica, one of the most magnificent competitions in which a human being can participate. It is so long and so difficult that it truly does draw out all that is best and remove all that is base in a person. Elaine Mariolle, one of the four women in the race, asked me at the starting line if I still got nervous about competing. My positive reply surprised her. But as Patton noted, his words altered here to apply to the race, "All men are afraid before a major competition like RAAM; the coward is the one who lets his fear overcome his ability to perform at his highest level."

Though eager to win, I can't help admitting that it was participation in such a major, exciting event that motivated me to enter the race. I remember a scene from the movie *Patton* in which he was racing through the heart of the front line of a battle with overturned jeeps, smoldering tanks, and bodies dotting the landscape as he turned to his aide in the jeep and noted, "Compared to war, all other forms of human endeavor shrink to insignificance. God, how I love it!"

As we began the race with a 60-mile parade through the heart of the Los Angeles basin, I turned to Haldeman and said, "Well, win, lose, or draw, this is going to be a great race." Lon just smiled and affirmed my feelings with a nod. For me, compared to the RAAM, all other forms of human endeavor shrink to insignificance. I love the participation, regardless of the outcome.

The 23 starters, 19 men and 4 women, rode through Los Angeles and surrounding cities at a leisurely speed up to the base of Cajon Pass in San Bernardino. We left LA after the greatest celebration in the three-year history of the event. In 1982 there were four riders and about 75 spectators at the Santa Monica Pier. In 1983 there were 12 starters and approximately 300 people at the same pier. Now, with a new starting location at the Huntington Beach Pier, and a weekend starting date of Sunday, August 19, over 5,000 people jammed the pier and adjoining streets to watch the 9:00 A.M. start.

The parade pace was painstakingly slow as my body was ready to go fast, but I reconciled myself with the fact that this would probably be the last time I would see most of the participants until we reached the boardwalk in Atlantic City, New Jersey, 3,047 miles away, and a 9 or 10 days' ride. I made use of the time to meet informally everyone I didn't already know.

From previous races were Dr. Bob Beeson, Mike Secrest, Pete Penseyres, John Marino, and the *campionissimo* (Italian for "champion of champions"), Lon Haldeman. While most of my fans and supporters had wished Lon were not participating, I reasoned that, if St. George had slain a dragonfly instead of a dragon, how great would his victory have been?

Others included the John Marino Open qualifier winner, Rick Bozeat; the Canadian transcontinental champion, Wayne Phillips; Belgian's ultra-marathon champion and five-time winner of the 750-mile Paris-Brest-Paris race, Herman DeMunk; Lon's training partner and wife, Susan Notorangelo; and 18-year-old Scott Fortner, the youngest contestant ever and a training partner of mine from southern California. The remainder of the field was drawn from the John Marino Open qualifying race.

With race director Bob Hustwit's resounding voice serving as the starting gun, the pace switched to a lung-searing, leg-burning speed as we began the 10-mile climb to the 4,000-foot Cajon Pass summit. Within seconds the pack began to spread out. Since drafting in the slipstream of another rider or vehicle is strictly prohibited in ultra-marathon cycling, your time to the top depended entirely on your ability to climb. Lon and I rode together for a while. Out of the saddle and passing riders right and left, we weaved our way to the top. Lon's pace was, however, relentless as always, and I wasn't anxious to become physically exhausted only 70 miles into a 3,000-mile bike race. Ironically, the first riders over the 4,000-foot summit would be those who were most competitive during the rest of the race. As anticipated, Pete Penseyres, being a slightly faster climber than I, caught and passed me near the top. As we crested and began the descent, however, I sprinted and caught Pete so we could ride together for a while. As we cruised along through the desert, the typical 30-mile-per-hour tailwinds made spinning in our highest gears easy enough to hold a casual conversation. Approaching Victorville, we were surprised to see Rick Bozeat flash past us a good 3–4 miles per hour faster on a bike that looked remarkably like those used in Olympic track racing. It had a smaller front wheel, a minimum number of spokes, and the shortened, aerodynamically designed, curved handlebars. It looked effective but terribly uncomfortable. If I have learned one thing in ultra-marathon cycling, it is that comfort and steadiness are paramount to staying strong and healthy for 10 days.

One of the greatest fears in the Race Across AMerica is that all the training, preparation, and organization that goes into an event of this magnitude will be washed out by the desert on the first day. Everyone prepares for it in his or her own way. Everyone is anxious about it at the start. It is an unspoken fear that is obvious as you observe your fellow riders: extra water bottles, white skin suits and jerseys, helmet covers, wet handkerchiefs around the neck, Arabian-style hoods covering the head and neck, white shoes, and plenty of sun block. It is rarely under 100 degrees at this time of year in Victorville. This year we were lucky. Weather is one of the many unpredictable factors in this event, and as I passed a bank in downtown Victorville whose time/temperature sign read 73 degrees, I knew this was going to be an unusual first day.

Beeson, the doctor from Indiana, was forced to abandon the race only 100 miles after the start due to a stomach virus that put him in a hospital.

It is the nature of competition for records to be broken, speeds to increase, and the lead to change hands as an event like the RAAM evolves. As we pedaled our way toward the first major landmark on the map, Las Vegas, Secrest held a small lead that quickly closed as he made a wrong turn and had to double back to the course, losing both time and placing. Getting lost is one of those variables of the race that can be controlled but is at times as unpredictable as the weather. It is the competitor's greatest fear in the race. Riding 3,047 miles is bad enough. Getting lost and having to pay for the same real estate twice is unbelievably frustrating. My turn came in Baker, at the base of the 22-mile climb toward Las Vegas. I missed the off ramp to go into Baker from Interstate 15. I then had to get into my support vehicle, drive to the next off-ramp, and double back on the interstate in the opposite direction in order to resume my northward course back to the correct off-ramp. It is a rule that you must cover every foot of road on the official course from the Pacific Coast to the Atlantic Coast, with no exceptions. I lost 30 minutes and a good number of placings.

I soon passed most of the people I lost ground to, and finally I passed Art Patten in downtown Las Vegas. As it turned out, he was the last rider I saw for the rest of the trip across the country. I was so upset about

PHOTO BY MICHAEL COLES

Some final words of wisdom from my step-father, Richard Godbold, who has not only supported me with vehicles from his Ford agency, but escorted me the final 500 miles in the last two RAAMs.

One of the greatest cyclists ever produced by the United States, Jonathon "Jock" Boyer rode out to meet me on the climb up Loveland Pass as he was there training for the world championships, to be held later that month. Jock was the first American to enter the famed Tour de France and has now raced in it four times. He is now considering the Race Across AMerica as his next challenge.

getting lost that I probably seemed a bit cold and aloof to Art since I just wanted to get up the highway as quickly as possible. I didn't realize that six days later I would be starving to see another competitor. Other than my crew and ABC Sports, it would be a solo trip from Las Vegas to Atlantic City.

At the beginning of any form of competition, all participants have in their mind how they can best win the contest. I am certain that as we lined up at the pier all 23 cyclists knew the fastest way they could pedal 3,047 miles.

My strategy this year was to run my own race. I have had enough experience now to know how to pace myself. I know when and where I

The quintessential element in ultra-marathon cycling: unbridled individual achievement made possible only by an efficient, professional support crew (left to right): John Hiner, navigator; Richard DeBernardis, navigator, Buck Peacock, mechanic; Janice Simmons, massage therapist; Karen Hiner, nutritionist; Christa Morones, assistant crew captain; Mike Morones, navigator; Michael Coles, crew captain; Ben Corrington, chiropractor.

will be tired, sleepy, and hungry. I also did some statistical studies from the past two races and realized that Lon's past successes were achieved by putting in two tremendous days at the beginning of the race, building himself a four- to five-hour lead, then sleeping for three hours. He gets up and back on the bike with a one- or two-hour lead but is relatively refreshed and back to riding strong. The rest of us, on the other hand, are playing catch-up and skip sleep to try to close the gap. The consequence of this is a loss in overall speed because, though ground is gained while the leader is sleeping, it is once again lost by riding more slowly when he is awake. In last year's race, for instance, I was only 1 hour and 16 minutes behind Lon at the 12,000-foot Loveland Pass in Colorado, 1,000 miles into the trip. But I paid a high price to get there: no sleep. I then proceeded to lose ground over the next four days so that by Illinois I was wasted, while Lon was strong.

Using my East and West Coast record rides as standards, I calculated that, if I could maintain the same pace in the RAAM that I did on those solo rides, then comparing those times to last year's standards of Lon's pace, I would be either in the lead or very near the leader in the race.

That was last year, however, and as our race director Bob Hustwit is fond of pointing out, every general in history knows how to win the last

Lon Haldeman cruises through one of the rare flat areas of Utah, near Cedar City. Though he was not to win this race, Lon is still considered by many to be the epitome of the professional endurance athlete. Lon has the most experience in years and competitive miles, as well as the greatest number of ultra-marathon records. Lon is a fierce competitor and yet a gentleman in every respect. He has earned every ounce of praise that has been showered on him.

Some cyclists dread riding at night. But this is the best time for me. Traffic is light, and the endless miles of highway and background scenery are invisible. Donning clear Gargoyle glasses, a reflective jacket, a hard-shell helmet, and a stereo Walkman, I can usually ride straight through the night and into the morning sunrise, which is always directly in my eyes when traveling east.

war—if only they could fight the last war now. Though my strategy was sound, I should have realized that it wasn't working after several days of falling behind the leaders. As General Patton noted, "Successful generals make plans to fit circumstances, but do not try to create circumstances to fit plans."

It is wise to have a strategy to begin with, but you must be ready to drop it if it isn't working. It is what Bob Hustwit calls the "Muhammad Ali Syndrome." Before every fight Ali would make bold predictions about what would happen in the fight. He would announce his strategy and predict in what round he would knock out his opponent. However, when the fight began, he would do whatever it took to win. He would change his strategy at will to fit the circumstances. He did not try to change the circumstances to fit his strategy. The classic case is his fight with George Foreman. When they climbed into the ring Ali realized that this guy was as strong as a bull and would kill him if he tried to stand toe to toe and match punches. Instead, Ali covered up on the ropes, let Foreman punch himself out until he was so tired he could hardly hold his arms up, then moved in for the kill. Ali later called this his "rope-a-dope" strategy. He created it in the ring as a strategy to win the race.

At Utah the race standings were becoming less flexible. There were five riders up front, with a gap between these and the rest of the field. The front five were Haldeman, Secrest, Penseyres, Elliot, and I. Though I was fifth, according to my strategy I was in good shape because I was keeping my pace while letting the four in front of me battle it out for first, thus wearing themselves down a la George Foreman—or at least so I thought. There was one rider in that four who didn't fall for the "rope-a-dope" of RAAM. Without my even realizing it, Pete Penseyres executed my strategy perfectly.

Unwilling to tangle with Haldeman, Secrest, and Elliot, Penseyres paced himself, got the right amount of sleep, and let the other three wear themselves down. As we approached the Colorado Rockies, I knew that I was carrying out my plans, and I assumed it was just a matter of time before the four in front would crack. I held on to my strategy.

First over the giant mountain that makes up the Continental Divide of North America was, to no one's surprise, Lon Haldeman. Lon was followed by Secrest, Penseyres, Elliot, and me. I was nearly three hours ahead of last year's pace at this point, but unbelievably Haldeman was over six hours ahead of his schedule last year. What a pace!

Now it became a race of flatlanders. Who could be best in the long stretches across the great plains of eastern Colorado, Kansas, Missouri, and Illinois? Smaller, leaner riders like Penseyres and me were battered about through the 400 miles of Kansas by 20- to 30-mile-per-hour headwinds. Haldeman was finally building his lead. Even though I had more supporters than ever before come out to cheer me on through the cities of Topeka, Lawrence, and Kansas City, the distance between me and the leaders was growing alarmingly large.

Even my annual visit from Harley Phillips of Hutchinson, Kansas, didn't bring the leaders any closer. By the time I reached the Mississippi River on the eastern side of St. Louis I was deeply concerned with catching Elliot, the rider in front of me, and was mounting attacks every night to try to close the distance. I do my best riding at night when it is cool and the wind is calm. I donned my portable cassette player and hammered from sundown to sunup. My crew captain, Michael Coles, would give me two reports daily, at approximately 8:00 A.M. and 6:00 P.M. My attacks, while effective in gaining ground by sunup, were usually nullified by the afternoon.

Not having seen a single rider since Las Vegas, I grew weary of chasing ghosts and images that seemed to exist only in my mind. No one was close enough from behind to pose a threat. No one was close enough in front for a sustained attack to succeed. I was bored. I was frustrated. I knew I was as good as Elliot, Secrest, and Penseyres, and I had beaten them all in the Spenco 500. Yet I was unable to catch them. Though I was turning in a personal best performance, it felt like a personal worst. Ten days is a long time to maintain a competitive edge against ghosts.

One answer to the mystery of why I wasn't able to catch the leaders came from Michael Coles and Christa Morones, both of whom had been on the Seattle–to–San Diego ride eight weeks prior to RAAM. They noted that my speed had dropped off considerably in the RAAM, compared to the corresponding distances covered on the West Coast ride. My split times for 10 miles, 25 miles, and 100 miles were slower than on the West Coast ride. My actual speed was down. I didn't have the snap and strength in my legs. This is such a demanding sport. Is it possible that eight weeks is not enough to recover from one race and come back

PHOTO BY JIM CALLAWAY

Crossing the Ohio border was significant, as this is where I was forced to abandon the race in 1983. This year I rolled on through and headed for the hills of West Virginia.

as strong for the next? In retrospect, I would have to answer affirmatively. I would not do two such events back to back in such a short span of time again.

Speed or no speed, the race continued. I plugged along on guts and fortitude, aided tremendously by my support crew, the finest I have ever had. Not only did they perform their professional duties with expertise and efficiency; they were fabulous at entertaining me. They realized I was growing weary of chasing ghost riders ahead. They sang to me, wrote poems to me, and played motivating music from a buzz box atop the support vehicle. Despite my occasional outbursts of emotion, directed mostly at Christa since I am closest to her, they all (especially Christa) understood what I was going through and were very understanding. Riding 22 hours a day and sleeping 90 minutes a day, allowing only 30 minutes for breaks per 24 hours, is trying both physically and emotionally. Ben Corrington, my chiropractor, and Janice Simmons, the massage therapist, did an exemplary job of keeping my body going. There were no neck problems, which had plagued me the year before. Thanks to the Spenco gloves and seat pad, I had virtually no paralysis or saddle sores. The carbon fiber Peugeot bike seemed to absorb more road vibration than the traditional steel-framed bikes. It was very comfortable. I hurt less that race than the year before. I just needed to go faster.

Those who think the Race Across AMerica is merely a matter of sleep deprivation and the winner is the one who sleeps the least are in error. Lon's secret in the past has been to get enough sleep to keep riding at a strong pace. Three hours of sleep may net you 18–20 miles per hour for the whole day. On the other hand, 90 minutes of sleep may leave you riding at 15 miles per hour or less, thus losing the ground you gained by not sleeping.

For example, in Indianapolis I had closed to within an hour of Elliot and had high hopes of catching him that morning, after a 40-hour sustained attack. When I reached the eastern borders of the city I was greatly in need of a quality break, as my longest before had been 90 minutes and I hadn't had one in 40 hours. I needed three hours. I took only 90 minutes because of the excitement of the prospect of catching Elliot. Dazed and confused after the short sleep, I wobbled down the highway, starting and stopping, taking nearly 10 hours to cover the next 100 miles. The crew finally put me down for three hours. While I awoke completely refreshed and recovered, I was once again six hours behind and motivationally defeated.

Up front, Lon was experiencing similar problems. Unwilling to

PHOTO BY JIM CASSIMUS

For my mother there was as much relief from worry as joy from finishing. Every year my parents have flown out from California, rented a car, and driven the final 500 miles to the finish with me. This type of support is very reinforcing in an event that is as trying psychologically as it is physically.

relinquish the lead, Lon hammered the pedals day after day, beating off attacks by Secrest and Elliot. Meanwhile, Penseyres paced himself, slept enough to maintain a steady speed, and waited for his chance. The opportunity finally came in West Virginia. Elliot and Secrest were exhausted and slowing. Lon had cramping legs and double vision. He was visibly shaken by his physical condition. Due to the double vision problem, he crashed in the hills of West Virginia and decided to take a four-hour sleep. He would awake in better shape but, for the first time in his career, in second place. Penseyres passed Lon and never looked back, stretching his lead to over six hours by the time he reached New Jersey.

What makes the RAAM particularly grueling is the last 500 miles. After 2,500 miles of beating your body to a pulp, the Appalachian Mountains, with the Allegheny and Shenandoah ranges, loom like castle walls before you. They seem almost impenetrable. The climbs aren't long, just steep and repetitive. The grades range from 6 to 12 percent, relentlessly hitting you mile after exhausting mile. The hills go on for literally hundreds of miles without a break. It is rarely flat until Gettysburg, in eastern Pennsylvania, is reached. Once you've made it past these mountains, the only obstacle remaining is Philadelphia. But Pennsylvania has its own rewards. Gettysburg is a historian's dream. The Amish country, including such towns as Bird-in-Hand and Intercourse, provide a time warp back to the 1700s, where fundamental religious beliefs prevent the use of such modern conveniences as electricity. As I was riding down Highway 222, I passed many horse-and-buggy vehicles cruising along at a mere 10 miles per hour. There is much farming in the area, and the highlight of the trip came as I was descending a gradual hill and happened to look to my right—before my eyes I saw a calf being born! It was unbelievable. Indeed, considering some of the bizarre hallucinations I have experienced in past rides, I queried my crew as to their observations on what I had just seen. They verified that it was indeed a reality, not fantasy.

I was somewhat surprised to find that I had no hallucinations on this trip. Nothing, at least, of the psychotic-like fantasy of aliens from another planet that I had experienced the year before. Nevertheless, there were many times when I awoke disoriented and confused. Upon occasion I felt I was back in California on a training ride, not in the RAAM. Particularly difficult were the hours from 3:00 A.M. to sunup. That is the time when people are normally doing their deepest sleeping, and it became very difficult to keep the eyes open. The sun rising from the east directly in my eyes made this especially difficult.

The end didn't come soon enough for me. At Philadelphia Elliot was too far ahead for me to catch. You wouldn't think that, after all we had been through, riding through a city could be too difficult. Philadelphia is the exception. This was by far the worst city I have ever ridden through. It made New York seem like a blessing. There were potholes three feet wide and two feet deep. There was construction on every corner. There were traffic lights, all of them seemingly red, every 100 yards. My motor home clipped a car, it was dark, and I was falling asleep. My projected arrival time of 1:00 A.M. was pushed back as I had to sleep for an hour in order to make the final 60 miles. Nothing could have been more frustrating. What was I doing, sleeping so close to the finish?

I couldn't help it. My mind had finally surrendered—it needed sleep. When I rolled in at 4:00 A.M. I was truly exhausted. I had ridden the race to the maximum of my ability. I had nothing left at the finish. This is how a race should be run. If you have something left in the end, you didn't do your best. It had been 10 days, 16 hours, and 30 minutes since I stood on the pier in Huntington Beach, California. I had beaten my previous transcontinental time by over three hours on a course much more difficult than the previous time was set on.

The surprise of the race was Penseyres's time of 9 days, 13 hours—a full 6 hours faster than Lon's 1982 record on a course 80 miles longer.

Competition has arrived in the Race Across AMerica. The standards are up, the pace is fast, and in the future anyone who makes the 36-hour cutoff at the Mississippi River will be a member of an elite group.

For purposes of race control there is a simple rule stating that, if you are more than 36 hours behind the lead cyclist by the time you reach the Mississippi River, you are dropped from the race. The first and only five finishers to make the cut this year were:

Pete Penseyres:	9 days, 13 hours, 13 minutes
Lon Haldeman:	9 days, 19 hours, 12 minutes
Mike Secrest:	10 days, 2 hours, 3 minutes
Jim Elliot:	10 days, 7 hours, 49 minutes
Michael Shermer:	10 days, 16 hours, 30 minutes

The first year all 4 entrants finished the race. The second year 6 out of 12 finished the race. This year the attrition was higher, with only 5 out of 23 making it. I am afraid that this trend is likely to continue as the competition continues to get tougher. Just to finish the ordeal is an accomplishment—a triumph.

The ordeal was over, and the triumph was in finishing and sharing the race experiences with competitors. The 1984 version of the world's longest race produced a new winner—41-year-old Pete Penseyres, a tenacious, yet gracious victor.

PHOTO BY MICHAEL COLES

APPENDIX I
COMING TO TERMS

Like all sports, cycling has a long list of terms, both technical and colloquial. Many of the terms are used throughout the text. Some are slang, heard only among cycling aficionados during races or training rides. Here is a guide to introduce you to the world of cycling jargon.

Aerobic: an intense level of exercise during which oxygen needs are continuously satisfied and the exercise can be continued for long periods of time.

Anaerobic: intense exercise endured even after the body can no longer dispose of the lactic acid produced and can no longer supply oxygen to the muscles. The exercise level is limited to a short period of time.

Anaerobic threshold: a level of exercise in which further increase in effort will cause more lactic acid to accumulate than can be readily eliminated.

Aerodynamic: the action of the air passing over or through the cyclist and the bike. Increasing aerodynamic efficiency reduces the wind drag on the cyclist or bike, allowing for greater speed and less energy expenditure.

Ankling: dropping and raising the heels in an alternate fashion through a pedal stroke to improve power and efficiency.

ANSI: American National Standards Institute, a body organized for the purpose of testing products; for instance, bicycle helmets.

Attack: a sudden attempt to get away from another rider or group of riders.

Bicycle, conventional: two wheels of equal size, no larger than 700 cm or 27.25 inches in diameter. A standard frame geometry, with the bicycle no longer than 2 meters, no wider than 75 cm, providing for a single rider in an upright position.

Bicycle, unconventional: all human-powered vehicles and others not meeting the requirements of the racing organization or sanctioning body.

Bicycle, recumbent: a bicycle of diverse design to be ridden while in a prone or recumbent position.

Bicycle, all-terrain: also known as a mountain bike, this is a conventional bicycle frame with modifications and special components allowing off-road riding.

Bicycle, BMX: a bike intended for bicycle motocross, or dirt track racing, of smaller size and with components designed for this form of racing.

Bicycle, tandem: two wheels of equal size and standard tandem frame geometry, providing for two riders in an upright position to power the bike, one rider behind the other. The rider in front is known as the *driver*; the rider behind is known as the *stoker*.

Big meat: the largest gears on a bike that a rider is using. Usually associated with high speeds obtained with the larger gears.

Blocking: a team strategy in road racing in which one rider gets in the way of other riders in order to prevent them from passing. Usually done to prevent cyclists behind from moving up to catch a leader.

Blow up: when a cyclist suddenly and dramatically decreases his pace due to overexertion.

Bonking: when a cyclist completely runs out of energy. This is also known as *hitting the wall*.

Boxing: when a team works together to box in a group of racers or a racer so that they cannot attack.

Breakaway: a cyclist or group of cyclists ahead of the main group. Also called the *break* or *lead break*.

Bridge: when a rider leaves one group of cyclists to catch up with the leaders or the next group ahead.

Carbohydrates: simple sugars and starches that provide a valuable source of muscle energy. They can be found in fruits, grains, potatoes, breads, and pasta and are stored in the liver in the form of glycogen.

Catch: when a rider or group of riders tries to catch up to the leaders or next group of riders or a rider.

Chainring: the rings attached to the pedals that turn the chain.

Chasers: cyclists who are trying to catch a breakaway group.

Chondromalacia: a disintegration of cartilage surfaces in the knee due to improper tracking of the kneecap or to extreme overuse. Symptoms are deep knee pain and a crunching sensation during bending. Surgery is frequently recommended.

Class: a quality in a rider consisting of good pedal action, position on the bicycle, and all-around bike handling skills.

Cleat: a metal, plastic, or other hard material fitting on the sole of a cycling shoe with a slot for fitting the shoe onto the pedal cage.

Clinchers: conventional tires with a separate inner tube.

Cluster: also known as the *freewheel* or *block,* it is the series of gear cogs attached to the rear wheel that the chain wraps around.

Cog: a gear of a freewheel; usually there are 5, 6, or 7.

Commuting: riding to and from the job.

Cramping: contraction of leg muscles due to loss of potassium and other minerals during excessive exercise and sweating.

Criterium: a multilap, short- to medium-distance race from 25 to 75 miles, conducted on a short, usually flat course no more than 1–4 miles long. These are excellent spectator races as the riders can easily be seen and the pace is fast with many sprints for special lap prizes called *primes,* and occasional crashes.

Derailleur: the mechanism for shifting gears by moving the chain from one cog or chainring to another. There are two on a bike, front and rear.

Drafting: riding in the slipstream or air pocket of another rider, which greatly attenuates the amount of energy needed by the following cyclist. Distances for drafting vary from 2 inches to 30 meters, depending on the speed and wind conditions. Drafting is the key to strategy in road and track racing. Drafting is not usually allowed in ultra-marathon cycling events.

Dropped: when one or more cyclists fall behind the lead group or main
  pack and are unable to catch up.

Drops: the part of the handlebars below the brakes that curve down and
  usually run parallel to the ground.

Echelon: a line of cyclists either single- or double-file, taking orderly
  turns at the bend in order to break the wind for riders
  behind. A pull at the front lasts from a few seconds to a
  minute.

Ergometer: an indoor, stationary bicycle device with adjustable pedal
  resistance used for training and physiological testing.

Fairing: any object attached to a bike that is designed to lower wind
  resistance.

Fartlek: a Swedish word meaning "speed play" that refers to training in
  intervals of alternate periods of sprinting and resting, with
  no structure for time, e.g. sprinting for city limit signs,
  telephone poles, etc.

Feeding: when riders are fed during a race either from a moving vehicle
  or from the side of the road. Liquids are passed via a water
  bottle while food is handed up in a musette bag. In road
  races there are usually designated feed zones or times,
  while in ultra-marathon races feeding is undertaken at the
  rider's request.

Field: also known as the *main pack* or *bunch*, this is the main group of
  cyclists in a race.

Field sprint: the final sprint of the main group of cyclists, not
  necessarily for first place if a break has escaped.

Fixed gear: a wheel with a cog locked in place, allowing only that cog to
  be used. Also known as a *single-gear bicycle*; no coasting or
  freewheeling is possible. When the wheel is turning the
  pedals are turning.

Forcing the pace: one or more cyclists picking up speed, forcing the
  others to follow or get dropped.

Fred: a word with negative connotations used by racing cyclists to
  describe a touring cyclist with hairy legs, pannier bags,
  and a helmet with a little mirror; one who rides for
  pleasure rather than competition.

GABR: the Great American Bike Race, the original name of the Race
  Across AMerica, featuring Lon Haldeman, John Howard,
  Michael Shermer, and John Marino. The race was held in
  August 1982.

Grand Masters: an age category in racing—55 years and older.

Hairnet helmet: made out of leather, this helmet usually meets the requirements of most cycling associations for protection in racing. The leather strips comprising the helmet are stuffed with foam or other soft materials. This helmet does not meet the ANSI Z90.4 crash tests.

Hammering: pedaling very quickly, producing a high speed. Also known as *jamming*.

Hanger: a cyclist who can stay with the group no matter how fast the pace becomes. Also known as a *stayer*.

Hang in: to stay with a pack of riders without attempting to take the lead.

Hardshell helmet: usually constructed of hard plastic shell with an expanded polystyrene or styrofoam liner. This helmet passes the ANSI Z90.4 crash tests and is recommended for use in competition, touring, and commuting.

Heat: a preliminary event that qualifies competitors for a main event.

Hillclimb: an uphill climbing race, usually in a time trial fashion. Each rider climbs individually against the clock, and drafting is not allowed. Occasionally a hillclimb is held at a road race.

Honking: to stand up and pedal hard, especially in climbing hills.

Hoods: the rubber coverings over the brake levers that provide improved grip.

Hook: one cyclist, either intentionally or accidentally, moves his back wheel against the front wheel of the rider behind, thus knocking the following cyclist down. This is not allowed in races.

Hooks: the part of the handlebars below the brakes that curves down and usually runs parallel to the ground.

Human-powered vehicle: any vehicle, bicycle or otherwise, powered solely by a person or persons. These vehicles are usually built aerodynamically and are not allowed in traditional bicycle races.

International Human-Powered Vehicle Association: the sanctioning body for competition among human-powered vehicles.

Intermediate: an age category in racing—from 13 to 15 years.

Jamming: pedaling very quickly, producing a high speed.

JMO: John Marino Open. This is the qualifier for entering the Race Across AMerica. It is named after the founder of ultramarathon cycling, John Marino.

Jump: to stand up out of the saddle with a sudden burst of speed.

Junior: an age category in racing—from 16-18 years.

Kick: a final burst of speed that provides the main acceleration for the sprint.

Lactic acid: a by-product of anaerobic exercise that accumulates in the muscles and causes pain and fatigue.

Lead-out: an intentional, tactical move in which one racer accelerates to give a head start or advantage to the racer behind, who can then come around the lead cyclist at an even faster speed to take the lead. This is a team tactic used in road racing.

LSD: long steady distance used for building endurance and a base of miles by riding at an even pace for several hours without intervals of speed or rest.

Manuped: a human-powered vehicle in which the rider uses just arms or arms and legs to provide power to the vehicle.

Masters: an age category in racing—from 45 to 54 years.

Match sprint: a track racing event in which two riders race each other head to head for three laps. The first two laps are usually slow, since each rider jockeys for position, while the last lap is a fast sprint.

Maximal oxygen consumption (max V0_2): the maximum amount of oxygen that a person can transfer from lungs to the cardiovascular system in one minute. It is generally predetermined genetically, though improvements can be made through a serious exercise program. It is considered a good indicator of potential in aerobic sports such as cycling.

Midget: an age category in racing—12 years and younger.

Miss-and-out: a track racing event in which a group of cyclists races around a velodrome, with the last rider of each lap being eliminated from the race. This goes on until there is a single winner or winners (sometimes the top three). This is also known as the *devil take the hindmost*.

Motorpace: riding behind a motorcycle or small car that breaks the wind in order to accomplish a faster, more intense workout.

Musette bag: the cloth bag used for feeding cyclists during a race.

Ominum: a group of several events at a track meet.

Orthotics: custom-made supports worn in shoes for arch defects or other biomechanical imbalances in the feet or legs.

Overgear: using a gear that is too big for the cyclist's conditioning level or for the prevailing conditions.

Overtraining: extreme fatigue caused by exercising at a level beyond the body's capabilities. It is related to stress.

Oxygen debt: the amount of oxygen that needs to be consumed during exercise in order to pay back the deficit incurred by the muscles in anaerobic work.

Pace car: the vehicle that follows directly behind a rider. It provides immediate support with food, water, and mechanical supplies.

Pace line: a single or double file of riders who take turns riding in front. *See* Echelon.

Paced: applies to Ultra-Marathon Cycling Association rules when two or more cyclists are involved. In certain UMCA events, these cyclists may draft, but crew and nonteam members may not be drafted.

Pack: this is the main group of cyclists in a race. *See* Field.

Pannier bags: bags attached to the bicycle for carrying goods and supplies. Usually used for touring.

Peloton: the main group of cyclists in a race. *See* Field and Pack.

Peak: a brief period of time when the body and mind are at their maximum performance level.

Points race: a velodrome, track racing event in which racers, beginning from a mass start, sprint for points on designated laps. The cyclist who accumulates the most points by the end of the race is the winner, though not necessarily the first racer across the finish line at the end.

Prime: pronounced "preem," this is a race within a race, in which riders sprint for points or special prizes to cross a designated prime line in various laps or distances of a long race.

Pull: an attempt to take the lead in a group and then to maintain this rate and position until the next rider takes his turn at the front.

Pull off: to move to one side so that the next racer can take a turn at the front.

Pursuit: an organized attack to catch the breakaway or pack. Also a velodrome event in which two cyclists, or two teams, chase each other around the track, each trying to catch the other or to be ahead at the end of a designated time period.

Pusher: a cyclist who prefers to pedal in a big gear. Though the cadence is usually low, the gear size produces the necessary speed.

Qualifier: a preliminary event that qualifies competitors for a main event. *See* Heat.

Quadriceps: the large muscles in front of the femur bone, or thigh; usually well developed in cyclists.

RAAM: Race Across AMerica, the longest and most prestigious ultra-marathon cycling event in the world. It is a 3,000-mile nonstop bike race from the Pacific Ocean on the West Coast in California to the Atlantic Ocean on the East Coast in New Jersey or New York. It spans 9–14 days, and once the clock has started it doesn't stop until the winner arrives at the designated finish line on the East Coast. The clock stops for nothing, including rain, winds, storms, traffic, detours, injuries, or sleep. The name Race Across AMerica is a registered trademark and the *M* in *AMerica* is always capitalized. The event is owned by John Marino, Michael Shermer, Lon Haldeman, and Robert Hustwit.

Repetition: an individual motion in a particular exercise in a weight training station. A set is a series of repetitions.

Road race: an event held on a long circuit or loop course, 6–20 miles long, or a point-to-point course, where the event usually ranges from 75 to 150 miles long.

Road rash: a skin abrasion caused by a fall on pavement. Sometimes called a *cherry*.

Rollers: an indoor training device that the bicycle balances on. One roller goes under the front wheel, and two rollers go under the rear wheel. Pedaling at medium to high cadence is required for balance.

Rolling a tire: when a tubular tire is not glued on the rim properly, it can roll off the rim when under pressure, such as when turning a corner, causing a cyclist to crash.

RV: recreational vehicle or motor home used in ultra-marathon cycling; equipped with cooking, bathing, and sleeping facilities.

Senior: an age category in racing, 19–30 years, broken into four categories (4, 3, 2, 1), 1 being highest, depending on experience and performance.

Set: a specific number of repetitions in a weight training program.

Side-by-side: a bicycle for two riders who ride next to each other as opposed to one in front of the other.

Silks: silk sew-ups or tubulars—constucted with silk threads in the casing, making the tire very light and expensive.

Sitting-in: to use the draft of another rider or riders without taking a turn pulling. *See* Hang-in.

Slipstream: the portion of moving air behind one rider that enables riders to draft behind the leader.

Snap: quick acceleration used in the jump.

Solo/unpaced: a UMCA category that most ultra-marathon cycling events are held under—a single cyclist on a conventional bicycle, riding without drafting.

Space cushion: the open space around a cyclist in which there is no other vehicle or moving object.

Speed work: doing intervals and fartleks and motorpacing for fast training.

Spinner: a rider who pedals with a high cadence in a medium to small gear. Spinning is recommended for recovery rides after races and for the development of good form on the bike.

Spinning: fluid, fast pedaling.

Sprint: a fast burst of speed by an individual or a group of racers for the finish line.

Sprinter's hill: a short, steep hill that can be climbed quickly out of the saddle; body weight and muscular bulk don't hinder the rider from climbing.

Squirrelly: an unstable or nervous rider.

Stage race: a series of different types of individual races—time trials, criteriums, and road races—all combined into one event that lasts a number of days. Each stage of the race presents cyclists with opportunities to gain scoring advantages, and it is quite possible for a racer to win the entire event without taking first place in any of the single stages of the race. The winner is the rider with the least accumulated time for the entire event. The longest stage race is the world-famous Tour de France, spanning 2,300–2,600 miles over the three-week-long course. The Coors Classic is the largest and most prestigious stage race in the United States.

Stayer: a rider who can maintain a steady, fast pace for long periods of time. One who is tough and can hang.

Straight block: a freewheel with cogs that increase in size in one-tooth increments.

Streamlined: bicycles designed with full fairings to reduce wind resistance to a minimum.

Suppleness: loose, smooth leg muscles of a quality that allows the cyclist to pedal with power and speed.

Support crew: a team of people who provide assistance to a cyclist. They may provide food, water, clothing, massage, moral support, directions, medical aid, advice—virtually anything other than actual assistance to the cyclist in moving the bicycle.

Support vehicle: a vehicle that accompanies a cyclist during a ride or race. The vehicle is driven and staffed by the support crew. This vehicle may be a motorcycle, car, van, truck, or motor home.

Take a flyer: to go off the front of the pack, usually alone, catching the other riders by surprise.

Team: two or more cyclists in a race working together to gain victory for themselves.

Team pursuit: two teams, of three or four riders each, chase each other around the track, trying to catch each other or take the lead at the end of a designated time period.

Time trial: a race against the clock. Drafting is not allowed.

Touring: a non-competitive form of cycling ranging in length from a few miles to thousands of miles; typically, all supplies are carried by the cyclist in pannier bags.

Track racing: held in a velodrome and involving the use of a fixed-gear bicycle; at least one rider at a time uses the track in such events as the pursuit, matched sprint, points race, team pursuit, and miss-and-out.

Tricycle: a three-wheeled cycle with two of the wheels in the rear. There are tricycle races in Europe in both road racing and ultra-marathon cycling.

Ultra-marathon cycling: *ultra* refers to the surpassing of a specific limit or range, exceeding what is common, moderate, or proper. *Marathon* is defined as a long-distance race, a contest of endurance. *Ultra-marathon cycling* is riding a bicycle a distance that is considered to be beyond moderate or common human limits, in the shortest time possible. The exact distance and elapsed time will vary. The characteristics of the event such as terrain, weather conditions, distance, along with age and physical condition of the competitor, must be taken into consideration. The Race Across AMerica is the longest, most prestigious ultra-marathon cycling event in the world. Other major ultra-marathon records include the Seattle–to–San Diego course, the Miami–to–Maine course, the Spenco 500, the English Land's End–to–John O'Groates course, the Bicycle Across Missouri, and the Paris–Brest–Paris race in France.

Unpaced: no drafting.

Veterans: an age category in racing—35 to 40 years.

Wheelsucker: a derogatory word for a cyclist who refuses to take a turn at the front of the pack or breakaway group.

Wind drag: a term in aerodynamics referring to the resistance produced by moving air.

Wind foil: an object attached to a bike that is designed to lower wind resistance.

Wind resistance: a term in aerodynamics referring to the resistance produced by moving air. *See* Wind drag.

Z-90.4: the current term for the standard set by ANSI for bicycle helmets.

APPENDIX II
BICYCLE PERIODICALS

The following is a list of bicycle periodicals, both consumer and trade, as well as other periodicals that are related to the sport or frequently cover cycling events. I have indicated after the title of the magazine whether it is consumer or trade. A trade publication is typically intended for the industry itself, in this case bicycle dealerships, manufacturers, distributors, and associations.

BICYCLE PERIODICALS

American Bicyclist (Trade)
80 Eighth Ave.
New York, NY 10031

Bicycle Business Journal (Trade)
Quinn Publications, Inc.
4915 West Freeway
PO Box 1570
Fort Worth, TX 76107

Bicycle Dealer Showcase (Trade)
1700 E. Dyer Rd.
Santa Ana, CA 92713

Bicycle Forum (Consumer)
PO Box 8311
Missoula, MO 59807

Bicycle Guide (Consumer)
128 N. 11th St.
Allentown, PA 18102

Bicycle Rider (Consumer)
29901 Agoura Rd.
Agoura, CA 91301

Bicycle USA (Consumer)
PO Box 988
Baltimore, MD 21203

Bicycling (Consumer)
33 E. Minor St.
Emmaus, PA 18049

Bicycling News Canada (Consumer)
101-1281 W. Georgia St.
Vancouver, BC, Canada V6E 3J7

Bicycling San Diego (Consumer)
1152 Oliver Ave. Suite #3
San Diego, CA 92109

California Bicyclist (Consumer)
1220 La Playa, #201
San Francisco, CA 94122

City Sports (Consumer)
PO Box 3693
San Francisco, CA 94119

Cycling (Consumer)
Currey House, 1 Thrawley Way
Sutton, Surrey SMa 4QQ
England

Cycling U.S.A. (Consumer)
PO Box 1069
Nevada City, CA 95959

Outside (Consumer)
1165 N. Clark St.
Chicago, IL 60610

Southern California Cycling Federation News (Consumer)
5040 Tujunga, #6
North Hollywood, CA 91601

Southwest Cycling (Consumer)
11684 Ventura Blvd., #213
Studio City, CA 91604

Velo-News (Consumer)
PO Box 1257
Brattleboro, VT 05301

Winning: Bicycle Racing Illustrated (Consumer)
1524 Linden St.
Allentown, PA 18102

RELATED PERIODICALS

Action Sports Retailer (Trade)
31652 Second Ave.
South Laguna, CA 92677

Athletic Journal (Trade)
1719 Howard St.
Evanston, IL 60202

The Runner (Consumer)
One Park Ave.
New York, NY 10016

Runner's World (Consumer)
1400 Stierlin Rd.
PO Box 355
Mountain View, CA 94043

Running News (Consumer)
PO Box 2822
La Jolla, CA 92038

Sierra (Consumer)
530 Bush St.
San Francisco, CA 94108

Sport (Consumer)
119 W. 40th St.
New York, NY 10018

Sportstyle (Trade)
Fairchild Publications, Inc.
7 E. 12th St.
New York, NY 10003

Tri-Athlete (Consumer)
1127 Hamilton St.
Allentown, PA 18102

Triathlon (Consumer)
PO Box 5901
Santa Monica, CA 90405

The Sporting Goods Dealer (Trade)
1212 N. Lindbergh Blvd.
St. Louis, MO 63166

Sports Merchandiser (Trade)
1760 Peachtree Rd., NW
Atlanta, GA 30357

Sports Retailer (Trade)
1699 Wall St.
Mt. Prospect, IL 60056

Ultrasport (Consumer)
PO Box 27938
San Diego, CA 92127

Women's Sports
PO Box 612
Holmes, PA 19043

APPENDIX III
SELECTED BIBLIOGRAPHY

Anderson, Robert. *Stretching*. Box 1002, Englewood, CO 80110, 1975.

Ballantine, Richard. *Richard's Bicycle Book*. New York: Ballantine Books, 1974.

Burke, Edmund. *Toward an Understanding of Human Performance*. Ithaca, NY: Movement Publications, 1977.

Colligan, Doug, and Teresi, Dick. *The Cyclist's Manual*. New York: Sterling Publishing Co., 1981.

de la Rosa, Denise, and Kolin, Michael. *The Custom Bicycle*. Emmaus, PA: Rodale Press, 1979.

——. *The Ten-Speed Bicycle*. Emmaus, PA: Rodale Press, 1979.

DeLong, Fred. *DeLong's Guide to Bicycles and Bicycling: The Art and Science*. Radnor, PA: Chilton, 1978.

Howard, John. *The Cyclist's Companion*. Brattleboro, VT: Stephen Green Press, 1984.

Kleeberg, Irene. *Bicycle Touring*. New York: Watts, 1975.

Leete, Harley. *The Best of Bicycling!* New York: Trident, 1970.

Marino, John. *John Marino's Bicycling Book*. Los Angeles: J. P. Tarcher, Inc., 1981.

Matheny, Fred. *Beginning Bicycle Racing*. Brattleboro, VT: Velo-News, 1981.

McCullagh, James C. *American Bicycle Racing*. Emmaus, PA: Rodale Press, 1976.

Merckx, Eddy. *The Fabulous World of Cycling*. Belgium: Andre Grisard, 1982.

Mirkin, G., and Hoffman, M. *The Sports Medicine Book*. Boston: Little, Brown & Co., 1978.

Mohn, Peter. *Bicycle Touring*. Mankato, MN: Crestwood House, 1975.

Rakowski, John. *Adventure Cycling in Europe*. Emmaus, PA: Rodale Press, 1981.

Rand, Ayn. *Atlas Shrugged*. New York: Random House, 1957.

Reynolds, Bill. *Complete Weight Training Book*. Mountain View, CA: World Publications, 1976.

Schwarz, Jack. *Voluntary Controls for Creative Meditation*. New York: E. P. Dutton, 1978.

Simes, Jack. *Winning Bicycle Racing*. Chicago: Contemporary Books, Inc., 1976.

Sloan, Eugene. *The Complete Book of Cycling*. New York: Trident, 1970.

Sutherland, Howard. *Sutherland's Handbook for Bicycle Mechanics*. Berkeley, CA: Sutherland, 1974.

———. *All About Bicycle Racing*. Mountain View, CA: World Publications, 1975.

———. *Food for Fitness*. Mountain View, CA: World Publications, 1975.

———. *Inside the Cyclist*. Brattleboro, VT: Velo-News, 1979.

APPENDIX IV
BICYCLE ASSOCIATIONS

ALETHEIA PSYCHO-PHYSICAL FOUNDATION
515 N.E. 8th St.
Grants Pass, OR 97525

AMERICAN YOUTH HOSTELS (AYH)
National Campus
Delaplane, VA 22025

ASSOCIATION FOR PROFESSIONAL TRIATHLETES
25108 B. Margarite Pkwy., #209
Mission Viejo, CA 92692

BIKECENTENNIAL
PO Box 8308
Missoula, MT 59807

CANADIAN CYCLING ASSOCIATION
333 River Rd.
Vanier, Ottawa, Canada, K11 8B9

LEAGUE OF AMERICAN WHEELMEN
PO Box 988
Baltimore, MD 21203

NATIONAL OFF-ROAD BICYCLE ASSOCIATION
2175 Holly Ln.
Solvang, CA 93463

PROFESSIONAL RACING ORGANIZATION
1524 Linden St.
Allentown, PA 18102

SOUTHERN CALIFORNIA CYCLING FEDERATION
5040 Tujunga, #6
North Hollywood, CA 91601

ULTRA-MARATHON CYCLING ASSOCIATION
3022 N. Hesperian
Santa Ana, CA 92706

UNITED STATES CYCLING FEDERATION
1750 E. Boulder St.
Colorado Springs, CO 80909

UNITED STATES TRIATHLON FEDERATION
PO Box 2461
Del Mar, CA 92014

WASHINGTON AREA BICYCLE ASSOCIATION
1332 Eye St., NW
Washington, DC 20005

APPENDIX V
ULTRA-MARATHON CYCLING RECORDS

The Ultra-Marathon Cycling Association (UMCA) is an organization designed to sanction, recognize, and promote the sport of ultra-marathon cycling in the United States. It was founded in 1980 by John Marino and Michael Shermer. John Marino, Michael Shermer, Lon Haldeman, and Race Across AMerica executive director Robert Hustwit head the new organization. The combined experience of Marino, Shermer, and Haldeman include over 50,000 miles of competitive marathon cycling.

The UMCA has established the following objectives:

1. Recognize ultra-marathon cycling as a bonafide sport.

2. Establish rules and regulations for specific events.

3. Categorize various classes of ultra-marathon cycling competition.

4. Promote and encourage participation in this new sport.

5. Reward personal achievement.

6. Judge and sanction ultra-marathon events.

7. Keep accurate records of all ultra-marathon accomplishments.

The membership of the UMCA is very exclusive. There are two

types of members—honored and associate. They are defined as follows:

Honored—Individuals who have attempted ultra-marathon events, with the intention of establishing or breaking a world record in the United States or achieving an admirable goal. Courage, determination, and a reasonable level of success are important. Setting a world record is not a prerequisite. As of January 1, 1985, there were fewer than 100 people qualified for induction. Invitations are extended to these select few. The dues are "a gallon of sweat and the will to succeed," which all these people have paid.

Associate—Individuals who have assisted in furthering ultra-marathon cycling by serving on a minimum of two support crews of honored members or by providing special contributions to the events.

Ultra-Marathon Cycling Events

The UMCA recognizes the following ultra-marathon events. (All records are from city hall to city hall. If there is no city hall, then the civic center or city courthouse may be used.)

Transcontinental

1. West Coast to East Coast: Los Angeles or San Francisco to New York or Atlantic City.
2. East Coast to West Coast: New York or Atlantic City to Los Angeles or San Francisco.

Double Transcontinental

1. West Coast to East Coast and back.
2. East Coast to West Coast and back.
3. Middle of U.S. to West Coast, to East Coast, then back to the starting point.

U.S. West Coast

1. Seattle to San Diego.
2. San Diego to Seattle.

U.S. East Coast

1. Miami, Florida, to Portland, Maine.
2. Portland, Maine, to Miami, Florida.

Ultra-Marathon Cycling Event Categories

1. Solo/Unpaced (no drafting)
   A. Single conventional bicycle, male and female divisions.
   B. Single conventional tandem, male, female, and mixed divisions.

2. Paced (drafting)
   A. Two single conventional bicycles, male, female, and mixed divisions.
   B. Two conventional tandems, male and female divisions.

3. Unconventional or Human-Powered Vehicle, male and female divisions.
   A. All human-powered vehicles except conventional single and tandem bicycles, including recumbents, triplets, unicycles, side-by-side tandem, tricycles, manupeds, high wheelers, streamliners, and any as yet unnamed garage machines.

Ultra-Marathon Cycling Records (USA)

Transcontinental (Solo/Unpaced), West to East, Men

4/02/72	Peter Duker	18 days, 2 hours, 30 minutes
3/15/73	Paul Cornish	13 days, 5 hours, 20 minutes
8/28/78	John Marino	13 days, 1 hour, 20 minutes
6/28/80	John Marino	12 days, 3 hours, 41 minutes
7/14/81	Lon Haldeman	10 days, 23 hours, 27 minutes
8/14/82	Lon Haldeman	9 days, 20 hours, 2 minutes
9/29/84	Pete Penseyres	9 days, 13 hours, 13 minutes

Transcontinental (Solo/Unpaced), West to East, Women

6/82	Ann Kovich	14 days, 14 hours, 54 minutes
7/13/82	Susan Notorangelo	11 days, 16 hours, 15 minutes

Transcontinental (Solo/Unpaced), East to West, Men

10/74	Victor Vincente of America	16 days, 8 hours, 25 minutes
7/21/81	Lon Haldeman	12 days, 18 hours, 49 minutes

Double Transcontinental (Solo/Unpaced)
East to West to East (or Vice Versa), Men

10/74 ·	Victor Vincente of America	36 days, 8 hours,
7/14/81	Lon Haldeman	24 days, 2 hours, 34 minutes

Transcontinental (Paced/Drafting, Single Bicycles), West to East, Men

8/9/77	Kevin Kvale Chris Kvale	14 days, 9 hours, 19 minutes

Transcontinental (Paced/Drafting, Two Tandem), West to East, Men

6/27/79	Pete Penseyres Rob Templin Bruce Hall Brooks McKinney	10 days, 21 hours, 49 minutes

Transcontinental (Unpaced, Tandem), West to East, Mixed

6/21/83	Lon Haldeman Susan Notorangelo	10 days, 20 hours, 23 minutes

Transcontinental (Unpaced, Tandem), West to East, Women

6/84	Estelle Grey Cheryl Marek	10 days, 22 hours, 48 minutes

Transcontinental (Solo/Unpaced, Unconventional), West to East, Men

7/7/81	Len Vreeland (recumbent)	14 days, 21 hours, 13 minutes

Seattle to San Diego (Solo/Unpaced), Men

9/23/80	Michael Shermer	7 days, 8 hours, 28 minutes
6/12/81	Doug Steward	4 days, 22 hours
6/29/81	Clint Worthington	4 days, 18 hours, 29 minutes
8/27/81	Michael Shermer	4 days, 14 hours, 15 minutes

9/18/82 Richard Clayton   4 days,   2 hours, 23 minutes
6/27/84 Michael Shermer   3 days, 23 hours, 49 minutes

Savannah, GA to San Diego, CA (solo/unpaced)

5/16/84 Michael Coles   11 days,   8 hours, 30 minutes

24-Hour Outdoor Track

5/23/81 Lon Haldeman   392.1 miles
9/22/81 Lon Haldeman   454.2 miles
4/02/84 Jim Elliott   502.3 miles

Miami to Maine (Portland) (Solo/Unpaced), Men

6/18/83 Michael Shermer   6 days,   1 hour,   55 minutes

1982 Great American Bike Race, Men

Lon Haldeman   9 days, 20 hours,   2 minutes
John Howard   10 days, 10 hours, 59 minutes
Michael Shermer   10 days, 19 hours, 54 minutes
John Marino   12 days,   7 hours, 37 minutes

Race Across AMerica
(Official Finishers—12 starters), Men

Lon Haldeman   10 days, 16 hours, 29 minutes
Pete Penseyres   10 days, 22 hours,   2 minutes
Michael Secrest   11 days,   6 hours, 30 minutes
Robert Beeson MD   11 days, 12 hours, 48 minutes
John Silker   11 days, 18 hours, 25 minutes
Gary DelNiro   12 days,   7 hours, 47 minutes

1984 Race Across AMerica (Official Finishers—23 starters)

MEN

Pete Penseyres   9 days, 13 hours, 13 minutes
Michael Secrest   10 days, 19 hours, 12 minutes
Jim Elliot   10 days,   7 hours, 49 minutes
Michael Shermer   10 days, 16 hours, 33 minutes

WOMEN

*Shelby Hayden-Clifton 12 days, 20 hours, 57 minutes
*Pat Hines   12 days, 20 hours, 57 minutes
Elaine Mariolle   13 days, 23 hours, 36 minutes
*Tie

APPENDIX VI
TRAINING/RACING LOG

The graph sheet provided here is for the purpose of logging weekly and monthly mileages. You may begin at any time of the year. If not on January 1, ignore the months and just use the numbered weeks, starting when you wish. Week one could be March 21 or October 10. Your "fiscal fitness year" would then begin and end with that date. Many riders like to begin their training year with spring training in March rather than in January, when such low mileage output can be discouraging to monitor.

I have left the miles/kilometers axis blank so you may plot mileage on it according to the type of riding you do. Marking the squares off in increments of 10 miles will result in a total bar length of 350 miles. Twenty-mile increments nets 700 miles. If greater distances are ridden, increase the distance between squares to 50 miles at the top of the bar. Psychologically speaking, it is best to use the entire area of the graph to plot values, giving the finished product a satisfying fullness. If you typically ride 200–300 miles per week, but the graph allows room for 700 miles, you will probably develop a sense of underachievement. On the other hand, it is very rewarding to fill in many squares of a bar when returning from a ride, knowing that you have trained well.

I suggest that you plot the graph with a colored pen—red or orange is a good color—as this attracts your attention and gives the psychological impression of having trained great distances. I also recommend that you fill in the appropriate number of squares after each ride. Not only does it act as a reinforcer to training, but it can also act as a negative reinforcer when you miss a day of riding that was not scheduled to be missed.

One trick to planning a schedule is to pencil in a mark on the bar graph in advance of the week to come as a motivation to get out there and ride so that you reach that goal. You can also do this in advance of the entire year, if you know your schedule well enough. Plot out the major races you want to do, then calculate how many miles you will need to ride in preparation in order to be in good shape to do well. Don't forget to restrict yourself to a lower mileage in the week following a big race that requires some physical or psychological recovery.

Having a completed graph at the end of the year is not only rewarding, but it can also help you determine your mistakes and successes. Maybe you need to add more miles here, subtract a few there. Perhaps you peaked too late for a big event, so the following year you can begin the heavy mileage weeks earlier. Feedback that is accurate and precise is critical in the improvement of a training program.

TRAINING/RACING LOG

Miles/Kilometers in 10 or 20 Intervals

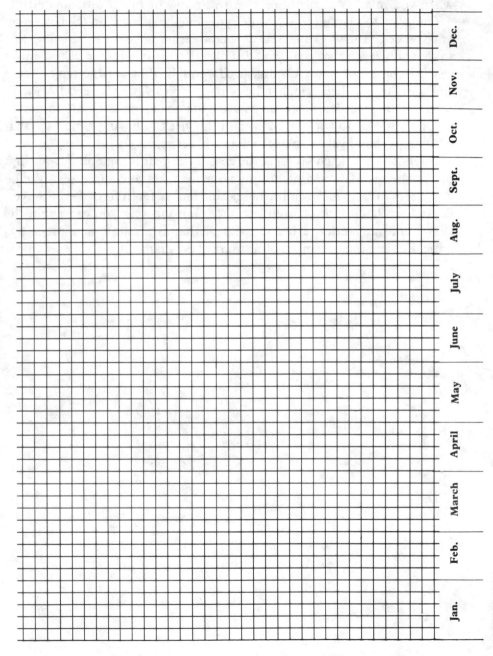

Time (Weeks per Month)

Jan.   Feb.   March   April   May   June   July   Aug.   Sept.   Oct.   Nov.   Dec.

APPENDIX VII
APPLICATION FOR ULTRA-MARATHON CYCLING EVENT

ULTRA-MARATHON CYCLING ASSOCIATION

ORGANIZED 1980

APPLICATION FOR ULTRA-MARATHON CYCLING EVENT

(Please print)

NAME OF CYCLIST_____

STREET ADDRESS_____

CITY_____ STATE_____ ZIP_____

TEL NO.(___)_____ AGE____ SEX____

BIRTH DATE_____

TITLE OF EVENT_____ TOTAL MILES _____

PLACE OF DEPARTURE_____ DESTINATION _____

DEPARTURE DATE AND TIME_____ EST. ARRIVAL_____

TYPE OF BICYCLE (TANDEM, RECUMBENT, CONVENTIONAL, ETC.) _____

EVENT CLASSIFICATION (SOLO, UNPACED, MOTORPACE, TEAM, ETC.)_____

HOW MANY CREW MEMBERS?___ HOW MANY SUPPORT VEHICLES?___

NAME AND ADDRESS OF CREW CHIEF_____

_____

_____

PHONE NUMBER(___)_____

PLEASE LIST ANY SPONSORS YOU HAVE FOR THIS EVENT

_____

_____

_____

COMMENTS:

SIGNATURE_____ DATE_____

INDEX

ABOUT THE AUTHOR

Michael Shermer is an instructor of psychology at Glendale Community College (California). He has a bachelor's degree in psychology from Pepperdine University and a master's degree in psychology from California State Univeristy, Fullerton. He has published articles in psychological journals as well as presented papers at professional psychological conventions. His area of specialty is motivation and goal orientation, and he is particularly interested in the psychology of individuals who push themselves to their physical or mental limits.

Michael is also a professional cyclist, holding numerous records:

1980: Seattle-to- San Diego, 1,500 miles—7 days, 8 hours, 28 minutes

1981: Seattle-to-San Diego, 1,325 miles—4 days, 14 hours, 15 minutes

1981: Hawaii Ironman Triathlon—Top third finish

1982: Great American Bike Race, LA–NY—3rd, 10 days, 19 hours, 34 minutes

1983: Miami-to-Maine, 1,900 miles—6 days, 1 hour, 55 minutes

1983: Race Across AMerica, LA–Atlantic City—DNF (injury), 2,600 miles

1984: Spenco 500, 520 Mile Texas Race—7th, 28 hours, 49 minutes

1984: Seattle-to-San Diego, 1,325 miles—3 days, 23 hours, 49 minutes

1984: Race Across AMerica, LA–Atlantic City—4th, 10 days, 16 hours

1985: San Francisco–LA, 401 miles—21 hours, 47 minutes

Shermer frequently lectures to audiences around the United States on psychology, health, fitness, and his world record rides. He has written many articles for bicycle and health-related magazines, and he was editor of a bicycle trade publication for three years. He frequently writes articles for bicycle magazines and has produced a 20-minute color documentary film on the 1981 Seattle-to-San Diego ride. He has appeared on ABC's "Wide World of Sports" in 1982, 1983, and 1984 in their coverage of the Race Across AMerica.

In business, Michael is an owner and director of the Race Across AMerica and the Ultra-Marathon Cycling Association. He also has a partnership in a bicycle shop, Shermer Cycles of America, in Arcadia, California. He is currently researching and writing other books on the underlying motivations behind successful athletes, stationary cycling, and a training log.